Keys to the Production Office

Opening a door to the real behind-the-scenes of a film or television show, this book explores the reality of working in the Production Office as an Office Production Assistant. Drawing on over 40 years' combined experience, authors Jennifer A. Haire and Gilana M. Lobel map out a career path into the industry by providing comprehensive practical information designed specifically for individuals pursuing the entry level role of the Office PA.

An invaluable tool for both breaking into the industry and on-the-job, the book is full of detailed "how to" information that not only provides an overview of the full scope of the industry, but also functions as a user's manual for Production Office operations. Haire and Lobel outline variations of the job of an Office PA nationwide, for both big- and small-budget feature films and television shows, and how you are a vital component of the Production team which can open the door to your future career. With coverage on how the Office PA supports the process of creating a show, the Production staff and crew, the practical day-to-day of the office, and developing your career, this is an essential resource for anyone wishing to take their first steps into the film and television industry. Featuring charts, graphics, diagrams, sample documents, templates, supplemental materials, and lighthearted cartoons throughout the book, the reader is immersed in real-world scenarios which create a solid foundation for how to be a professional in the workplace.

This is an inspiring and practical manual that reveals what is beyond the behind-the-scenes of film and television production. It's ideal for aspiring film and TV professionals with little to no experience working in Physical Production as well as readers studying film and television production courses and industry training programs.

Jennifer A. Haire is a Line Producer and DGA Production Manager with global feature film and television experience. Proud to be a "Fighting Pickle," she earned her BFA in filmmaking at the University of North Carolina School of the Arts. Her commitment to the industry includes serving on the Board of Directors for the Producers Guild of America, IATSE Local 871, and launching international Production crew training and Production safety education workshops.

Gilana M. Lobel is a New York-based Producer and DGA Production Manager. A graduate of the University of North Carolina School of the Arts, School of Filmmaking, her experience with the Production Office comes from working on major feature films and television shows in various capacities. She is dedicated to telling diverse stories and creating a more inclusive work environment by collaborating with industry organizations to encourage upward mobility in film and television.

Keys to the Production Office

Unlocking Success as an Office Production Assistant in Film & Television

Jennifer A. Haire and Gilana M. Lobel

LONDON AND NEW YORK

Cover image: © Getty Images

First published 2022
by Routledge
4 Park Square, Milton Park, Abingdon, Oxon OX14 4RN

and by Routledge
605 Third Avenue, New York, NY 10158

Routledge is an imprint of the Taylor & Francis Group, an informa business

© 2022 Jennifer A. Haire & Gilana M. Lobel

The right of Jennifer A. Haire & Gilana M. Lobel to be identified as authors of this work has been asserted in accordance with sections 77 and 78 of the Copyright, Designs and Patents Act 1988.

All rights reserved. No part of this book may be reprinted or reproduced or utilised in any form or by any electronic, mechanical, or other means, now known or hereafter invented, including photocopying and recording, or in any information storage or retrieval system, without permission in writing from the publishers.

Trademark notice: Product or corporate names may be trademarks or registered trademarks, and are used only for identification and explanation without intent to infringe.

British Library Cataloguing-in-Publication Data
A catalogue record for this book is available from the British Library

Library of Congress Cataloging-in-Publication Data
A catalog record has been requested for this book

ISBN: 978-1-032-18095-3 (hbk)
ISBN: 978-1-032-18098-4 (pbk)
ISBN: 978-1-003-25282-5 (ebk)

DOI: 10.4324/9781003252825

Typeset in Avenir
by KnowledgeWorks Global Ltd.

Contents

Dedication ix
Authors' Preface x
Introduction xii

1 YOU ARE HERE 1
PHASES OF A SHOW *1*
WHERE ARE YOU? *3*
    Production Hubs *3*
    Production Office vs. On-Set *5*
NUANCES OF PRODUCTION HUBS *7*
CREW STRUCTURE AND MANAGEMENT *8*
KEYS TO SECTION 1 *12*

2 WELCOME TO THE PRODUCTION OFFICE 13
THE PRODUCTION STAFF *14*
    Office Staff Responsibilities *18*
    Who's the Boss? *19*
WHAT THE PRODUCTION OFFICE DOES.... *20*
    Why the Production Office Is Necessary *22*
    The Production Pyramid *23*
KEYS TO SECTION 2 *24*

3 UNLOCKING THE ROLE OF THE OFFICE PA 25
RESPONSIBILITIES OF THE OFFICE PA *25*
    How Long Is the Job of an Office PA? *27*
THE PRODUCTION OFFICE CYCLES *29*
    Prep → Film → Wrap → Repeat *30*
WORKING HOURS *31*
JOB SKILLS AND TOOLS *33*
THE PRODUCTION CREW *33*
    "On" and "Off" Production Departments *34*
KEYS TO SECTION 3 *35*

4 MAKING IT HAPPEN, BEHIND THE SCENES 37
PRODUCTION OFFICE SETUP AND WRAP *37*
    Furniture and Workspace *37*
    Office Machines *38*

File Storage *39*
Keys *39*
Office Supplies *39*
First Aid *39*
Vendor Services *40*
Distribution *40*
Office Signage *42*
Craft Services Setup *43*
Parking, Public Transportation, and Production Vehicles *44*
PRODUCTION FILING *44*
Production File Labels *45*
DIGITAL WORKFLOWS *47*
DOCUMENT DISTRIBUTION *48*
Hard Copy Distribution *49*
Electronic Distribution *51*
Tracking and Managing Document Distribution *53*
OFFICE OPERATIONS *57*
Office Equipment *57*
Runs *59*
Meetings, Greetings, and Scouts *65*
That's Lunch! *70*
Craft Services *74*
Research *76*
The AD Kit *78*
SCRIPT REVISIONS AND SIDES *79*
Revisions *79*
Script Collating *81*
Sides *82*
DAILY CHECKLIST *86*
BASIC ACCOUNTING *91*
Purchase Orders *91*
Petty Cash/Purchasing Cards (P-Card) *93*
Check Requests *95*
SUPPORTING CAST AND CREW TRAVEL *98*
KEYS TO SECTION 4 *102*

5 TURNING THE PAGE ON PRODUCTION PAPERWORK   **103**
FROM THE SCRIPT TO THE FILM SET (VIA PAPERWORK) *105*
CONTACT LISTS *106*
SCHEDULES *107*
SCRIPTS *114*
REPORTING DOCUMENTS *115*
POST PRODUCTION/EDITORIAL NEEDS *118*
FINANCIAL *119*
OTHER *121*
KEYS TO SECTION 5 *122*

6 MASTERING THE ART OF WORKPLACE PERFORMANCE — 123
IMPRESSIONS AND PERCEPTIONS *123*
ASK QUESTIONS. TAKE NOTES. *124*
LISTENING AND COMMUNICATING *125*
INITIATIVE AND FOLLOW THROUGH *128*
BEING ONE STEP AHEAD *129*
OFFICE ETIQUETTE *131*
PHONE ETIQUETTE *133*
   How to Give Good Phone **134**
   Cell Phones and Texting **138**
APPROPRIATE VS. NOT APPROPRIATE *138*
PROFESSIONAL CODE OF CONDUCT *140*
KEYS TO SECTION 6 *143*

7 REEL LIFE, UNHINGED — 144
TO FREELANCE OR NOT TO FREELANCE *144*
GETTING PAID *145*
   PA Pay Rates **145**
   Start Paperwork **146**
UNEMPLOYMENT *150*
ON THE JOB *151*
   Safeguards **151**
   Day 1 / Your First Day **154**
   Lessons Learned on the Job **155**
CLIMBING THE PYRAMID *158*
   Inspirational Stories **161**
UNIONS AND GUILDS *162*
KEYS TO SECTION 7 *164*

8 RESPONSIBLE PRODUCTION INITIATIVES — 165
PRODUCTION SAFETY *165*
   Types of Safety Plans **166**
   Production Safety and You **168**
   Employer Responsibilities **170**
   Pandemic Safety **174**
HARASSMENT AND DISCRIMINATION *174*
   Harassment **174**
   Discrimination **176**
GREEN PRODUCTION INITIATIVES *176*
KEYS TO SECTION 8 *179*

9 THE BIG SCREEN VS. THE SMALL SCREEN — 180
PRODUCTION PATTERNS AND SCHEDULES *180*
RELEASE PLATFORMS AND SCHEDULES *187*
PA WORK LIFESPAN ON A SHOW *189*
KEYS TO SECTION 9 *191*

10 WHERE YOUR STORY BEGINS   192
   NETWORKING *192*
   OTHER JOB SEARCH TIPS *194*
   YOU DON'T KNOW WHAT YOU DON'T KNOW *196*
      Internships 197
      Educational Programs 198
      Mentors 199
   LANDING THE JOB *199*
      The Resume 199
      Your Online Presence 201
      The Interview 201
   COMPETITION *203*
   REFERRALS AND RECOMMENDATIONS *204*
   KEYS TO SECTION 10 *205*

Conclusion	206
Coordinator Corner	208
Acknowledgments	210
Appendix	212
A.1 – Crew List	213
A.2 – Office Supply List	228
A.3 – Production File Organization Chart	229
A.4 – Day File Labels	230
A.5 – Production File Labels	231
A.6 – Mileage Log	232
A.7 – Script Title Page	233
A.8 – Script Revisions	234
A.9 – Phone Activity: Answering Common Calls	238
Glossary	246
Index	254

Dedication

This book is dedicated to the countless passionate and hardworking Office Production Assistants we've had over the years, without whom we would have had to do all the work.

Authors' Preface

> Some are born great, some achieve greatness, and some have greatness thrust upon them.
> – William Shakespeare.

The entertainment industry is built by people who want to tell stories that shape our world; however, people work in the industry for many different reasons. Some are passionate storytellers, some seek a quick road to fame and fortune, and some may have been raised in it as if it was the family business. For others still, it may be the notion of being part of a team that creates content which influences others, where someone might laugh or cry or even view the world just a little differently. Whether you know right now that this is the career path for you and are ready to get started, or you simply want to know more, we have no doubt that *Keys to the Production Office* will guide you. With a little bit of knowledge and practice, anyone can get their start in the film and television industry, it's not as far out of reach as you may think.

We wrote this book to help you develop skills to put you on a path in the industry. Many prestigious Writers, Producers, Directors, and even Cinematographers began their journey in the Production Office. This is your map; you pick the career destination. This book is designed primarily for use in **physical production** on a feature film or television show, with a focus on the Production Office and the entry level role of an **Office Production Assistant**. On a very basic level, working in the Production Office is very similar to working in any office environment, just a bit more nuanced. Adopting these skills is essential for success in any job; however, they can also be applied to your everyday life. We've designed *Keys to the Production Office* to be an invaluable resource of extremely detailed information that not only provides an overview of the full scope of the industry but also takes you behind-the-scenes of the behind-the-scenes, to the control tower of the entire show: the Production Office.

We will explore the step-by-step processes of how to do specific tasks and assignments you'll be asked to do on the job. Consider this book a user's manual for working as an Office PA, and this is the first time it has ever been put together in a comprehensive guide available to the public. In the past, this information could only be acquired on the job. You had to already have the job to get the information! We've leveled the playing field and made it available to everyone.

How will you know if this is the right path for you? After putting in long hours each day, each week, each month, and for potentially years, every now and then you will find a moment when the phones have stopped ringing, the script has been handed out, and the coffee is brewing. The stage is set, the lights are hung, the camera is rolling, the Actors are in position, and just before the Director calls "Action" …. you'll know you are in the right place. Whatever your reason, whatever your story, it is this moment that will make your heart swell with pride, and there is no place in the world you'd rather be. This book is the culmination of our 40+ combined years of experience and our journey through the Production Office, having started as Office PAs. We've seen what works, what doesn't, and what could be better. We've trained countless PAs who have successfully advanced in their careers. This book strives to make the industry practices more accessible. Now it's up to you. We can't wait to have you on the team.

Introduction

There are two ways to navigate the unknown. One door holds fear and doubt, and the other holds courage and confidence. Knowledge is the key; it can lock away the fear and doubt and open the door to exciting opportunities.

When considering a career in the film and television industry, it can be both scary and exhilarating. There is no right way to the top and no one path to ultimate success. Success is measured in different ways for different people, and the only measurement of that success is by your own standard. If you don't take the chance, you'll never know what could be achieved. The key to opportunity is maintaining consistent and good work, to always try to be better, and not to compare your work to those around you. Be the best version of yourself in all your actions, at work, and in life. If you show up every day, work hard, and express your passion through your commitment to quality work, there is nothing you can't accomplish in time.

This book is a guide to prepare you for that long journey pursuing a successful career in the film business, and a great way is through the Production Office. Be open to different pathways and manage your expectations, as one opportunity can lead you in many directions. You may aspire to be a Writer, Director, Producer, Studio Executive (we've seen it happen for our PAs!), but perhaps along the way, find you excel and become impassioned in another production field. Maybe you end up preferring Post Production or the Art department? Or perhaps you decide you don't want to work in film and television but prefer another career path entirely? That's okay, too; many of the "how to's" in this book apply to other work environments as well! Working in the Production Office can lead to interactions with every department and give you a full scope of what film and television career options may lie ahead. Many individuals get tossed into the job without the first clue as to what is expected of them. Nor do they have a sense of what to expect of the job itself. This book will remedy that. Working as an Office PA is a rare type of job where you can get hired and not know anything about the work you'll be doing! Some get frustrated and discouraged by what they perceived the job to be; others are so overly enthusiastic they get carried away. Your goal should be to perform the job so well that you become too valuable to remain as an Office PA and promotion is inevitable. We're here to help you navigate those challenges.

Production *Assistant*, as a job title, is self-explanatory. You are an *assistant*, hired to *assist* any and all aspects of the production as a whole. We think this role is so vital to the success of a project, an entire book was created for you! PAs fill in the gaps while holding the show together. As a point of clarification, the term "PA" or "production assistant" is used to describe an entry level film and television position, and it's important to note that many departments on a show may have their own "PA." Those PAs will be assigned responsibilities associated with the specific department they are working in. For the purposes of this book, we've added the word "office" in order to define that the job is part of the Production Office team. It is a real job, with real impact every day. This book is designed to produce Office PAs who are efficient, informed, office-ready, an asset to the production from day one, and on a path to future success.

Throughout this book, the term "**production**" will be referenced often. Essentially, production is the period of time, once a film has been financed, when it is creatively prepared and physically produced. That means a screenplay has been **greenlit**, a Director has been hired, and together with a crew of creative and skilled craftspeople, they film Actors performing roles in order to tell a story. Production includes **pre-production** and **principal photography**. After filming, we **wrap**, and Post Production takes over and we all go on to the next film. Production is also the period of time an Office PA is employed.

Working for the Production department can be dually referred to as *On Set* production, as part of the Assistant Director team and where principal photography is physically taking place, or in the *Production Office*, which, among many other things, supports the needs of the set. The Office PA works in the Production Office, *not on set*. It is important to clarify this, as they are two very distinct roles with very different job responsibilities, both crucial to the success of the project. In either case, you are an element of production and truly the core of any show.

With this book you will learn applicable "Filmmaking 101" basics, such as the phases of the **content** creation process, the size, scope, and structure of the **production crew**, and the roles they perform, as well as the ways different types of productions operate. We'll walk you through common paperwork and documents you'll handle each day. We will go in depth about the function of the Production Office and the team that makes it run. In order to make sure you know exactly what you are committing to, we are giving you a thorough description of the type of work, hours, and the tasks you'll be asked to perform. We've included "how-to" checklists for job tasks as well as general best practices. The information presented is as "hands-on" as you can get from a book! By perfecting the concepts within, you'll be prepared for anything that comes your way. Working safely and using "green" practices are also part of any job. Here you'll learn how they are adapted to filmmaking. Finally, we'll walk you through the ways to navigate freelance employment: how to get the job, efficiently go from job to job, and ways to look out for yourself. Go ahead and tell your mom you don't have to move to California, because there are domestic **production hubs** where film production is thriving, not just in Hollywood. Unlike other entertainment-industry related books, this book will not teach you how to write your screenplay, produce an award-winning show, direct Actors, or create a YouTube channel. Most of your creativity will go toward problem solving. This book is a practical, no-BS guide on how to conquer being an Office PA.

There are a zillion ways to produce content. The production practices referred to in this book will focus on scripted narrative content. Commercials and nonfiction/docuseries content will have similarities to the processes we describe. The skills you learn from this book will adapt to any type of content creation and can be considered "**Hollywood Industry Standard**" processes. This simply means it is a practice that has become most common within the industry in America. There are exceptions to every rule, but basic aspects will hold true. The industry standard for a particular type of show will determine the extent in which the practices can be applied. The Hollywood Industry Standard is very structured and routine, but this does not mean there isn't a better way to do something. Consider the information on the following pages as guidelines. Never stop trying to improve. There are no right or wrong ways to make movies, just ways and better ways.

Filmmaking has its own language. Call it "movie speak," call it "production lingo," but no need to go looking for a language app. After one week on the job, you too will be telling your dog to "standby" or telling your roommate you've got to go on a "run" (and you don't mean exercise). When your mom tells you that your uncle is flying in for a visit, you'll respond with "copy that," ask her for the travel memo, and not think twice about it. There will be terms used throughout this book that are unfamiliar, or familiar but used in a less traditional way. No need to fret, we've provided a glossary of terms at the back of the book to help you along. Very soon they will no longer be "movie speak," but simply part of your regular vocabulary.

One final note to mention: the terms "motion picture," "feature film," and "filming" are industry standard language and refer to when content was captured on film stock. Many productions now film entirely on digital formats. In traditional industry vernacular it is common to use the word "shoot" when referring to the process of principal photography in the production process. You are "shooting a film," "prepping the shoot," "on shoot day 27," or just plain "shooting." In consideration of the current social and political climate, we have elected to use the word "film" in lieu of "shoot" in order to discourage the association with war and gun violence. Often film production is compared to the military due to the structure, hierarchy, regiment, and discipline required to complete a project. But making a film or television show is not a war, and we want to discourage the association with acts of violence, even if the film or television show is about acts of violence.

Use this book to excel at your first job, improve at your second, and inspire others by your third. It may not have the answers to all your questions but will guide you where to find them. We hope this book helps you open the door to a career in the film and television industry, because with the right knowledge and dedication, it is possible. We're giving you the keys.

1 YOU ARE HERE

The film and television universe is vast. In order to find your place, it helps to have a basic understanding of the process of how a project comes together, where a majority of shows film and why, where your work will actually take place, and how your role fits in the whole of the system. This section will help you gain a frame of reference for how these puzzle pieces come together, from a wide view of the production process, narrowed all the way down to where your office might be!

PHASES OF A SHOW

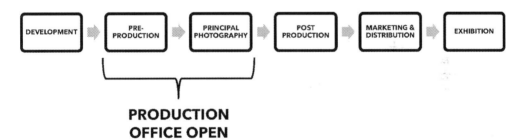

Diagram 1.1 The phases of production in which an Office PA works.

The phases of a show consist of six main steps, as outlined in Diagram 1.1. For all intents and purposes, throughout this book, we will refer to the types of content production – TV series, feature films, **new media** – as "shows," "productions," or "projects." These phases apply to all of them in varying degrees. The Production Office PA, i.e., YOU, will work in phase 2, Pre-Production, and phase 3, Principal Photography, which includes wrap.

Explore what interests you within each aspect of the industry. Learn as much as you can. There are many exhaustive books, videos, classes, etc. that go in depth on each of these phases. You don't have to decide your path right now. This book is focused on training you for the Production Office, and thus a basic understanding of each phase is acceptable. What is essential is that you understand where you fit in the grand scheme of the industry when starting out.

DOI: 10.4324/9781003252825-1

Table 1.2 Phases of a Show – Descriptions and Translations

1. Development and Financing	
Formally: The first stages of a new project, asks: What is the product being made? This is the "business" of show business.	**Translation:** What story do I want to tell? How will I pay for it?
Includes: Finding and securing the rights to a story	Has this story ever been told? I need to get permission to tell a true story.
Hiring the screenwriter/writing the **script**	I need a script to film. Who will write it?
Attaching **elements**	Who is going to star in it? Can I get my favorite celebrity to act in it and the director of my favorite movie to direct?
Securing **pre-sales** and financing	Maybe some foreign country will give me money in advance if I can get Tom Cruise to star. Can I get an advance on my inheritance?
2. Pre-Production	
Formally: The process of formulating the plan for how the project will be created.	**Translation:** How are we going to film this thing? Plan your work, work your plan.
Includes: Building a schedule and budget	How much does this cost to make and how long will it take to film?
Casting	Who's playing the role of the taxi driver?
Hiring crew	Who is going to help bring this project to life?
Creating the look of the show	How are we going to make Brooklyn look like the 1940s?
Finding filming locations	Where will the project be filmed?
Setting up the Production Office	We'll need desks, phones, Internet, coffee…
Renting equipment	Cameras, lights, lighting support, trailers, etc.
Creating the production plan to complete principal photography	What is the most efficient way to capture this story while maintaining creative integrity? How do we film this with the team we have on this budget?
3. Principal Photography	
Formally: The process of filming the script.	**Translation:** "Roll camera… Action!"
Includes: Ongoing prep, support of principal photography, and wrap	Facilitating the needs of the set, continual advance work for the upcoming days/weeks of filming, and, when finished, closing down anything that has been completed.
Navigating challenges	Putting out fires, managing egos, making sure the camera can keep rolling
4. Post Production	
Formally: The processes of finishing a film. Telling the final story.	**Translation:** Piecing together everything that was filmed, creating anything that wasn't, removing anything that isn't needed or wasn't supposed to be filmed and adding color, sound, and music.

Continued

Table 1.2 Phases of a Show – Descriptions and Translations (Continued)

Includes: Picture Editing	Piecing the story together scene by scene.
Sound Design and Sound Editing	Fixing any sound problems, adding "real life" sounds, creating the complete audio/listening experience.
Music score and rights	Creating emotion through music. Cue the orchestra! Can we get permission to use that hit song?
Visual Effects	Wow! Did they really film this in outer space? No, we didn't actually film on Mars, it's computer-generated.
Color Correction	Adding atmosphere and emotion to shots through color. Fixing the color of the images to match or look more stylistic.
Final delivery	Ok, we're done. It's a masterpiece. "I'd like to thank the …"
5. Marketing and Distribution	
Formally: Determining the best marketing campaign to advertise the project to audiences. AND Selling or licensing the film to worldwide release or distribution platforms (theater chain owners, streaming services, television broadcast networks).	**Translation:** "That Instagram ad for a free slushie totally made me want to see that movie, you know, the one with the snow … and cold." Or, "Gosh, every city bus seems to have that Big Actor's face all over it. Maybe I should go see their movie." Where the film can be seen. Who is buying the show?
6. Exhibition	
Formally: The show is available to viewers on a specific date, platform, and for a duration of time.	**Translation:** Meet me at Big Movie Complex at 7 p.m. to see the movie! Or let's stay in and binge *Hit TV Drama* when it drops on Sunday.

WHERE ARE YOU?

Production Hubs

Content is produced globally, and over the past two decades, states and countries alike have created film and television **tax incentives** designed to lure productions to them. More and more shows now opt to film nationwide and internationally rather than solely in Hollywood, California, the home of the US film industry. Studios want more bang for their buck and states want the influx of revenue (not to mention prestige) that is generated by the productions spending money in their state. This has led to a growth of production hubs, all with varying degrees of support **infrastructure** to make filming in that state as user-friendly as possible. Demand for local skilled crew labor has increased, including the need for *you* when a show comes to your town. This is where being a knowledgeable Office PA is crucial. You can be an invaluable asset to out-of-state crews, because you are familiar with the city and have personal connections. Graphic 1.3 reveals the largest current production centers where the most filmmaking is currently taking place in the US. While movies would lead us to believe that the show was filmed on the moon, you don't have to live there to find work.

Where Are You?

Graphic 1.3 Globe from moon to world to USA to Production City.

As of this publication, the leading domestic production centers are:

Albuquerque and Santa Fe, New Mexico
Atlanta, Georgia
Chicago, Illinois
Los Angeles, California
New Orleans, Louisiana
New York, New York

There is some sort of content creation happening wherever you live. Whether it's the local news, commercials, industrial corporate videos, etc., finding consistent work in the entertainment industry will be a challenge if the state you live in isn't offering an incentive. You won't need to up and move to sunny California or the Big Apple, but you should consider what production hub is closest to where you reside and is the best fit for the production life you want to lead.

Once you've found your way from the moon to the city or region that makes the most sense for you to find work, now you might ask, "How close am I to *action*?" Other than a few exceptions, most every show will have a "home base" or Production Office that is the center of all production activities. We will expand on this in depth in

Section 2, but for the purposes of explaining your proximity to the Big Time Director and "Roll Camera," allow us to clarify: *What and where is the Production Office?*

Production Office vs. On-Set

The office is the point of off-site operations for the set and all production departments. Working as an Office PA, you are part of the production department, in the Production *Office*, not on the set. The **set** is where principal photography takes place and cameras roll. It is run by the Assistant Director staff, the AD department, which is also often referred to as production.

Graphic 1.4 shows an example of the location of the physical Production Office in relation to the practical filming location for that day. The Production Office is in Culver City, California and the set is 30 miles north in Santa Clarita. If you are asked to make a run to the set, it could easily take one to two hours one way depending on the time of day, traffic, and other factors. Some productions film on a soundstage, and many soundstages have office space, which allows the production to be based out of the same Studio lot they are filming. Rather than driving two hours and 30 miles to the set, you

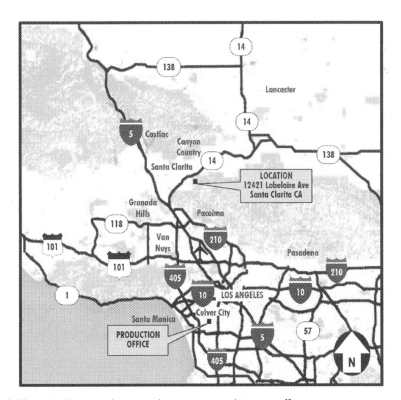

Graphic 1.4 Map with directional arrows showing set in relation to office.

6   You are Here

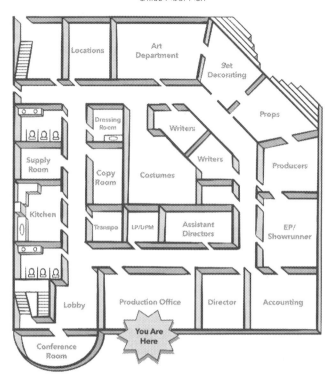

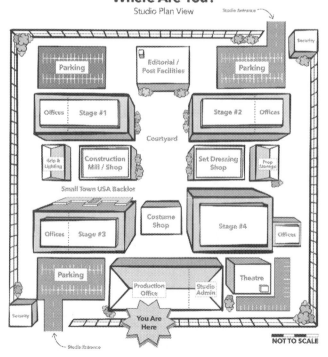

Graphic 1.5A and B Floor plan of a Production Office location in an office and where on a Studio lot the office is located.

may only be walking ten minutes and a quarter of a mile across the lot. In a place like New York City, you may be taking a taxi or riding the subway between office and set. It varies from city to city, and it is important for you to know your general working radius.

The Production Office can physically be located in an office building on the Studio lot, across town, in another state, or even in another country. However, where you are actually filming the show (the set) could be in another place entirely separate from the office location. Maybe it's on a soundstage at the Studio lot nearby, such as in Graphics 1.5A and B, all the way across town, in the mountains of another state, or on a remote island country (still not the moon....yet). The Production Office may be set up in an unused office space in Midtown Manhattan, a community center outside of Winston-Salem, North Carolina; a hotel room in Carmel, Indiana; or a barn filled with folding tables in Bartlesville, Oklahoma. Whatever the location, the office will adapt, production will find a way.

The physical location of the Production Office depends on a variety of factors that make the most logistical sense to support that particular show. It is unlikely there would be more than one main Production Office but satellite offices could be set up if a show is filming in multiple states or countries, and they need to coordinate locally.

NUANCES OF PRODUCTION HUBS

Across the nation, general production operations are relatively consistent when filming (remember the Hollywood Industry Standard?). Before you decide to move to one of these production hubs (also known as production centers), familiarize yourself with what that region offers and the scale of the industry in that area. Recognizing these differences and how they affect your work will put you ahead of the game when working in a production hub.

For the purposes of this book, we identify five aspects that could potentially adjust how you perform the role of an Office PA in these particular cities.

About the City – consider general information about the size and makeup of the city itself. Is it a major city with lots of people and traffic, or smaller with fewer production resources?

Larger cities are naturally equipped to provide an abundance of goods and services to their residents, but the trade-off may be having to navigate through traffic congestion. In a smaller city, getting across town might be a breeze, but you may find that the store you need is two towns away. Where is the city located geographically? Are there direct flights to/from it and relatively short travel time from nearby states? Or does it take a full day of travel to get there no matter where you are traveling from?

Climate/Seasons – What's the weather like? What are the common natural hazards for that area? This doesn't mean knowing whether it may rain occasionally, or even what the average annual rainfall is. However, it is helpful to know if a region experiences extreme weather, such as hurricanes and hailstorms that can directly impact a show's ability to maintain their **production schedule.**

Infrastructure – What are the support resources that enable production operations? Things like soundstages, equipment vendors, and a collaborative local film office are all ways a production hub sets itself apart. When the Director of Photography (DP) needs a camera crane the next day, can it be sourced within the state, or would it need to be shipped in, potentially not arriving in time? By encouraging industry businesses to set up shop in their region, it entices producers to bring their shows and easily launch their productions.

Crew base – How many simultaneous productions can be staffed with local crew members living in the area?

While it may seem like everyone wants to work in the movies, they don't. When you consider that a standard production crew size is anywhere from 75 to 200 people, finding experienced, skilled labor available locally or crew willing to travel away from home in order to work will be an ongoing process. You are part of the local crew base, wherever you choose to reside.

Other Production considerations – When working in this production hub, what are the main factors to consider that will affect your work and/or the production?

Will you need a car to get around or is public transportation sufficient? Are there any major annual events that cause road closures and an influx of tourists to the area? Is there a saturation of productions where opportunities are plentiful or are shows scarce?

Working in a Non-Production Hub

Working in a city where film and television production is a familiar practice means crew and support resources are usually readily available and do not take much difficulty to source. The cities and residents have become accustomed to seeing movie crews around town and are either excited or savvy. However, it is not unrealistic to find yourself working in a remote town in Montana where the nearest crew lives 30 miles away and finding a copy machine to rent means asking city hall where they got theirs.

When a production comes to your town, they could be filming the next huge superhero movie, *The Fighting Pickle*, its spinoff series, *Fighting Pickle and Friends*, or the low-budget independent feature, *In a Pickle*. The responsibilities needed of the Office PA will be the same. However, finding solutions may require more out-of-the-box problem-solving. If you happen to live in or near one of these non-production cities and a production does come to town, your day-to-day knowledge is what can make you a superhero and a local celebrity.

CREW STRUCTURE AND MANAGEMENT

This section is called "You Are Here" because not only do you need to have an understanding of the physical Production Office location (still not the moon) versus the film set, you also need to know your place within the overall crew structure. Interacting with the production team will be part of your everyday routine, and knowing where you fit is just as vital as knowing where all the other crew members fit as well.

Like the Office PA, everyone working on the show has a very specific job title with very specific responsibilities. Diagram 1.6 lays out a traditional "Hollywood Industry Standard" crew organizational chart. There is a very clear reporting hierarchy within each department and throughout the crew. In many cases full sub-departments will fall under larger creative oversight departments led by a key member of the creative team. For example, the Construction department falls under the Art department, which is led by the Production Designer.

Within each department there are levels of management. Just as you wouldn't take an internal departmental problem such as one person's need for a new desk chair to the CEO of a multi-million-dollar company, you wouldn't report a paper jam to the producer of the show (more than likely, they will come to you to fix it!). Following the chain of command when relaying information will save you and others potential embarrassment and upset. Make sure you know and understand the chain of command in your department (more on this in later sections).

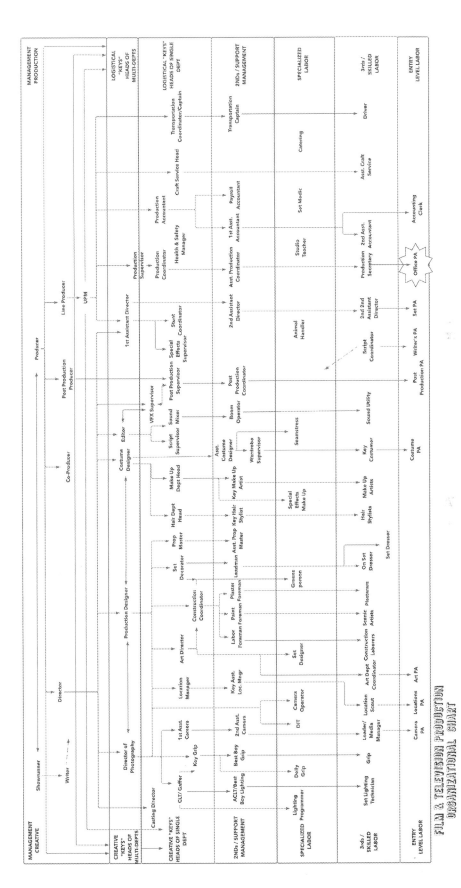

Diagram 1.6 Production crew organizational chart.

The responsibilities of the production crew can be broken down into the following six basic categories, some roles may fall into more than one:

1. *The Creative Team* is responsible for the overall look and aesthetic of the project. Everything from how it will be filmed, what the sets will look like, who are the best actors for the roles, the style of costumes, and on the post production end, how the story best pieces together. In feature films, the final creative decisions generally stop with the Director. In television, the final say will usually be with the Executive Producer/Showrunner. In a corporate structure, this would be considered an executive, such as a CEO.

2. *Management* – These heads of departments, such as the Production Designer and Location Manager, are responsible for supporting the creative team and are managers of multiple or single departments. They manage budgets, negotiate with **vendors**, find the right locations, source **set dressing**, and manufacture the **props**. This may also involve creating a character's look, ensuring equipment and trucks are where they are supposed to be, or making sure the cleanest sound is being recorded. Department heads are responsible for equipping the Director and Director of Photography with the tools needed to achieve the desired shots. Some of these roles allow for creative input. Every aspect of their job is to ensure the creative team can deliver the vision for the show.

3. *Support Management* – This team comprises the right-hand direct supports to the heads of departments, including the Assistant Prop Master and Wardrobe Supervisor. Often, they are tasked with managing internal departmental budgets, sourcing specialty equipment and supplies, labor hiring, as well as ensuring their individual department is delivering their work on time and within budget. Responsibilities can also be at the discretion of the head of the department.

4. *Specialized Labor* – These individuals have a unique skill set that may require technical skill, certifications, licenses, or training, or they are simply experienced and knowledgeable individuals in a specific field. At times they may constitute their own sub-department, such as a Set Medic or Special Effects Makeup Artist.

5. *Skilled Labor* – These individuals have demonstrated the skills required for a specific craft, offer vital experience to the team, and can be found in almost every department on set.

6. *Entry Level Labor* – This includes relative newcomers to the field who are looking to expand their skills. It can also be the entry level position for the department, such as the Office PA. These roles could be considered assistants and associates both inside and outside the film industry, such as an Executive Assistant or Sales Associate.

Graphic 1.7 shows the management structure within the production crew. As you move toward the outside of the circle, the rings grow larger to represent those who have the most influence on the project. Table 1.8 shows the same relationship in a more structured layout.

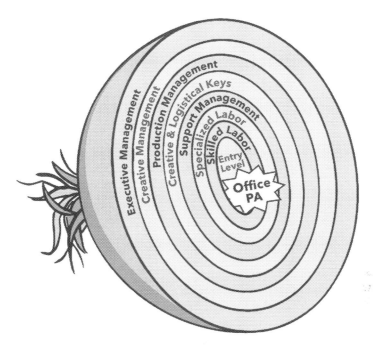

Graphic 1.7 Crew structure layers.

TABLE 1.8 Crew Management Structure Relating Hierarchical Layer to Job Titles

Hierarchical Layers	Job Titles
EXECUTIVE MANAGEMENT	Executive Producers/Studios/Networks
CREATIVE MANAGEMENT	Producers, Showrunner, Director, Writers
PRODUCTION MANAGEMENT	Co-Producers, Line Producers, Production Managers, Post Production Producer
HEADS OF DEPARTMENTS/ CREATIVE KEYS	Director of Photography, Casting Director, Production Designer, Costume Designer, Editor, Makeup and Hair department heads, VFX Supervisor
HEADS OF DEPARTMENTS/ LOGISTICAL KEYS	1st Assistant Director, Location Manager, Production Coordinator, Set Decorator, Prop Master, Production Accountant, Key Grip, Gaffer, Sound Mixer, Transportation Coordinator, Transportation Captain, Script Supervisor, Stunt Coordinator, Special Effects Supervisor, Art Director
SUPPORT MANAGEMENT	2nd Assistant Director, 1st Assistant Camera, Best Boy Grip, Best Boy Lighting, Leadman, Assistant Location Manager, Assistant Prop Master, 1st Assistant Accountant, Assistant Production Coordinator, Construction Coordinator, Assistant Costume Designer, Wardrobe Supervisor, Craft Service/Catering department heads, Labor Foreperson
SPECIALIZED LABOR	DIT, Paint Foreperson, Plaster Foreperson, Greensperson, Set Medic, Studio Teachers, Animal Handlers, Special Effects Makeup, Dolly Grip, Lighting Programmer, Set Designer, Health and Safety Manager, Armorer

Continued

TABLE 1.8 Crew Management Structure Relating Hierarchical Layer to Job Titles (Continued)

Hierarchical Layers	Job Titles
SKILLED LABOR	2nd Assistant Director, Payroll Accountant, Key Makeup Artist, Key Hair Stylist, Key Costumer, On-Set Dresser, Art Department Coordinator, Scenic Artist, Driver, Set Dressers, Grips, Set Lighting Technicians, Construction Laborers, Plasterers, Painters, Hair Stylists, Makeup Artists, Seamstress, Boom Operator, 2nd Assistant Camera, etc.
ENTRY-LEVEL LABOR	Office Production Assistant, Set Production Assistant, Accounting Clerks, Art Production Assistant, Costume Production Assistant, Post Production Assistant, Locations Unit Production Assistant, Writer's Production Assistant, other departmental production assistants, Interns

Some shows have over 200 or more production crew members. You are not expected to know all the titles and responsibilities of every single role, but knowing the basics of what each department is responsible for and that each department has a hierarchy is crucial. Not every type of production will maintain the same hierarchy. The size and budget will dictate the amount of crew hired. By observing how professional crews work together you'll better understand your place in the system, and this will allow you to provide the best service in the Production Office to support the show. A sample **crew list** in the appendix outlines the basic core job positions and defines their roles on the production. Get to know them and strengthen your understanding of the team it takes to create a show.

KEYS TO SECTION 1

- Production consists of six phases: Finance and Development, Pre-Production, Principal Photography, Post Production, Marketing and Distribution, and Exhibition. The Office PA is employed in the Pre-Production and Principal Photography phases.
- Content creation is global. Consider what production hub could offer you the most continued employment.
- The term "production" refers to both the on-set Assistant Directing department as well as the Production Office. The Office PA works in the Production Office, not on set.
- Know what production resources are available closest to where you live and work.
- The production crew comprised to bring a show to life is extensive, with clearly defined roles and responsibilities. This applies to the Office PA as well, who has a specific and vital role to play within the crew hierarchy.

2 WELCOME TO THE PRODUCTION OFFICE

The Production Office is the hub for the entire show, the "control tower" of information. The crew who work here are the behind-the-scenes of the behind-the-scenes. When ideas and creative concepts are generated, and before they can be executed on the set, proper pre-production must be done. This **production plan** comes together in the Production Office and is shepherded by the Production Office team. During principal photography, the office is continually planning for tomorrow, cleaning up yesterday, and putting out the small fires that come up throughout each day. The Production Office must stay one step ahead, anticipating the needs of the production as a whole, as well as be on top of the day-to-day minutiae. Almost all cast and crew members will have a need to interact with the Production Office for one reason or another. Whether they need a question answered or assistance with a task, the office is there to help.

The purpose of the Production Office is to provide information, resources, and support so that every department and crew member has what they need to do their job. They are the center of **distribution** to the **Studio, Network,** Producers, **cast,** and crew. The office staff is responsible for disseminating crucial production-related information that each department requires for principal photography. The Office Production Assistant (PA) is a vital part of the team and a position that keeps an entire show running.

If the Production Office does their job correctly, they should be able to:

Anticipate the needs of other departments.

Have an ear in everything that is happening and changing, so they are ready to move into action.

Answer questions. The office might not have all the answers all of the time, but they can get them because they know the right people to ask.

Find and *offer possible solutions* to every challenge.

It is the mission of the Production Office to ensure everyone else can focus on doing their work, knowing the office will always be on top of it!

Let's meet the Production Office team!

DOI: 10.4324/9781003252825-2

THE PRODUCTION STAFF

The crew organizational chart in Section 1 provides the complete scope of the production team on a show, including the department hierarchy. In general, most departments are made of a **department head** or **"key,"** a **second**, and **thirds**. Chart 2.1 breaks down the particulars of the Production Office reporting structure

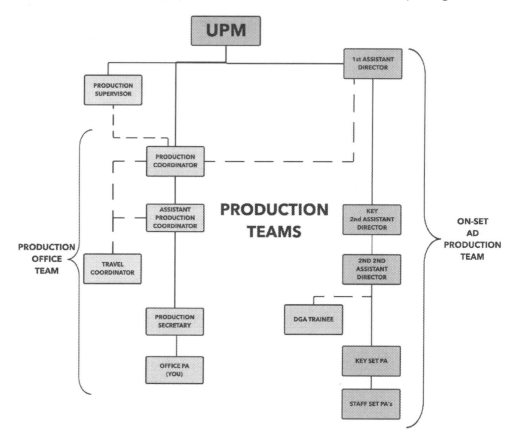

Chart 2.1 Production Office and Assistant Director organizational chart.

further. Depending on the scope of the project and budget, some offices may or may not employ every title listed. Other than a few exceptions, such as very low-budget independent films where a formal Production Office isn't put into place, 99% of the time Office PAs will be hired to support the office team.

Here are the roles of the Production Office staff. Responsibilities may vary slightly from one office to another, but the overall scope will be the same.

Production Coordinator

The Production Coordinator (PC) is the department head overseeing the Production Office. This person will assign responsibilities to the office staff. It is also the Production Coordinator who is held accountable for everything that happens within the Production Office.

The Production Coordinator reports to the Unit Production Manager (UPM) and/or Line Producer and to the Production Supervisor for shows staffed with one.

Direct Reports:
Assistant Production Coordinator (APC)
Production Secretary
Office Production Assistant(s)

General job description

The Production Coordinator facilitates production logistics assigned by members of the producing team. This involves any or all aspects of the production, from pre-production, principal photography, and through wrap. They function as an information clearinghouse and crisis manager for the production and are instrumental in the smooth flow of communications between the Studio, the Producers, the office, set, cast, and both the **"on"** and **"off" production** crew departments.

Based in the Production Office, the Production Coordinator serves as a liaison between the show and film community. They have a working general knowledge of Unions and their contracts (**DGA, SAG-AFTRA, IATSE, Teamsters**), equipment, and equipment houses, including all varieties of production equipment, shipping companies, customs brokers, and travel agents. The Production Coordinators' relationship with industry vendors is key in setting up accounts and negotiating deals and terms. They work closely with the Production Manager to stay within budgetary constraints for each department.

On each production, the requirements of this position can vary slightly. Some Production Managers need a more involved Production Coordinator who might assist in handling things like Union signatory paperwork for the Guilds, such as SAG-AFTRA and DGA, making calls for hiring crew, negotiating rental packages, handling insurance, and reviewing agreements with the legal department. Just as the office staff responsibilities are at the discretion of the Production Coordinator the responsibilities of the Coordinator can vary as delegated by the Production Manager.

In general, the Production Coordinator is responsible for ensuring that the Production Office staff facilitates the needs of all departments on a show. They will usually interface with the Studio production executives and must be prepared to answer their inquiries. A Production Coordinator must be ready to rapidly switch gears for any and all production needs that might occur and crisis-manage calmly and efficiently should the need arise. This position is generally considered **"on-call,"** and work hours may extend beyond the standard 10–12-hour workday. The Production Coordinator will have a strong, skilled staff to help keep the office running smoothly even when they are not physically present. That staff includes you.

Assistant Production Coordinator

The Assistant Production Coordinator reports to the Production Coordinator.

Direct Reports:
Production Secretary
Office PA(s)

The Assistant Production Coordinator is the first line of support for the Production Coordinator. This person is generally tasked with running the day-to-day office so the Production Coordinator can focus on the more overarching demands of the production. The APC should have a working knowledge of everything the Production

Coordinator does. They are responsible for the department when the Production Coordinator is not available.

Travel coordinator

Many productions require cast and crew to travel between multiple cities, states, or countries. Larger shows will hire a dedicated Travel Coordinator. This person will work closely with the Production Coordinator and a travel agency or the Studio travel department to ensure the necessary employees are traveled and housed appropriately for the show. They focus solely on booking and tracking travel movements and costs. They will research housing for cast, directors, writers, and crew as well as schedule flights as needed to move them between their homes and production cities or to international filming locations. Often, if there is no Travel Coordinator, this responsibility falls to the office staff.

Production secretary

The Production Secretary reports first to the APC and then the Production Coordinator.

> Direct Reports:
> Office PAs

Production staffing may vary from job to job, and not all productions hire a Production Secretary. However, often the primary responsibility for this position is managing document distribution. As we'll continue to unravel in this handbook, the volume of paperwork generated by a production in order to disseminate crucial information is vast. Tracking to whom, and how a document was distributed to a cast or crew member is an ongoing job. Most productions are transitioning to digital, email, or online distribution, which makes tracking easier. Originals or hard copies of some production paperwork, such as contracts, need to be scanned and organized in files for final delivery to the Studio. The Production Secretary will oversee the "virtual Production Office" and all digital filing.

The role of the Production Secretary can be one of the most challenging in the office. There is a lot of paperwork to be managed, maintained, and distributed. The Office PAs directly support this role, and they work together as a team.

Office Production Assistant (YOU!)

The Office PA reports first to the Production Secretary, then the APC, and then the PC.

> Direct Reports: None

Production Assistants are quite possibly the most versatile element of the production pyramid, and they can serve in various departments on a film or television show: Accounting, Art, Costumes, Construction, Camera, Casting, Locations/Unit, Post Production, Writers, and, of course, the Assistant Director department as a "Set" PA. As the entry level position in the Production Office, the Office PA may be assigned a wide range of very specific tasks as well as be responsible for general office functions and routine. At times it may require helping to resolve a crisis, researching a hard-to-find item for production personnel, or driving the lead actress to the set and delivering a script to the Director's house. Every day will be different from the previous, which keeps the job exciting and you on your toes. Depending on the size of the show, there may be one, two, or three designated Office PAs, and the tasks may be shared between them or divided up. They might seem like simple things, but without someone answering the phones, making sure everyone has a current schedule copy, and keeping the coffee fresh, the show would be in chaos. Since this book is dedicated to the role of the Office PA, the next chapters deep dive into your job specifics.

The Set PA (Not You)

The Set PA is not a Production Office staff position, but it is the other most common PA position you'll hear about in production. The role of the Office PA varies greatly from that of a Set PA, and in order to give you perspective on how different but vital these two roles are to keeping the show together, we've elected to include a description here.

The key distinction is that each type of PA is designated by their work location and department – the Office PA works out of the Production Office, and the Set PA works on the film set. Set PAs are part of the Assistant Director staff and are an extension of the 1st Assistant Director. They are assigned tasks and given directions that support the completion of each day's work as scheduled to help production and the crew "make their day." Equipped with a walkie talkie, surveillance mic, multiple pens, a flashlight, gloves, multi-tool, gum, sharpies, **sides**, call sheets, foul weather gear, and a myriad of other essential items on their person, they are ready for any on-set challenge. Set PAs may be designated to specific tasks, such as the managing and handing out of walkie talkies, assisting with getting cast through **the works**, helping with background actors, and attending to **1st team** on the set. These assignments are primarily given to full-time Staff PAs booked for the run of the show, who are hired as a "Walkie PA," "Basecamp PA," "Background PA," or "1st Team PA." In New York, there is commonly a "Paperwork PA" who is responsible for assisting with the completion of the various daily paperwork generated by the AD team during the course of a filming day. This designee will work most directly with the office staff. The Key Set PA works closely with the 1st AD and 2nd 2nd AD to oversee these designated PA roles, including assigning "lock ups" on stage and on location for each shot to ensure only what is meant to be captured on camera is in the frame. Additional PAs may be hired to join the department on days where more complex work is happening and help is needed to wrangle all the moving pieces. In general, all Set PAs are responsible for:

1. Doing lock ups. This may be on a city street to keep pedestrians from walking into the camera frame, or just outside the stage door to keep crew from disrupting the take.
2. Loudly shouting "rolling," "cut," and a variety of other phrases that let the rest of the crew know exactly what is happening as each shot is preparing to film, during filming, and when they are moving on to the next one.
3. Keeping chatty cast and crew members quiet during takes. Set PAs are masters of the "shush."
4. Finding people. They often have to be professional people wranglers, locating the leading lady who may have wandered over to craft services or spotting the DP who just returned from **10-1** (the bathroom).

The AD department will hire a greater quantity of Set PAs compared to the number of Office PAs, as they have a larger footprint to cover. They may need to be directly on set, in basecamp passing out call sheets, or in holding helping direct background performers to lunch. However, Set PAs don't file paperwork, answer office phones, or place expendable orders with vendors, and rarely do runs beyond the occasional one to Starbucks. They are on their feet for 12–16 hours a day and battling the elements, rain or shine. If you want to get your steps in, being a Set PA is a way to do it! There are lots of books, websites, and workshops that go in depth into the role and work required of the Set PA and what life is like on set. We encourage you to learn more about it, so your knowledge can be well-rounded. But not right now, right now you are learning about how to be a rock star Office PA!

Office Staff Responsibilities

Table 2.2 shows a general guide of how specific tasks might be designated to the individual members of the office staff. Assignments may vary from show to show, Production Office to Production Office, and regionally there may be nuances to how the work is assigned. They may be assigned based on proven competency or are sometimes dictated by staggered work shifts, in which case the tasks fall to the available office staff member.

Table 2.2 Office Staff Responsibilities by Position

Production Coordinator	Assistant Production Coordinator	Production Secretary	Office PAs
Hiring and managing office staff	Daily Production Reports	Paperwork distribution	Office phones
Ordering equipment packages	Expendables and supply orders	Crew list upkeep	Production filing
Cast related: contracts, travel, housing	Vehicle rental log	Vendor list upkeep	PO/check requests
Daily Production Reports	Vendor accounts and rental agreements	Production file management	Office supply orders
Vendor accounts and rental agreements	Crew list upkeep	Distribution logs	Craft Services replenishing
SAG-AFTRA and DGA reporting	Vendor list upkeep	PO/check requests	Trash/recycling
Pre-pro schedule	Parking lot accounts	Office supply orders	Paperwork distribution
Child Performer permits	Cast and crew travel	Craft Services orders	Email blasts
Trucks/vehicle rentals	Insurance certificates	Trash/recycling oversight	Manage copier supplies and maintenance
Tracking office spending	Lunch/wrap reports	Email blasts	Research
Insurance and workers' compensation claims	Pre-pro schedule	ID badges	Mail/packages distribution
PO/Check requests	Paperwork distribution	Sides	Sides
	ID badges	Meal orders	Meal orders
	Facilities liaison	Drive-on passes for Studio lots	General office upkeep
	PO/Check requests		Runs
			Meeting setup

Who's the Boss?

Line Producer

The Line Producer reports to the Producer.

> Direct Reports:
> Unit Production Manager
> Production Coordinator
> Heads of Departments

See also Unit Production Manager

The term "Line Producer" is used to describe the producer who manages production elements that fall both "**above-the-line**" and "**below- the-line**" in the budget. This can include handling cast issues as well as departmental needs and may also extend into post production. The Line Producer and UPM often have similar responsibilities and may be a combined or hybrid role on some productions. As separate roles, the responsibilities are often at the discretion of the Producer, the Line Producer, and the UPM. The title "Line Producer" is not a Union-covered position.

Unit Production Manager

The Unit Production Manager reports first to the Line Producer, then the Producer.

> Direct Reports:
> Production Supervisor
> Production Coordinator
> Heads of Departments

The UPM is the manager of the production as a whole from pre-production through wrap. They are in charge of all organizational, administrative, financial, and logistical aspects and must collaborate accordingly with the Executive Producer, Producer, Line Producer, Production Accountant, Director, and Studio.

Essentially, the Production Manager is responsible for delivering the show on time and on budget. They determine how much it will cost to make the project, over how many days, hire the Heads of Departments, and generally oversee that all production operations are equipped with what they need to execute the creative vision. On shows that are **signatory** to the Directors Guild of America, this is a Union position.

Production Supervisor

The Production Supervisor reports to the Production Manager.

> Direct Reports:
> Varies by production

This position is the right hand to the Production Manager, though it is not yet an industry standard on all shows and is sometimes an Assistant Unit Production Manager

(AUPM). Responsibilities vary per the discretion of the UPM. However, they are often the on-set representation for the Production Manager when they are needed in the office. The assignments can be similar to the responsibilities outlined under the UPM or more similar to some of the tasks assigned to the Production Coordinator. As with all members of the production staff, hiring of this position is based on need and if the budget allows.

WHAT THE PRODUCTION OFFICE DOES….

….Everything.

The Production Office does things like make sure that the crew has lunch every day, the lead actress can find a dog walker, or the Director can see a chiropractor in between takes on set. They make sure the crane shows up on the right day, with the right technician, to the right location. In short, they take care of everyone on the production, sometimes without them even knowing.

Here is an overview of the how the Production Coordinator leads the Production Office team to manage the following responsibilities. In the absence of one of the positions mentioned previously, the responsibilities will be reassigned within the team as the work will still need to be completed.

1. Manages all aspects of the Production Office.
    a. Sets it up, keeps it going, tears it down.
        - Arranges for office machine rentals (computers, printers, copiers, fax machines, phones).
        - Coordinates vendors for things like utilities, trash, recycling, Internet.
        - Buys office supplies.
        - Is the key master, the repair person, and the janitor.
        - Saves parking spaces.
        - Makes sure there is always water, snacks, and coffee.
    b. Seeks out and books support workspaces.
        - Where is the rehearsal taking place?
        - What room is the production meeting in?
        - Where are we storing the 42 wardrobe boxes?
    c. Staffs the office team.
        - Hires (sometimes fires).
        - Trains (using *Keys to the Production Office!*).

2. Gatekeepers of all production information sharing.
    a. Creates and updates production documents, including but not limited to the crew list, cast list, vendor list, production calendars, prep schedules, etc. (more on these in Section 5!).
    b. Distributes production documents, including but not limited to:
        - Contact lists.
        - Schedules.

- Scripts.
- Reporting.
- Financial.
- Post production/Editorial.
- Other (deal memos, contracts, breakdowns and director plans, etc.).

c. Copies, scans, and files production documents.
- Submits Union reports and deal memos.
- Hard copy and digital filing of all production paperwork required for the Studios, Producers, cast, and crew.
- Coordinates the collection of department final show files.
- Stores and tracks all assets.

3. Need something? Say something. How can we help?
- Assists the AD department with pre-production meeting arrangements.
- Directly supports the accounting department.
- Arranges wrap gifts, wrap parties, and cast and crew personal requests.
- Orders production equipment, supplies, and **expendables** (Camera, Grip, Electric, Hair, Makeup, Sound, Wardrobe, etc.).
- Requests quotes for rentals or purchases.
- Facilitates transportation of pickups and deliveries.

4. Uses all the tools to follow the rules.
  a. Liaison for production insurance and workers' compensation matters.
   - Arranges for insurance physicals for primary cast members.
   - Provides **insurance certificates** to vendors.
   - Reports and submits paperwork for insurance claims (theft, damage, illness, or injury/workers' comp).
   - Secures specialty insurance as needed for stunts, animals, helicopters, planes, watercrafts, spacecrafts.
   - Deals with workers' compensation claims.
  b. Stays informed of civil, state, and federal mandates regarding employment policies and health and safety regulations.
  c. Employment eligibility and worker compliance.
   - Permits for child performers.
   - In California, ensures that all cast and crew members are in good standing with their labor Unions. *Not applicable to all production hubs.*
  d. Studio compliance.
   - Ensures the production follows Studio and Network policies and guidelines.
   - Contract approvals through legal and risk management departments.

5. Planes, Trains, and Automobiles.
    - Arranges for travel of cast and crew if needed.
    - Negotiates group rates for hotels and researches airfare costs.
    - Creates and tracks travel using travel itineraries, travel logs, and travel memos.

Why the Production Office Is Necessary

Graphic 2.3 is an exaggerated example of how the production could go awry without the Production Office.

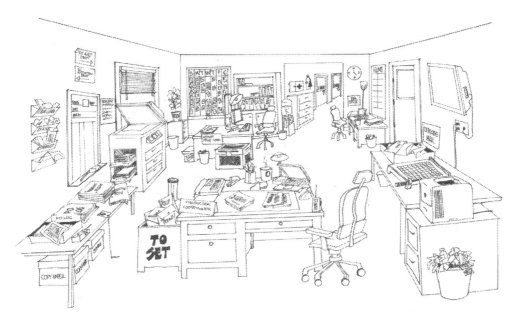

Graphic 2.3 Cartoon of a Production Office.

The crew reported to the Studio, but NO ONE COULD GET ONTO THE LOT because there was no one to notify security.
The Script Supervisor has not arrived, but THERE IS NO CREW LIST to call her.
The Director wants to rehearse with the actors, but NO ONE HAS RECEIVED A SCRIPT.
The scene is rehearsed, but the lighting and grip crew DON'T HAVE ANY EQUIPMENT because there wasn't a purchase order number to release it.
There is nothing for the cast to wear because the wardrobe department DIDN'T HAVE ANY CAST INFO for fittings.
First team needs to go through hair and makeup, but NO SUPPLIES WERE ORDERED. The scene is lit, but THE CAMERA PACKAGE IS STILL AT THE RENTAL HOUSE, waiting for pickup.
The AD is calling for sides, but THEY HAVENT BEEN PULLED, COPIED, OR DISTRIBUTED.
The sound department needs to wire the actors, but THERE ARE NO BATTERIES for their microphones.

The camera has its marks, but THE HARD DRIVES WEREN'T ORDERED to store the recordings.
It's lunchtime, but THE CATERER WASN'T BOOKED.
The show is filming a daytime exterior in the bright sun, and there is no shade because THE POP-UP TENTS WEREN'T RENTED.
Everyone is shouting at each other on set because THE WALKIE TALKIES WEREN'T ORDERED.
It's wrap, but THERE WAS NO PRINTER FOR THE CALL SHEET.
In the end, no one reported to set anyway because THERE WAS NO INTERNET TO SEND THE CALL SHEET.
…and there actually isn't any script, because THERE WERE NO MACHINES TO MAKE COPIES, but that doesn't matter since there wasn't any COPY PAPER, and there was NO FRESH COFFEE in the kitchen so the writer couldn't write anything anyway.

The Production Pyramid

Graphic 2.4 represents your place within the hierarchy of both the Production Office and the overall production team. As you can see, the Office PA is vital to keeping

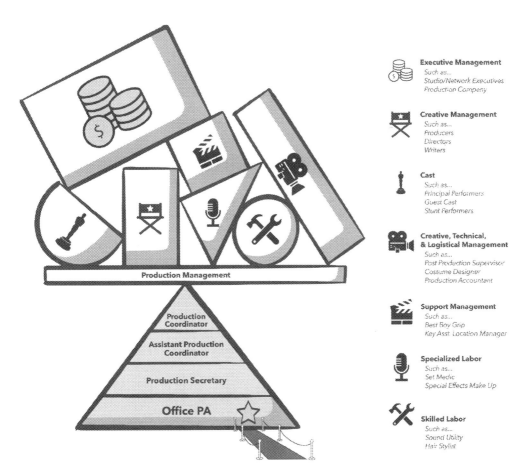

Graphic 2.4 Production pyramid.

everything stable and providing the foundation to support the entire show and all the responsibilities it encompasses! There are many opportunities to grow your career – the only way is UP!

The Production Office sustains the environment for the show to run smoothly. It is the support net, the communication hub, and the comforting embrace of a warm blanket that holds the show together. Your role as an Office PA is a critical component to this team. Practical experience is the best education, and with a realistic understanding of the commitment, responsibilities, and collaborations that contribute to a successful Production Office, you will earn your place among the stars.

KEYS TO SECTION 2

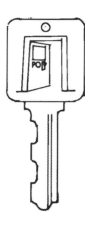

- The Office PA is responsible for supporting the Production Office. The Production Office is responsible for supporting every aspect of the production.
- There are clearly defined roles and responsibilities dedicated to the Production Office and its staff. Whether you are the Production Coordinator or the Office PA, always be conscious of what responsibilities have been assigned to whom.
- Your counterpart is the Set PA, and collaboration is essential.
- Not all shows have a physical Production Office, and Production Office staffing may vary.
- Production Offices need an Office PA in order to efficiently support the film crew.

3 UNLOCKING THE ROLE OF THE OFFICE PA

As an Office PA, you'll be asked to do a myriad of assignments to keep the production moving forward. Your task could directly affect whether the show can continue filming for the day, such as delivering a new lens to set for the Camera department. Or it could be a support task, like placing an office supply order for the Accounting department so they can focus on a more pressing matter. No two days will be exactly the same, but the general responsibilities assigned to the Office PA will be consistent from office to office. You should expect to work at a desk, often in front of a computer and phone, in an office that may not even have a window or door. However, the job may also require you to be out of the office from time to time, taking care of pickups, drop-offs, and purchases. These **runs** might be done on foot or in a vehicle, but within the course of a day you could find yourself crisscrossing the city, taking a trip to the set, to the wardrobe office across town, or to the office supply store, all before even stepping foot in the office for the day. Expect the unexpected and plan for change.

What exactly is the job of an Office PA? In short, you are the assistant to *everything on the production*. Sounds like a big job, right? It absolutely is. Your work hours will vary, and days will be long. An Office PA is not a 9 a.m. to 5 p.m. job. You'll interact with almost every production crew member, so knowing the departments that comprise the crew and the positions within them is required. There are some really great and unique aspects of the role of an Office PA that are not found in other lines of work. An Office PA job isn't for life, it's for the life of the show (hopefully). How long can the job last? Do you need any special skills? What kind of work will you be expected to do? Clerical? Will you need to be a delivery person or a research maven? Copy master or logistics expert? Customer service representative? Snack provider? Yes. It is all these things, and more. And without you, the entire production system can break down.

RESPONSIBILITIES OF THE OFFICE PA

Here are some of the most common and necessary responsibilities of the Office PA.

1. TO BE THE FIRST LINE OF DEFENSE
   This includes answering the phone as well as greeting and assisting visitors to the Production Office.
2. TO FACILITATE COMMUNICATION
   Including distribution of production paperwork, via hard copies and email, relaying messages, and other information you have been delegated to share.

3. **TO GO ON RUNS**
   Pickups, drop-offs, delivering items from point A to point B (often from the set to the office or vice versa), making various purchases, doing airport transfers, etc.

4. **TO NOTIFY, SET UP, AND STRIKE MEETINGS AND APPOINTMENTS**
   Production is notorious for holding many, many...many meetings. For larger meetings, you may be responsible for notifying and reminding attendees of the meetings as well as setup and strike. You might also be asked to make appointments and schedule smaller meetings or make reservations and set up virtual meeting platforms.

5. **TO COPY AND SCAN**
   Making photocopies of documents needed for distribution and scanning documents for storage in the digital production files.

6. **TO FILE ALL THE THINGS**
   All production paperwork must be filed for easy access, both hard copy and digitally. Maintaining organized files is imperative. Know your alphabet!

7. **TO BUY SNACKS! (MAINTAIN CRAFT SERVICE)**
   A perk of working on a film or television production is the common practice for both the office and set to provide snacks and beverages throughout the day to all working crew. On the set, there is a dedicated **Craft Services** department to ensure the filming crew has sustenance. In the Production Office, the office staff must manage their own. A large responsibility of the Office PA will be purchasing, maintaining, and cleaning up craft service items and organizing the designated kitchen space. Yes, this means making coffee. This also includes preparing coolers of snacks and beverages to travel in vans that are taking crews on various location scouts.

8. **TO KEEP THE OFFICE TIDY, STOCKED, AND FUNCTIONING**
   When the copier is jammed, the Internet is down, the phones aren't programmed, or the producer needs a printer driver installed, it's the Office PA to the rescue! A little tech savvy will go a long way. The Office PA will also be tasked with making sure the office space is always tidy and presentable and stocked with office supplies. Remember, almost everyone on the production will stop by at some point or another. Make your parents proud, treat the office like they are coming to visit tomorrow, keep it clean and organized.

9. **TO DO RESEARCH**
   The office staff and crew rely on the Office PA to research best options for various purchases, rentals, and services. Don't underestimate the skill of navigating the information superhighway (aka the Internet!) to solve problems. The Office PA will be asked to research any number of items, from where to purchase water in glass bottles from Iceland, how best to recycle rolling office chairs, or find the top poodle grooming place for the lead actress's favorite pet.

10. **TO ORDER MEALS**
    The boss can't live on Chex Mix and Red Vines forever. The Office PA will be responsible for collection of and placing meal orders. The PC will generally have their own office lunch ordering system in place to manage meal requests.

11. **TO LEAP TALL BUILDINGS IN A SINGLE BOUND!**
    Okay, no, you don't have to be a superhero. However, the ability to lift up to 50 pounds will be an asset to the job. Provided you are physically capable, you

may need to carry tables and chairs from a storage facility to a conference room, assemble a bookcase, or help rearrange furniture. There will always be a need for a little bit of heavy lifting.

12. TO PROVIDE SERVICE WITH A SMILE
    Sometimes the Production Office will be asked to assist with personal requests from cast members, Producers, or Directors who may not have assistants. The PC will direct you to help complete these requests and determine what is urgent and how best to handle them. By doing these kinds of tasks, you've helped make sure the production has not been delayed.
13. TO DISTRIBUTE MAIL AND PACKAGES
    All day, every day the Production Office will receive mail and shipments for all of the departments. Logging them and ensuring they are delivered to the right department is critical.
14. TO BE ON TOP OF IT
    Tasks and assignments will be ongoing. Your job is to willingly complete the assignment as instructed and with a sense of urgency. You got this! And that too, and that, and maybe that over there....
15. TO LEARN
    Take advantage of the fact that you are working in the nucleus of a production. Absorb the process, the interactions, the collaborations, and the problem-solving. Learning on the job is essential, and every show provides a unique opportunity.

You will continue learning to navigate the responsibilities of your role throughout your career, even beyond your work as an Office PA. These are not one-time tasks but evolving and cyclical. Assignments in each Production Office will be nuanced, and you will have to adapt on each new show. As your career advances, your knowledge of these basic job functions will allow you to be a better manager.

Even with all the things that make being an Office PA so awesome, you might find that your passion ultimately isn't in an office setting, and that's okay! It's still a great foundation of experience that can lead you to a job on the set or can be applied to another career entirely.

How Long Is the Job of an Office PA?

Production is booming. This means many opportunities for you to find work in a Production Office!

The number of days, weeks, or months it takes a show to progress through the start of pre-production through post production is called the production schedule. Most content can be defined in two categories: television programming or a theatrical motion picture. A **one-hour primetime episodic television drama** will have a different production schedule than a **half-hour episodic television sitcom**. Broadcast Networks often order more episodes per **season** than a streaming platform. The more episodes in a season, the longer the potential employment period. Feature films will also maintain their own unique production schedules based on the time of year, location, cast availability, or story needs. Knowing what type of project you will be working on will determine how long you can potentially expect to be employed. It could range from a few months on a television **pilot** or independent feature, to up to a year or more on a Network TV series or big budget feature film. We will expand more on this in

28 Unlocking the Role of the Office PA

Graphic 3.1 Why being an Office PA is awesome!

Section 9. Production schedules vary, and this means the pace and workload for you and the Production Office will need to adapt along with them.

There is no guaranteed timeline for employment from show to show. Some larger shows will prep for weeks and months and could be in principal photography for 80 days or more with a few wrap weeks on the end. Smaller shows such as a television pilot may only prep for a month, film for a couple of weeks, and wrap in a week or two. On a television series, the show is in a constant state of prepping, filming, and wrapping as you move through the episodes to be completed for the season. There are also times when a show may shut down, be it due to lack of financing, cast availability, or simply a Network cancellation, and you may find yourself unexpectedly unemployed. However, there is no lack of production in major hubs, and you'll hopefully be hired on the next show.

Employment on a film or television production is considered **"freelance,"** and you are typically hired as an "at will" employee, meaning you can leave the job at any time, and at any time the job can leave you. You could find yourself working on as many as 20 different productions within a year, or just one. This is the nature of the work, and it can be a challenging adjustment from a more traditionally stable career path. Section 7 goes more in depth on navigating this type of employment.

THE PRODUCTION OFFICE CYCLES

Office PAs are some of the first crew hired onto a production and usually the last to be released after filming is complete. Unlike a Set Production Assistant, who is only employed for principal photography, the Office PA is needed in pre-production and for wrap once principal photography has been completed. This timeline is determined by the PC and the budget dictated by the UPM based on the needs of the show.

In Section 1 we identified in which aspects of the production process an Office PA would be employed: pre-production and principal photography, commonly referred to as prep, filming, and wrap. Each step follows a specific daily schedule that dictates what is intended to happen each day.

"PREP"/PRE-PRODUCTION – The beginning of the production process, formulating the plan for how the project will be created. This includes departmental meetings and location scouting as well as casting and script revising. Office space is secured and outfitted for work, crew are hired and begin their involvement, and vendor deals for equipment and other rentals are secured. Outside of the office, the sets are being built, rigged with equipment, and being dressed to look like "real" life or fiction.

In order to keep everyone on the same page and where they need to be, a daily pre-production schedule (prep schedule) is issued by the Production Office. It is created in collaboration with the 1st AD to track meetings, scouts, fittings, and other production-related events that occur solely during the prep period.

"FILMING"/PRINCIPAL PHOTOGRAPHY – The process of filming the script. Cameras are rolling, actors are performing, and every day pages of the script are recorded and making their way onto the screen.

The **one line schedule** and daily **call sheet** are generated by the AD department for and during principal photography, which dictates the scenes scheduled for each day of filming.

"WRAP" – This is the end of the production process. Crew complete their work, ensuring there are no loose ends, and provide a clear road map of how their work is documented. Office space is broken down, and equipment and other rentals are returned to vendors. Production documents and materials are handed over to post production and the Studio. While there is no formal document that dictates the daily wrap schedule, crew will have a finite amount of days to complete their work. This will determine the pace of the wrap process.

Prep → Film → Wrap → Repeat

At different points during the production schedule, the responsibilities of your job will be focused on either pre-production, principal photography, or wrap. Most of the time you'll be dealing with aspects of all three.

The process that happens in order to create the production plan in prep, maintain support of the filming crew during principal photography, and then to eventually wrap out the show, is essentially the same from project to project. This is the production's workflow. On a feature film, the majority of pre-production will happen before filming begins, versus on a television series, which may cycle every seven to ten days, and the pre-production steps start over for the next episode.

Feature films will generally complete one workflow cycle of pre-production, filming, and wrap. However, on most television shows, the production process will be a continuous cycle. Each episode is prepped, filmed, and wrapped, one after another until all of the episodes have been filmed. As episode 2 wraps filming, you will simultaneously be finishing prep for episode 3; as you are filming episode 3, you are prepping episode 4 and in post production on episode 2. During principal photography, some shows will **cross-board** episodes. This means filming scenes from multiple episodes grouped together, similar to how a feature film is scheduled, instead of one episode at a time. There may also be days where two episodes are filming on the same day. This is called a "double up" or "tandem" day and means the previous episode is finishing as the next episode is starting, all within the same filming day. Sometimes this will require two units working simultaneously in different locations. Each episode requires its own dedicated prep period, which includes a pre-production meeting, location scouts, production meeting, table read, and a tech scout, all of which the Production Office must coordinate with the AD department. In addition, you can anticipate new drafts of scripts, schedules, and other production paperwork to be issued continuously throughout the prep and filming periods. While your job assignments won't change based on a particular production schedule, the workload will need to adapt to the particulars of the show type. More on show types in Section 9.

Each department will have their own process to address the needs of each new episode in the show's production cycle. This may include guest cast hires, costume fittings, special equipment rentals, new sets (either found in a practical location or by having one built), equipment rigging/striking, set dressing, etc. The Production Office supports all these processes.

Often in television, guest directors are brought in for each episode. The Director of Photography, 1st AD, and Editor may also rotate between every other episode, creating an "even episode" team and an "odd episode" team. This means that it is imperative you pay close attention to who needs to receive specific paperwork distribution for each episode.

Diagram 3.2 represents how a feature film or episodic television show progresses through prep, filming, and wrap, from the perspective of the Production Office. They anticipate what needs to be done to support each part of the process. In this diagram, four key components are identified: script, schedules, meetings, and scouts. Each of these elements will require specific actions, such as distribution of script revisions

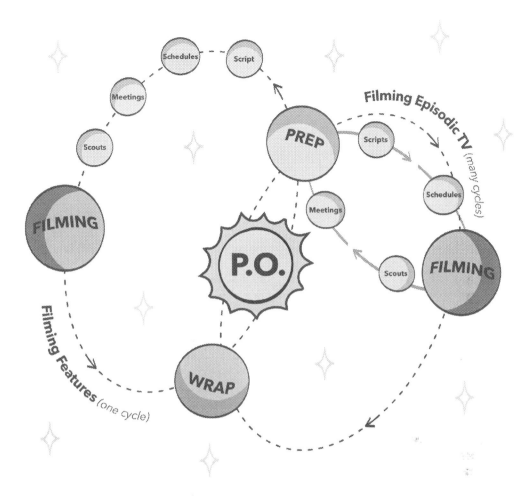

Production Office Cycles

Diagram 3.2 Solar system represents cycles of filming.

and schedules, setup and **strike** of meetings, and preparing for scouts. Often, these will occur simultaneously. The office collaborates with other departments within each phase of the prep-filming-wrap production cycle to ensure the production needs are met. The Office PA is assigned specific tasks to support each of these components. What these tasks include and how to successfully complete them are detailed in Section 4: "Making It Happen, Behind the Scenes."

WORKING HOURS

When you take a job as an Office PA, it is important that you are aware of the time commitment expected of you daily and over the course of the show. Work weeks on a film or television production are usually based on 60 hours. In a five-day week, it breaks down to 12 hours each day. You are considered an hourly employee, and generally your minimum pay will be based on a 12.5-hour workday, allowing for a 30-minute lunch break, which may or may not be a working lunch. Fortunately, some productions will provide lunch, an unusual perk. There are days you may be asked to work longer hours, and on rare occasions, usually in prep or wrap, your workday may be shorter.

The general start time for the film crew to report to work on set each day is the **crew call**. This will vary throughout the week in order to ensure the cast and crew have enough rest from one day of filming to the next, or due to production needs such as a scene that needs to be filmed at night. There are numerous Union and Guild regulations for rest periods, which will also dictate **turnaround time** from one day to the next.

The Production Office supports the needs of the production, no matter what time of day. Thus, the office is typically open at least one hour prior to crew call, but no later than 9 a.m., and remains open at least an hour after the company completes filming or wraps for the day. As a rule, the office will need to be open during regular 9 a.m. to 5 p.m. business hours in order to conduct business with vendors. What happens when the crew call is 12 noon? Does that mean that your day would start at 9 a.m. and continue until the company has wrapped for the day, which at best will be 1 a.m.? In a Production Office that is appropriately staffed, no. Your workday will most often stick to the 12 hours.

If the company is filming nights, it is up to the discretion of the UPM whether the office will remain staffed overnight. There are two schools of thought on overnight Production Office staffing. One approach is that there isn't a lot the office can do at 3 a.m. that can't also be done by the production team on set. Thus, the office may close at midnight or after crew is back from lunch. Conversely, if an emergency should arise, then the office is there to support them no matter the hour.

Typically, the Production Office staff will have staggered **call times** with an early, mid-, and late shift to avoid working anyone over 12 hours. Chart 3.3 demonstrates an example where crew call is 12 noon and the Production Office is staffed with two Office PAs, a Production Secretary, an Assistant Production Coordinator, and a Production Coordinator. The early shift would arrive one hour before crew call and handles any prep needs for the day. The mid-shift arrives at crew call to support the early staff and any immediate needs. The late shift could arrive up to two hours after crew call and handles wrap. Work shifts are at the discretion of the Production Coordinator based on the needs of the show.

Within the work week, start and end times will adjust with the call time. Some coordinators may opt to rotate the PA shifts from week to week, so no one is stuck on the same shift for weeks in a row, giving them a chance to deal with personal life matters during non-working business hours. If you are the "late PA" that week, your shift may start at 2 p.m. on Monday and slide to as late as 7 p.m. or 8 p.m. by Friday if the filming company is transitioning into overnight filming and requires overnight staffing. When the company is filming overnight from a Friday into a Saturday, it is jokingly referred to as a "Fraterday," implying that your Friday blends into your Saturday.

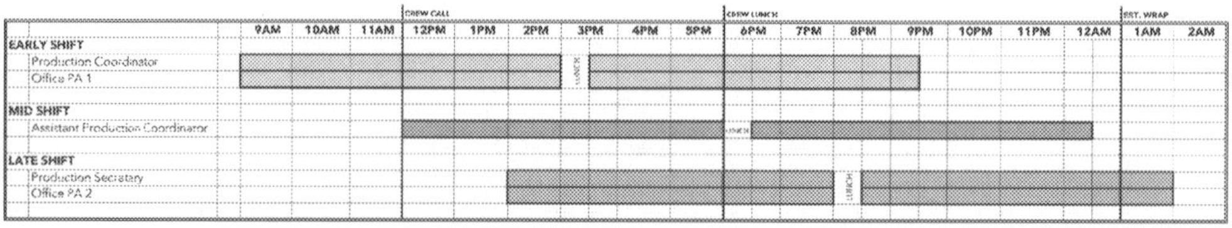

Chart 3.3 Sample work shifts of office staff.

JOB SKILLS AND TOOLS

As an entry level position, the skills needed to be an Office PA do not require certifications or specific education. Working the job itself will be your training, and you'll learn as you go. The job will inherently become "PA school," but rather than being lectured to in a classroom, you'll be thrown day one into the production machine, spinning 90 miles an hour, and be expected to speak, act, and think as if you already know what you are doing. Good thing you have this book!

A majority of the work you'll be performing will be at a computer. So basic computer skills are needed. You'll need to know how to present information clearly and concisely, possibly by creating a spreadsheet, writing a memo, and/or composing a competent email. Programs like Microsoft Excel, Numbers, Microsoft Word, Pages, and how to create and edit a PDF will be necessary for the job. Being able to navigate email programs like Gmail or Outlook as well as use digital filing programs such as Dropbox or Google Drive will also come in handy. In your proverbial toolbox, you should be equipped with skills in problem-solving, time management, organization, and planning. It is beneficial to have non-office-based skills, as well as being a good driver, knowing how to read a map, being detail-oriented, and having the ability to juggle tasks.

You will also be expected to provide and know how to use the tools needed to perform the job. This could be a laptop computer, as well as a cell phone and/or a reliable car with car insurance.

THE PRODUCTION CREW

When you watch the end credits for a movie, there are hundreds of names scrolling past (eventually yours will be up there too!) of cast and crew members who contributed their time, energy, blood, sweat, and tears to making the film. Each one deserves to have their name credited and respect given for the work they've provided. Just as a quarterback needs to know the names of all their teammates, the same goes for knowing your film crew, thus the importance of the crew list. You'll want to know who you are working with so when you need to deliver a package, you know who to go to. It is also important for them to know you. However, as we previously mentioned, the amount of production crew can be extensive, so while best efforts should be made to learn each and every person's name, knowing what they do is a good start.

Each phase of production (as diagrammed in Section 1) is responsible for tracking employees who deserve to receive credit for their work. During the production period, one way we keep track of those who contributed their time to the production is with a contact list known as the crew list. In addition to the crew employed for principal photography, often this list will include Editorial/Post Production, and sometimes a section for the **Production Company**, Studio, and Network contacts.

The crew list in the Appendix is an example of a relatively standard template. It lists the most primary roles and general job descriptions for the crew members in each of the various departments. This way you can avoid going to the costume department when you are looking for a Set Dresser. Depending on region, some shows may have a variation on the titles listed. Unlike the hierarchy organizational chart from Section 1, the crew list is traditionally organized alphabetically. With exceptions that the Producers, the Director, the Writers, and the production team are listed first. Learn the departments and positions, and as many names as possible on the crew

34 Unlocking the Role of the Office PA

with whom you work. It's a sign of respect if you can greet them by name. You are all part of the same team.

"On" and "Off" Production Departments

As we mentioned in Section 1, the Production Office is not just the well-oiled team behind-the-scenes, but also the physical location where many departments operate in the pre-production period. Working in the Production Office, you will cross paths daily with crew members from other departments and will need to know how to appropriately support them.

Once principal photography starts, the crew will be considered either "on" production or "off" production. The "on" production crew are the ones actively working on the set where principal photography is taking place. They are facilitating the needs for each shot in real time. These are departments such as Camera, Sound, Lighting, Grip, Hair, Makeup, and the Assistant Directors.

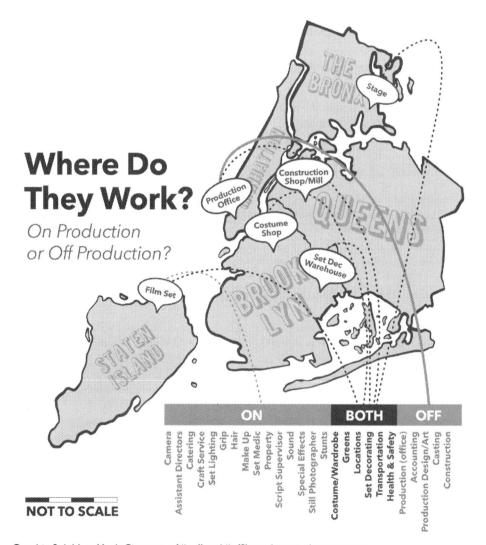

Graphic 3.4 New York City map of "on" and "off" production departments.

Unlocking the Role of the Office PA   35

The "off" production crew are the ones taking care of everything that was just completed or is coming up. They are not working directly with the filming crew but are making sure the next set is built and dressed, the lights are pre-hung, the trailers are parked, or the crew is paid. Some departments have a combination of both "on" and "off" production crew within them, such as Wardrobe, who will have "Set" Costumers, and Set Decoration, who will have an "On-Set" Dresser. You'll learn these intricacies over time as you gain experience with working crews, Graphic 3.4 gives you a glimpse of what the production footprint may look like.

The Production Office is considered part of the "off" production team, since they are not actively working on set, as are Set Designers, the Construction department, and Accounting. Most of the "off" production departments will be the ones with offices in the Production Office space. They are the ones employed on the project for a prep and wrap period and therefore need space to work more long term. You will likely be interfacing with these departments most often simply due to proximity. They are working down the hall. The scope of office care will extend to them as well. When they need another desk lamp, office supplies, or have an issue with an office machine, they will come to the Production Office staff for help. Knowing what departments have an office workspace is crucial for communicating information. Some paperwork will be distributed within the office at a centralized mail station, and some will need to be delivered to set. Lost paperwork due to incorrect distribution can cause problems.

Though the "on" and "off" production crew may be in physically different locations, they still rely on a close collaboration and work together to maintain schedules and coordinate production needs.

KEYS TO SECTION 3

- You don't have to be a superhero to be an Office PA.
- Office PAs are hired for pre-production, principal photography, and wrap. They are some of the first crew hired on and last to be released after filming has completed.
- Being an Office PA is essentially being the entire production's assistant, and you're there to help.
- The skills needed to be an Office PA can be applied to almost any job.
- Knowing the production crew and the job responsibilities for each department will help to avoid distribution errors and miscommunication.
- Learning on the job is expected.

We get it, starting out as an Office PA doesn't seem like the glamorous Hollywood career you were dreaming about when you decided to join the moviemaking circus. But this is just the ground floor, and an entry level job isn't forever. Whether it was a favorite movie when you were a kid, or a burning desire to tell stories that led you to this point, remember why you went looking for the key to get you in the door. It's up to you to turn the key. Every day you get to be a part of something bigger that could inspire the next you to come knocking on Hollywood's door. Now that you know what the job is, let's learn how to do it.

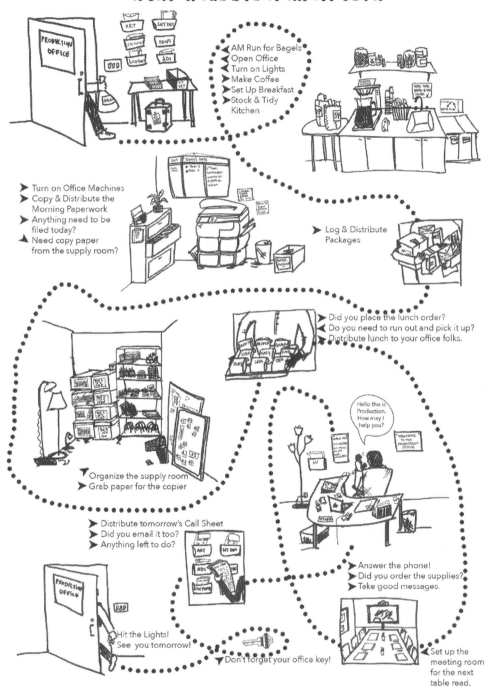

Graphic 4.1 A day in the life of an Office PA.

4 MAKING IT HAPPEN, BEHIND THE SCENES

Everything the Production Office does ultimately supports how the show functions as a whole. However, some aspects are focused more on internal Production Office operations, such as the actual setup of the office space, and others are focused on external production support, such as document distribution and assisting with cast and crew travel. Now that you know the purpose of the Production Office, where your work will take place, the commitment expected of you, and what the responsibilities consist of, let's break it down. Moving forward, we will explore the very specific tasks of the job with the step-by-step processes involved in successfully completing each one. Every single day will require your attention to detail, use of common sense, and efficient completion of the work described here in order to support the office and the production.

Production Coordinators may have their own preferred approach to how these tasks are completed. However, in general, these basics will apply.

PRODUCTION OFFICE SETUP AND WRAP

The setup, organization, and upkeep of the Production Office are at the discretion of the Production Coordinator. Their first responsibility when they are hired onto a show will be to set up the Production Office. Often, an Office PA will also be hired to start at this early stage, because setting up a Production Office is a big job. The Production Office space may be **"turn-key"** where most of the infrastructure is already in place, i.e., furniture, phones, Internet, etc.; or the office could be completely empty aside from its four walls and will need to be outfitted to function as an office. It could be an empty warehouse or a series of hotel rooms. The office space itself will have been secured before you start on the project, and your Coordinator and UPM will have devised a plan for setup, which you are there to help make a reality.

Here are the areas and potential tasks you may be assigned during the initial Production Office setup.

Furniture and Workspace

Will the furniture be purchased or rented?

You may be asked to assist the Production Coordinator in determining quantities needed. Who will be working in the office space, and how many people need to be accommodated? Remember that most "off" production departments will have an office workspace. Rented furniture will be delivered and installed by a company.

DOI: 10.4324/9781003252825-4

If the show opted to purchase furniture, you will be called on to help assemble and place furniture in offices. Having a knowledge of how to read IKEA instructions will be helpful!

What kind of furniture is needed?

A typical single office setup will include a desk, desk chair, one to two guest chairs, a bookcase, a filing cabinet, and likely additional lighting. The Production Coordinator will determine what will ultimately be required. However, you may be asked to assist with reaching out to department heads and asking if there is any specific furniture they require. Six-foot or eight-foot tabletops are incredibly useful and allow work to be spread out, unlike a single desk. The Production Office will need tabletop workspace for daily operations. Other departments may require this as well. Never underestimate the infinite need for a traditional folding table.

When you've been asked to assist with placing furniture in offices, think through the need and purpose of the furniture to make sure it is ready for use. A desk without a chair or a lamp without a light bulb isn't functional.

What is the workspace?

Another thing to consider when acquiring furniture is the type of workspace needed. Production Offices will traditionally have a combination of workspaces. This usually consists of private offices, larger departmental offices that will house multiple members of a single department, a separate bullpen area, a copy room, a kitchen, and a conference room or meeting space. Not all workspace is an office; some areas may need storage cabinets or additional shelving to accommodate various storage needs, like craft services and office supplies. Setting up the various workspaces may fall to you. Graphic 1.5A provides an example of a Production Office floor plan.

When does everything need to be set up?

Often crew will have staggered start dates. That's good news for you, because trying to set up 11+ offices in a day would be a bit of a challenge! Work with the Production Coordinator to prioritize what departments will need offices first and focus on them.

Office Machines

What office machines are needed? Will they be rented or purchased?

If an office is turnkey, it may already have some office machines in place. Your Production Coordinator will determine what supplemental machines are needed. It may be more cost-effective for the show to purchase printers, televisions, and computers rather than rent them long term. Copy machines and phone systems will almost always be rented. You may be asked to help research vendors for both rental and purchase options.

Who needs an office machine?

Some individual offices may require their own printer or computer. Often executive offices, Accounting, and the Art department need a dedicated setup. Accounting needs secure systems to confidentially process payroll and bank transactions. The Art department may need a dedicated color printer for printing on-camera visuals. And yes, it's a good idea to consider giving the Executives a dedicated printer rather than having to calm a frustrated Producer who is unable to print. You'll work with the Production Coordinator to determine the needs for each department.

How does it work?

In the instance the production has chosen to purchase office machines, and even sometimes with rentals, you'll be asked to assist with driver installations, machine settings, and ensuring they always have support items like paper and toner. Phone systems will need programming. If the production is acquiring cable television or setting up a streaming service, you'll need to know how to navigate it.

File Storage

Whether it is a bankers box or a filing cabinet, a file storage system must be set up to hold crucial original production documents. How office files are organized will be up to the Production Coordinator. An example of file organization structure and sample standard file names and label templates is located in the Appendix as "Day File Labels," "Production File Labels," and "Production File Organization" chart. You will likely be responsible for building the files. How to create production files is expanded on later.

Keys

The Production Office is responsible for distributing office keys and will keep a copy of every door key in the Production Office. You'll work with the Production Coordinator to determine quantities, make copies, and log and distribute keys to the various departments. Some departments may also need keys to offices other than their own, such as to the Production Office. Transportation and the Assistant Directors (ADs) may need to access the office when it isn't open to collect items for the set. This applies to key cards or door codes if your office has a more sophisticated locking system.

Office Supplies

The Production Office will always keep a stock of basic office supplies on hand. An initial bulk order will be placed in prep, and departments can request items be ordered as needed throughout prep, production, and wrap. Supplies will need to be stored in a location that is easily accessible, such as a centrally located storage cabinet or shelving. It may need to be able to be locked to avoid theft. The Office PA will be responsible for supply organization, inventory, and ordering. A general sample office supply order can be found in the Appendix "Office Supply List".

First Aid

Paper cuts, headaches, or stubbed toes are all potential hazards in the Production Office. Keep a stocked first aid kit on hand.

Vendor Services

Utilities

Utilities are things like phone lines, Internet, power, and water. While it is unlikely, you'll need to assist with anything power- and water-related, you may be called upon to meet a vendor for installation or for work orders early in pre-production. Work with the Production Coordinator to determine what utilities are not part of the office rental and need to be set up. You may also be asked to assist in determining the number of phone lines and Internet connections each office needs. What office machines need to be connected to a wireless port? Where are the routers located? How does each office connect to the Wi-Fi or hard-lined Internet? This will be the first question you'll be asked when a new crew member starts.

Trash and recycling

Check with the Production Coordinator regarding the office trash and recycling program. Is there a janitorial service that comes in daily or weekly? Will you be responsible for taking out the trash and recycling each day? Where does it go? Know the process. In addition, you'll be responsible for making sure each desk as well as the common areas have a trash can and recycling bin.

Distribution

Wall pockets

Even with the push for digital, some Production Offices will still have a central "mail station" where departments can check for any paperwork that has been distributed. Traditionally it is made up of either plastic pockets or paper 10" x 12" envelope "wall pockets" labeled and adhered to the wall. You will likely be asked to create this central mail distribution area if your office chooses to set one up. Each department should have a dedicated pocket labeled with the department name. Some departments may request their wall pocket be placed outside of their office door. Consult with the PC regarding your course of action. If a department has documents piling up in their mailbox, offer to take it to their office or give them a call so they know to come get it.

General distro

Some documents distributed on a production have specific regulated distribution assignments, but many will be made available to the general crew. These include:

- Crew list
- Pre-production schedule
- One line schedule
- **Day Out of Days**
- **Shooting schedule**
- Call sheets
- Location maps/directions

These documents may live on a labeled bookcase shelf or in a designated wall pocket filled with copies. You will be responsible for making sure there are copies of these items available for any crew member in need. Photo 4.2 is an example of wall pockets in a production office.

Photo 4.2 Photograph of wall pockets.

To Set Box

The Production Office will have a single dedicated location where items that need to go to set, such as expendables, actor contracts, and other paperwork, will be dropped until they can be delivered. This is the **"to set" box** (photo 4.3), and departments know to look for it in the Production Office if they need something to get to the set. It should be in a secure yet visible place in the office. You will be responsible for creating this (often out of a paper or large shipping box) and checking it for distro every so often.

Photo 4.3 Different types of to set boxes.

Mail and shipments

A basket for outgoing mail should be placed in a central location. This includes USPS mail as well as shippers such as FedEx and UPS. The Production Office (you) will be responsible for making sure the mail gets to a drop-off location each day.

Research what times the delivery services make their daily rounds to your office and investigate where the nearest FedEx, UPS, USPS, and DHL drop locations are and their hours and cutoff times for next-day delivery. Make sure all the office staff have this information, and consider posting a sign that tells when the last drop-off time is above the basket.

When shipping anything from the Production Office, always double-check the address and zip code an item is being sent to. Call the vendor or recipient if clarification is needed. We discuss shipping logs later in this section. You will likely be responsible for creating the log itself.

Office Signage

In the first day or so of opening an office, one of your first tasks might be to make wall signage. There are various kinds of signage needed to assist cast, crew, and visitors to the office: directional signage, identification signage, nameplates, and informational signage. Each type has a specific purpose, but all serve to make a visit to the Production Office as smooth as possible. If your PC allows, don't be afraid to be creative and colorful with your signage. Be sure you have approval to adhere to the wall before applying any signage.

Directional signage

This helps the crew navigate the office. You'll want to walk the office from the entry and identify the best placement for directional arrow signage. For instance, there should be a sign pointing to the Production Office from the hallway, a sign to the bathroom, and signs to the building exits if they don't already exist.

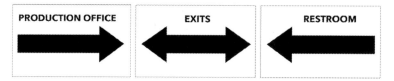

Graphic 4.4 Sample directional signage with arrows.

Identification signage

An identification wall sign can be just a piece of paper, with a border or without. BATHROOM, COPY ROOM, PRODUCTION OFFICE, and KITCHEN are some examples. It is also customary to put a sign outside of each department office so they know where they have been assigned and so other departments can find them. Your Coordinator might already have a template where you can just change the show name and hit "print."

| ACCOUNTING OFFICE | WRITER'S ROOM | CRAFT SERVICE AREA |

Graphic 4.5 Sample identification signage.

Nameplates

These provide the name and title of each person working in a particular office. Often, these are created for each department and for each crew member with a desk. Part of this is so everyone can find each other easily on day one, but also, it's a confidence boost, a sign of respect. Everyone gets a nameplate with their position on it, and it makes them feel important and a recognized part of the team. Everyone is important.

Graphic 4.6 Sample nameplates with names and titles.

Informational signage

Signage will be necessary throughout the office that provides the most commonly requested information. This includes the Production Office contact information, such as show name, Production Company name, address, phone, and production email. This is a helpful reference for crew members who may need it for shipping or supplying a phone number to a vendor. Signage with the Wi-Fi password and IP address should also be placed around the office. You will be responsible for generating and applying these signs.

The Fighting Pickle	**Printer Instructions:**	**Emergency Contact Info:**
c/o Company	How to connect via wifi	
123 Street Address	IP Address:	**HR Contact:**
City, State, Zip	Network Name:	
212.555.5555		**Production Safety Hotline:**

Graphic 4.7 Sample informational signage with addresses and contact numbers.

Some PC's prefer that wall signs and nameplates also have the Production Company or show name on them, some don't. It just depends; you'll be instructed accordingly.

Craft Services Setup

In regard to office startup, you'll need to make sure there is a locked storage space where office snack back stock can be stored (and find a secret hiding place for the key!). Ideally you don't want to be operating "item to item," and whenever possible, extra drinks and non-perishable food items should be stored on hand in order to restock the kitchen as needed. In addition, the Production Coordinator will likely arrange for water and coffee delivery services. Be sure you know when the deliveries happen each week and what supplies are scheduled for delivery.

The initial set up of the kitchen or craft service space will likely be dictated by the Production Coordinator and is worth careful consideration. Depending on the type of space your office has designated for craft services, be it a full kitchen, a break room, or a folding table, you may opt to purchase shelving or bins to store food. Some bulk food items can be transferred from their original container into a stay-fresh and refillable one. Other non-food craft service items you'll need to make sure to have on hand include plates (disposable or non), flatware or plasticware, mugs, hot and cold cups, bowls, napkins, and paper towels, as well as general kitchenware such as knives and scissors. It is also generally a good idea to make sure there is ice on hand. Hopefully, the infrastructure in your office allows for a sink, though this may not always be the case.

Kitchen appliances

When possible, the kitchen space should always include:

- Coffee maker
- Hot- and cold-water dispenser
- Refrigerator
- Toaster/toaster oven
- Microwave

Parking, Public Transportation, and Production Vehicles

What is the parking situation at the office? Is there parking available on site at the property? Are special arrangements needed for cast and crew to access the office or parking? Do they need a **drive on** pass? Is there space for VIP parking? Will spaces be assigned? To whom? Do delivery trucks have access to a loading bay? What public transportation systems can you use to get to the office? Does it run on a limited schedule? Research and scout out these answers so you can better prepare for when crew start reporting to work. Check with the Production Coordinator so you can help facilitate and relay this information when asked.

When the production is providing shared or individually rented passenger vehicles for daily production use, it may become the responsibility of the Production Office to manage them. This means ensuring vehicle keys are signed in and out before and after each use, there is a safe but 24/7-accessible location for the keys to be kept, and a way to communicate where the vehicle is parked. In addition, some shows may elect to label or "name" the vehicles in some way, such as with a sign in the window. For security reasons, using the name of the production isn't recommended; however, some shows have fun with it and come up with themes or use character names from iconic TV shows.

When cast or crew are being provided individual rental cars for work and personal use (such as when they are traveled to a distant location), they are responsible for their rental car during the course of the show. However, the Production Office, in collaboration with the Travel Coordinator, is responsible for keeping a vehicle rental log to track all personal passenger vehicles being rented.

Wrap

Everything that was brought in and set up in the Production Office will need to be removed. This may include discontinuing services, returning rentals, forwarding mail, collecting keys, boxing production files, selling purchases, or inventorying and storing assets. You'll be directly involved in assisting this process when the time comes.

PRODUCTION FILING

Production has no shortage of paperwork, and each document will have its place and purpose in the grand scheme of the show. The types and purpose of each are outlined in a later section. Whether generated and distributed digitally or via hard copy, these documents will need to be systematically filed and organized for reference and future use. The alphabet is a good guide for organizing a filing system both within your digital workflow server or in hard copy files. Filing preferences will be at the discretion of the Production Coordinator, and you will be expected to navigate the files so that nothing gets lost.

Both digital and hard copy files will be divided into sections and subsections according to their category and the type of document. You may have sections designated for the Art department, Production Office, vendors, etc., and within those sections you will have folders for set plans, templates, vendor-specific files and so on. The file structure setup may vary depending on whether you are on a feature film or an episodic series. It isn't uncommon to have general production files and episodic files in addition to day files. Sometimes the Studio or Production Company will provide an outline for how they expect the files to be organized and how the file names are to be labeled. Other times it's up to the Coordinator. A sample file organization and file-name guide can be found in the Appendix "Production File Organization" chart.

Every show will have specific files for each day of filming where you collect daily paperwork. These are referred to as **day files**. In Section 5, we will review the types of daily paperwork found in these files. It may be necessary down the line to refer to something that was filmed on a specific day during principal photography; hence, day files are commonly used in Production Office filing.

Graphic 4.8 is one example of how some production files might be laid out. Again, file structure will be at the preference and discretion of your Production Coordinator.

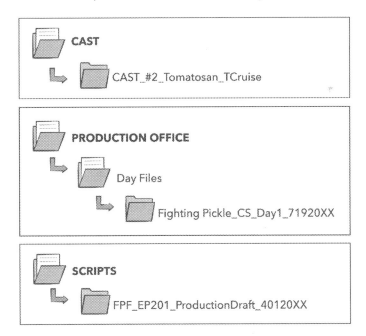

Graphic 4.8 Sample production file layout.

Production File Labels

Hard copy production files consist of two types of folders. You'll have the "hanging file" that identifies the main file category, which houses internal folders, each with a tab that identifies the individual folder content. Graphic 4.9 demonstrates this. For example, the hanging file might be labeled CAST, but one of the internal files might be labeled

PRODUCTION FILE ORGANIZATION

GENERAL (HARD COPY) PRODUCTION FILES

With approval from the Production Coordinator, this can be used as a general guide for initial production files set up.

CAST
- CAST LIST
- CONTRACTS
- DEAL MEMOS

CREW LIST
- (BY REVISION COLOR)

DAY FILES
- CALLSHEETS
- PRODUCTION REPORTS
- CAMERA REPORTS/DIT LOG
- SCRIPT SUPER REPORTS
- SOUND REPORTS
- SKINS/BACKGROUND BREAKDOWN

LOCATIONS
- MAPS
- LOCATION CONTACT LIST
- LOCATION AGREEMENTS
- PERMITS

MISC
- STANDARDS & PRACTICES

SCHEDULES
- ONE LINE SCHEDULE
- DOOD
- SHOOTING SCHEDULE

SCRIPT
- PRE-PRODUCTION DRAFT
- PRODUCTION DRAFT
- REVISIONS
- FULLY COLLATED

LEGAL
- APPEARANCE RELEASES
- CLEARANCES
- PRODUCT/MATERIALS RELEASES

VENDORS
- VENDOR LIST
- A-M
- N-Z

INSURANCE
- WORKER'S COMP CLAIMS

Graphic 4.9 Hard copy file organization.

CAST LIST. You will need to create a file label to adhere to the file folder; this will help easily and alphabetically identify the filed items. Most file labels will need to have as much identifying information as space and clarity allow. This might mean including the production and episode name as well as the season, in addition to the name of the document going in that folder. Sample labels ("Production File Organization" chart, "Day File Labels," and "Production File Labels." can be found in the Appendix.

How to Build a Bankers Box

At some point, when principal photography is over and it's time to wrap up the Production Office, you'll need to build a bankers box (Graphic 4.10) to store the files. It's exciting, you made it through the whole show, and now it's over. All you have to do is this final task – Build. A. Box. For some reason, it's not as easy as it looks, even though the directions are in fact on the side of the box.

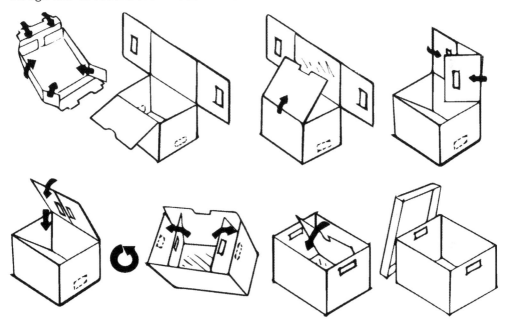

Graphic 4.10 How to build a bankers box.

Once files have been added to the box, don't forget to label the boxes with the production name and contents so they can be found later.

DIGITAL WORKFLOWS

Under the direction of their Studio or Production Company, many shows adopt digital platforms to manage document distribution and general production file organization, also known as a Virtual Production Office (**VPO**). A variety of software programs have been developed that emulate a basic email distribution and digital filing system; however, each program allows for additional customizations and features, such as adding watermarks to documents and generating production sides. Your Production Coordinator will advise you as to which system the office will use and what your involvement will need to be with utilizing that system. Some of your tasks may require learning the software and understanding how the office digitally manages documents and information.

One of the primary functions of the digital workflow is file sharing. Often if the Studio doesn't have a designated server, programs such as Dropbox or Google Drive will be used, and files will be shared internally between the Production Office staff. This way the team has access to the same documents no matter who is on duty or available. File organization will be dictated by the Production Coordinator. The files shared internally within the Production Office may include office templates such as logs, wall signs, and printer information sheets. It may include a master digital script to be used for sides, digital copies of sides for each day of filming, the production day files, the master crew list and vendor lists, and a master PO log, to name a few. This will be the place to come if you need to print fresh copies of interoffice documents or if you are tasked with updating any of them, and these files need to be kept up-to-date. This digital filing system will mimic any hard copy files you may keep in the Production Office and should be labeled to match. Refer to the electronic production files document in the Appendix "Production File Organization" chart. If a show is using a VPO system, it can be expected that all departments will be allowed access to use it. One of the features of digital file sharing is being able to assign access to specific folders of information to individual members of the cast and crew. For instance, the cast doesn't need access to the internal Production Office working documents, nor would you want them to have it. They would be restricted to access only the files and folders designated for them, such as scripts or call sheets. Some departments, like art and locations, may have their own department folders. The Production Office may be responsible for tracking and assigning access interdepartmentally to crew members for files they need.

Some Studios and Production Companies are using fee-based cloud storage services, which allow for more digital functions to support Production Office operations. These digital platforms help the office not only file documents digitally in the cloud so that the Studio can access them when they need to, but they also allow for Studio and crew to be direct-distributed documents on a daily basis. This takes email distribution to the next level, rather than it coming from an individual email account, distribution comes from the production cloud. Programs such as Scenechronize, Set Keeper, Prodicle, Yamdu, and numerous others exist to help support group distribution of documents. There are variations in the specific functionality of each program that are not expanded upon here. Your Production Coordinator will help you navigate using the system if it becomes part of your daily tasks.

Additionally, continuing the effort to go paperless, some Accounting departments are using similar digital systems to help manage the production accounting needs and workflow. These are often proprietary to the payroll company or a particular vendor whose services are being used on the production and may link with the payroll company's accounting software. We'll get into basic accounting later in the section, but you may need to become familiar with using web-based programs to file accounting paperwork, such as purchase orders, check requests, p-card expense logs, and even your timecard.

DOCUMENT DISTRIBUTION

Let's distribute some documents! This is exactly what it sounds like and means physically handing out or emailing production-related documents to the cast, crew, Studio, Network, Producers, and the Production Company. Often referred to in shorthand as "distro," distribution is a key function of the Production Office. It is ongoing from prep day one through principal photography. This includes everything from scripts to crew lists to **safety memos** and call sheets. If it contains information pertaining to the show, it needs to **fly** (be distributed). How documents are distributed varies from show to show. As a faster means of communication, many shows operate entirely digitally, either via a standard email program (like Gmail) or using VPOs. However, there are still many cases where a physical hard copy of a document is necessary, and you need to know how both are expected to be distributed. You might be thinking, "how hard is it to hand someone a piece of paper, send an email, or make a photocopy?" And you would be correct that common sense would be the logical course of action. However, this is film production, and we like to take the nuances a step further. Let's face it, step by step "how to's" exist because at some point along the way, common sense failed.

Each Production Coordinator will establish protocols for how documents and information are distributed. This will be based on preferences of the cast and crew members as well as what is dictated by the Studio, Network and/or Production Company. Confidentiality can also be a factor where certain types of distribution require specific security measures such as **watermarking**.

Below are the general practices regarding various types of document distribution.

Hard Copy Distribution

Hard copies are the traditional, non-eco-friendly distribution method. It requires lots of photocopying, collating, stapling, paper-clipping, hole-punching, labeling, logs, and physical delivery of documents to everyone working on the production. Not to mention the paper jams, toner explosions, and paper cuts you will inevitably have to contend with. In short, it's time consuming. All this is in addition to the digital distribution of these same documents.

As the Office PA, making copies is a primary assignment that must be done accurately. Missing pages or cut off information will lead to confusion and frustration to those receiving the document, and it will be your responsibility to ensure the copies are distributed correctly.

Not all documents are treated equal. Some have smaller "limited" distribution, such as only to department heads; other documents will distro "wide" to all cast, crew, etc.

Making copies

Before you set out to make the copies you've been assigned, be sure you understand the instructions. Know the following:

1. HOW MANY?
   The Assistant Coordinator or Production Secretary should be able to give you a count of how many copies of a document you'll need to run.
2. WHAT REVISION COLOR?
   You'll need to know what color paper you are copying the document on. Are the revision color and date clearly marked on the document? We'll discuss revision colors later.

3. TYPE OF FINISHING?
   Should the document be stapled? Three-hole-punched? Paper-clipped?
4. DOUBLE/SINGLE-SIDED?
   Can the document be copied double-sided? Does it need to be single-sided? Do some need to be double- and some single-sided?
5. DOES IT NEED TO BE SCANNED?
   Most documents for distribution are received by the office digitally. However, there may be the rare instance where a document needs to go out for distribution that is an original hard copy. In this instance, it is essential to make an extra copy and scan of the original. This way there is a backup should the original get lost or if it needs to be returned to the owner. The backup will need to be stored in the virtual and hard copy production files and will be used to make additional copies as needed.

Good copy habits:

- Run a test copy first. This way you can make sure all the copier settings are right. Sometimes important information at the edge of a page can be cut off or a hole punch will go right through crucial information. You don't want to run 75 copies before you notice an error. (It may be necessary to shrink the document slightly or reset a margin.)
- Consider marking the original with a yellow highlighter. Yellow highlighter does not photocopy. This way you can ensure you always know which one is the original document. However, legal documents or documents with original signatures should never be marked with yellow highlighter.
- Always save the master document from which you make copies. It should never be stapled or hole-punched (binder clips work great) and should be scanned and filed for repeated use. You may have to make the same copies again!
- Always remove colored paper from the machine after making copies, and clear all copy settings for the next person!

The recipients

Once the copies have been run or are in progress, delivery will usually be tracked by one of two traditional methods:

A LOG – A list of all recipients to receive that particular document. You'll check off a person's name once it has been delivered, or the recipient signs off upon receipt. This provides proof that each person received their assigned documents. (This is more common on shows with confidentiality issues.)

NAME LABELS – Some productions may opt to use a sticky name label that has been preprinted with the name and department or position of the recipient. Each label is then placed on the document being distributed to ensure each person receives the document assigned to them. Some PC's may have designated labels for each type of document. When adhering name labels, be sure they do not cover any information.

There are also instances when the Production Coordinator may elect for the office to operate on a "print on demand" system to maintain a more eco-friendly environment.

In this case, a crew member can receive a hard copy of the document upon request only. You will likely be tasked will filling this print request and documenting to whom it was given. Of course, they always have the option to print the document themselves if they received it via email.

Delivery

In Section 3 we discussed "on" and "off" production crew. This is where knowing whether someone is working on set or in an office will come into play. You may be asked to deliver something directly to a departmental office, have it sent to set, or it may go to a central distribution pickup area. This distribution area is often in the Production Office, and each department is responsible for checking in throughout the day to see if anything new has been released to their "mailbox" or wall pocket.

When sending distribution to set, you can use the designated to set box where distro lives temporarily until it can be delivered. Be sure to label the items with the person's name and department. Do not send distro to set that is meant for someone working "off" production. This will lead to the item either being returned to the office by a frustrated Set PA, or it will get lost on set, and that person won't receive their document.

There are times when certain documents being distributed will have confidential information on them, such as a cast contact list. This means the paperwork needs to be treated differently from other documents. It may be necessary to distribute them in sealed, labeled envelopes or face down on a desk. In no way should confidential information from these types of documents be given to anyone other than approved production team members.

Priorities

Production moves extremely quickly, and often cast and crew are urgently waiting on a script or schedule revision to be released so they can start or adapt their work to the changes. Prioritize the distribution to those who may need the document immediately, such as department heads or those who are designated VIP's such as Producers and cast. Some offices will have a distribution log or list that outlines the priority of who should receive documents first. When in doubt, check with the Production Secretary.

Electronic Distribution

Email is the most common and preferred form of information distribution. Many Production Offices will set up one dedicated production email account that the office staff will have access to use to send and receive information to/from the crew. Rather than having official production communication coming from an individual's personal account, this is a centralized email account managed by the team for that particular show. This also keeps the correspondence in one place. The Production Coordinator will dictate by whom and how this email account is monitored and managed. As an Office PA, this responsibility may come to you. Many VPO systems offer email distribution internally and operate much like an email account. Whether you are using Gmail, Yahoo!, Mac, Outlook, etc. or a web-based VPO, cast and crew contact information will need to be input, updated, and maintained frequently to stay up-to-date with the ever-changing production team.

Virtual setup

Groups – Batch email groups should be created within the digital system you're using (email account or web-based VPO) for easy selection when doing large e-blasts. Rather than having to type in a ton of individual email addresses every time a document needs to fly, one click to a group will do the trick. When entering email addresses, be sure to double-check spelling! Group categories can be general such as: CREW, CAST, DEPARTMENT HEADS, or more specific to document types: SCRIPT, ONE LINE SCHEDULES, CREW LIST, CAST LISTS. This will make it quick and easy when you need to send a specific document to a certain group of people, such as the Studio.

Labels – It helps to keep the email account organized. That means labeling and filing emails within the account under specific label headings such as: VENDORS, CREW, RESUMES, SOLICITATIONS, INVOICES, EPISODE 2, etc. An organized account allows for any member of the office team to easily access information at any given time.

Composing emails

- Header/Subject – the subject of the email should be clear and specific as to what is being sent. It should include the show name (or initials for longer titles), the production document name, and the date. Each PC will have guidelines as to how they or the Studio prefer email headers be listed.

- Signature – Use the email account settings to create a signature that has all of the Production Office contact information so that crew and vendors can reach the office. It should include the PRODUCTION NAME, PHONE, and EMAIL ADDRESS. If you are sending production paperwork via email, it may not be necessary to sign the email with your personal name and position – though it's a nice way for the crew to start identifying you. However, you should always sign your name if you're emailing phone messages or corresponding with individual crew and vendors. That way if there is a question, everyone knows who to call for the answer!

  For security reasons, we do not recommend including the physical address of your Production Office; however, some productions do elect to provide that information. Consult your PC regarding this decision.

- Content Language – If you have been designated to generate, read, or respond to production emails, make sure the PC has approved the language used so that all information is clear, concise, and formatted per their requirements. In most cases, short and to the point is best. Avoid trying to be too casual, cute, and funny; it can be perceived as unprofessional and is unnecessary. You'll also need to be aware of what information you are authorized to share. Consult with your Coordinator before including information such as filming locations and names of cast or crew.

- Attachments – Don't forget to attach the document! It should be labeled to correspond with the email subject header. Consistency is key. With so much information flying constantly, it is important that there is no question what the document is so it can be easily identified.

Graphic 4.11 is a sample email an Office PA may need to send.

Making it Happen, Behind the Scenes   53

```
┌─────────────────────────────────────────────────────────┐
│ NEW MESSAGE                                      _  X   │
├─────────────────────────────────────────────────────────┤
│ To:                                                     │
│ Cc: / Bcc:  Crew                                        │
│ From: FPProduction@email.com                            │
│ Subject: FIGHTING PICKLE - BLUE REVISED ONE LINE SCHEDULE a/o 5/04/20XX │
│                                                         │
│ Dear Crew!                                              │
│                                                         │
│ Please find the BLUE ONE LINE SCHEDULE as of 5/04/20XX, for │
│ "The Fighting Pickle" attached for your information and review. │
│                                                         │
│ Please contact the AD Department with any schedule questions. │
│                                                         │
│ Thank You,                                              │
│ *** (signature example)                                 │
│                                                         │
│ Production Office                                       │
│ "The Fighting Pickle"                                   │
│ 212.555.5555 phone                                      │
│ FPProduction@email.com                                  │
│                                                         │
│ [ + Attachment: FP_BlueRevOneLine_50420XX ]             │
└─────────────────────────────────────────────────────────┘
```

Graphic 4.11 Sample email with language.

Sending and receiving emails

One very important aspect when sending and receiving emails is the proper use of CC and BCC, "Carbon Copy" and "Blind Carbon Copy," respectively. When you "CC" someone, this means you are openly copying them on the email so that they, and the recipient, know everyone who received the message, and they can easily respond to the group. Your PC or APC may request to be "CC-ed" on all of your emails so they can stay informed of your correspondence. They may also "CC" you on emails that include information you may need to know. The "BCC" is usually used when you must send to multiple people on an email (as in most electronic document distributions) and do not want to reveal all the persons receiving the message. You may need to keep the email addresses confidential (such as with cast members), or there are just too many email addresses that show up in a chain. This also prevents the notorious "reply all's" that clog up email inboxes, by only allowing a reply to go to the sender. One person accidentally hitting "reply all" rather than just replying to you has now started a chain of 30 people responding to the 200 people who were CC-ed rather than BCC-ed on the email. As a general rule of thumb, it is better to BCC any email going to a large group of people.

When your PC, APC, or any crew member or vendor emails you directly – REPLY. Even if it's only to say "Copy," "Received," or "I'm on top of it!" It is important to verify you have received a message and are responding to it. If you are "CC-ed" on an email, be sure to REPLY ALL. Whether the email was just for your information or is a task to complete, you want to make sure everyone knows you have received the information and are reacting.

Tracking and Managing Document Distribution

A common phrase you'll hear from a cast or crew member is, "I never got it." Let's call this "distro amnesia." Despite the fact that the script was hand-delivered to a doorstep, emailed directly to the recipient, and a notification text was sent, someone will always claim theirs is nowhere to be found. Email distribution has made document tracking easier, and signature logs can prove receipt, but not loss once received. Ensuring logs, labels, email groups, and email addresses are continually updated and accurate will help prevent distro amnesia, as there is proof of the effort made, but managing distro is an ever-evolving game that can sometimes never be won. Good news! Most cases of distro amnesia can be cured with a new copy, another email, and a smile.

Recently it has become common practice that the process of script distribution has been delegated to the Script Coordinator on a show. While this is a relatively new position, it is more common in television than on features. They are part of the writing staff and responsible for managing script revisions, including working with the staff Writers and Showrunner / Executive Producers regarding formatting, copyedits, proofreading for writing style, story continuity, and historical accuracy. The Script Coordinator will also work with Production Legal to address potential clearance issues in the script. The email and/or physical hard copy distribution of scripts and script revisions is often assigned to the Script Coordinator. This can prove invaluable on shows where scripts are being revised daily and helps alleviate the demand on the Production Office.

Distribution logbooks

Distribution logs are a way to track both packages and documents that come in and out of the Production Office. They are generated by the Production Office and record names, dates, and to/from information as items are distributed between departments. Distribution logs are often still used, and some are managed digitally. The PC will dictate what documents need to be tracked and how to track them.

It is general practice that most departments will have their items shipped to the Production Office. For shows that are filming in more remote locations, this will become a necessity, as there may be fewer places to shop locally, and more online ordering will be required. There could be 16 or more departments placing orders that will be arriving daily! Logging every package that is delivered to the office and then whom it was distributed to becomes increasingly important. If a package goes missing, the logbook might help track it down. If a crewmember claims they did not receive a script, the log will reveal to whom the script was given or who signed off on receipt. The process can be tedious, but it's the best way to cover the communal office ass. You may be asked to create these documents in Excel, or your PC will provide templates.

Tables 4.12–4.15 are some of the types of logs that an office would create.

Key Log: To track who is given copies of office keys. Some office buildings will charge a lost key fee if all office keys are not returned at the end of the production. It is also imperative to know who has access to which office spaces for safety and security.

Table 4.12 Sample Distro Log – Key

Key Log					
Key Issued To	Room Number	Date	Total Number of Keys	Initials	Date of Return
F. Pickle	203	5/4/20XX	2	FP	

Making it Happen, Behind the Scenes 55

Shipping Log – Incoming: To track packages that arrive TO the office.

Table 4.13 Sample Distro Log – Incoming Shipment

\multicolumn{7}{c	}{Incoming Shipment}
Date Received	Packaged Received For	Department	Shipped From	Tracking #	Shipping Co. (Fedex/UPS/USPS)	Logged By
5/04/20XX	Luke S.	Art	Tatooine	7901202811X	FedEx	GL

Shipping Log – Outgoing: To track packages that are shipped FROM the office.

Table 4.14 Sample Distro Log – Outgoing Shipment

\multicolumn{7}{c	}{Outgoing Shipment}
Date Received	Packaged Received For	Department	Shipped From	Tracking #	Shipping Co. (Fedex/UPS/USPS)	Logged By
5/04/20XX	Tatooine	Art	Luke S.	072019830Z	UPS	JH

Your office may utilize this log to track packages from the office that are sent to set. This log is a way to identify when items are sent out and by whom (often you, but possibly via the transportation department) so they can easily be traced in the event the package did not reach its recipient. You should become accustomed to logging "to set" items just as you would FedEx or UPS packages.

To Set Log: To track any paperwork or packages that leave the office for SET.

Table 4.15 Sample Distro Log – To Set

\multicolumn{7}{c	}{To Set Log}
Date	To	Department	From	Item	Time Sent to Set	Sent to Set With
7/20/20XX	R. Two (Key Make-up)	Make-up	The MU Store (via package)	Expendables	10:59AM	Office PA

Script Distro Log (Graphic 4.16): To show who received which versions of the script, script revisions, when and by what method (i.e., delivery, email, etc.). This type of document-specific log may also be applied to other documents being distributed.

Cast Contact Info Log (such as **cast lists** and **cast deal memos**): To check off who was given confidential cast information. This log may look similar to the script distro log template.

Morning Distro Log (Graphic 4.17): To track the distribution of the paperwork received in the **football** every morning for the previous day of filming.

The amount of tracking logs that can be used is endless. Consult with your PC regarding the extent deemed necessary for your show.

56   Making it Happen, Behind the Scenes

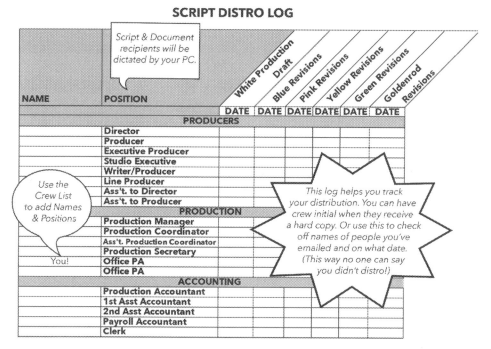

Graphic 4.16 Sample script distro log.

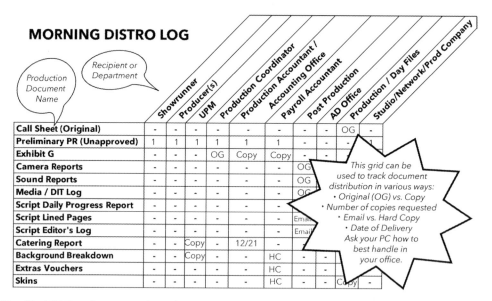

Graphic 4.17 Sample morning distro log.

OFFICE OPERATIONS

Office operations is essentially the support the Production Office provides to the other departments in order to facilitate their work and to help the show operate efficiently. This means providing services to departments through disseminating information, maintaining office machines, assisting with runs, greeting visitors, and the set up and strike of meetings and scouts. It is also to ensure snacks and lunches are procured. Each day will include some aspect of these support tasks, and the Office PA will be essential in completing them.

Office Equipment

Photocopy machines! Printers! Computers! And…. telephones! While it is not a traditional office machine, let's throw televisions in here as well. You don't have to be a professional copy machine technician, but you will need to gain a basic understanding for how the machines in your office operate, how to best maintain them, and know when they are in need of repair. Here are some key tasks associated with your everyday machines.

The copy machine

Most copy machines today are multi-function. They will photocopy, scan, staple, sort, hole-punch, remote-print, buy you dinner, play music, and compliment your outfit. Okay, maybe not the last three, but they certainly do a lot of the work for you. Knowing the scope of what your machine can do and how to use it will save you time. Why staple by hand if the machine can do it? Out of three-hole paper? That's okay, the machine can punch it for you.

We discussed copying in "Document Distribution"; however, here are some additional helpful common-sense reminders when working with the copy machine.

- Post a general "How To" informational sign next to the copier. This machine will likely be shared by everyone on the production. Help other departments out by posting some basics. This could include what paper is assigned to what drawer, tips on which way to feed a document, and whom to contact for help.
- Does your copy machine print wirelessly? Most copiers will be networked using your Internet to allow users to print remotely to the machine. Understand if/how the copier is networked for access by all office crew. You may need to help others connect to the copier for printing. A "how to connect to the copier" guide posted around the office showing the IP address of the machine and the differences if connecting a Mac computer vs. a PC will be invaluable.
- Paper, like people, comes in all shapes and sizes. Your copier may have multiple paper trays to allow for various size options. Scripts and schedules will be copied on traditional 8 ½" × 11" letter paper. Call sheets will generally print on 8 ½" × 14" legal-size paper, with a few exceptions. The Art department will print larger-scale "director set plans" on 11" × 17" paper. Be sure the correct paper is in each drawer of the machine and each drawer is well-stocked.

- Figure out how to clear a paper jam. A gentle touch is usually best when trying to remove paper lodged in places of a machine that paper should never be lodged.
- What supplies does the machine need? Are there spare staples? What is the inventory of copy paper? Is there enough of each size and revision color? What about toner? Nothing is more frustrating than a copy machine out of toner. Most machines will let you know when they are running low. Keep an eye on it. Always have backup toner on hand and know where to get more. Does it come from the rental vendor? Does it need to be purchased online?
- Always reset the copier settings once you complete a job. You may have just run 50 double-sided, stapled documents. If you just walk away, the next person needing a single one-page copy might not check the settings and end up with a mess of wasted paper. One helpful factor, though, is machines will usually reset on their own after a short time has passed.
- Always remove any color paper used when you finish a copy job.
- When running big copy jobs, consider others in the office who may also need access to the machine. If you have a job running for 30 minutes, that could create a problem, especially if it is the only copier or printer shared by the entire office.
- Help stop the spread of germs. A few times a day, take a cleaning wipe to the touch points on the machine.
- Some departments may have their own designated copy machine. You will be asked to assist with it in the same manner as well.

Office printers

When department offices are spread out over an office building, individual printers may be needed to support personal offices. These may be rented or purchased, depending on the production. Either way, you'll be asked to assist with them. Stay on top of this by:

- Making a log of who has printers throughout the office. What brand and model are they?
- Document what toner they take and where is it purchased from.
- Post connection instructions above each. Are all office printers networked? How do you identify a particular printer in your computer printer options?
- Check office printers daily to make sure they have paper and ink.
- Manage clutter. Any unclaimed printouts left on printers being used by multiple users can be set aside for their owner to claim but should be recycled at the end of each day.

Fax/E-fax

Faxing has mostly become obsolete in Production Office operations. Generally, offices no longer have a separate machine devoted to this capability; however, they may have an online digital fax account in place.

Phones

Other than projects that may opt to go without a landline, a phone system will be rented and installed as part of the Production Office setup (if not pre-existing in a turnkey-type office). You'll be asked how the phones function and will need to become an expert.

- Learn how to program specific speed dials.
- Learn how to put someone on hold and then retrieve the call without hanging up on them.
- Learn how to transfer calls, including forwarding to a cell phone.
- Learn how to connect a conference call.
- What phones have speakerphone capability? Some phones may need a special hardware installed for this function.
- What offices have separate **direct dial** outside lines (vs. an internal extension)? What are the numbers? Often, direct dial lines are assigned to specific departments where extensive calls are expected and may become cumbersome to filter through the Production Office. Direct dial numbers may be assigned to the main Production Office line as well as departments like Accounting, Transportation, and the Producers.
- Create and distribute a phone extension list or make sure phone extensions are listed on the crew list. Phone extensions are a set of numbers that allow you to connect to an individual's office landline and may be part of their direct dial number. List the department direct dial and extension when applicable.
- Learn how to set up, listen to, and change the voicemail from within the office and outside the office. You are responsible for checking the voicemail throughout the day and distributing messages.

Section 6 elaborates further on phone etiquette.

Computers

For the most part, other than maybe the Accounting department for confidentiality reasons, everyone who needs a computer on a show supplies their own. Having a general tech knowledge of both Mac and Microsoft computer operating systems and being able to assist with things like Internet connections, printer hookups, software upgrades, device compatibility, and contacts integration will be the most common asks.

Televisions

Television operations is likely something you've already mastered in your personal life. In the Production Office, you may be asked to assist with purchasing a television or setting up cable, streaming, or Internet service connections. Or simply help locate the remote control.

Runs

Errands, or as referred to in the industry simply as "runs," are assigned to the Office PA. Runs cover all manner of responsibilities from transporting people, picking up/dropping off equipment, or replenishing an urgent stock of peanut butter-filled pretzels. This also includes making runs to the film set to drop off important items and pick up paperwork; it will be a daily reoccurring event. You'll be asked to make many runs during your time as a Production Assistant. In Los Angeles, having a car will be a requirement for any Office PA job, but in other cities you may need a solid understanding of public transportation options.

Some offices have a "runs" board where they keep an ongoing list of necessary errands that need to be completed throughout a day or during the week. Keep an eye on it, maybe ask the PC or APC to assign you some runs. If you see a run that needs to be done – offer to do it! Many PAs really enjoy doing runs, as it is a chance to get out of the office for a bit. Runs are a part of our daily personal lives and likely second nature, but as with everything in this section, there is a specific way you will be expected to perform them for production.

Before you go

Before heading out on a run, make sure you have done your homework regarding all aspects of the task and are prepared for any circumstance that may arise.

1. *Notification* – Make sure your supervisor knows you are departing for a run. Don't just get up and leave the office.
2. *Destination* – Know where you are going. Review directions before leaving the office so you can estimate the length of time it will take you to complete the trip in traffic. Do not rely solely on your GPS. For some runs, calling ahead to find out about available parking, if they have the item you need, or if there are any specific instructions upon arrival is a good idea.
3. *Know the assignment* – What is the run? Are you doing a pickup? A drop-off? A purchase? Are you going to set? This will dictate any additional steps you need to take.
4. *What to take*:
    a. A form of payment. If you are making a purchase how are you paying for it? Petty cash? P-Card? Is it on a vendor account? Will you need quarters for a parking meter?
    b. A method of navigation. Whether you prefer a paper map or a navigation app on your cell phone, have a way to follow directions.
    c. Proper identification. This should go without saying, but make sure you have a current driver's license and car insurance.
    d. The item. If you are doing a delivery or item swap, do you have the item? Is it ready to go?
    e. A cell phone, fully charged, and a charging device.
    f. A contact list. Make sure you have a copy of the crew list and **vendor list** with you so you always have contact information if you need to reach the person you are doing the run for or if you need to reach the vendor.
    g. The individual. Are you transporting a person to a location or picking them up? Where are they? Do they need your assistance with anything regarding the run before you can leave?
    h. A list. If you are purchasing supplies such as craft services or office supplies, do you have a list of exactly what to purchase?
    i. Water. Keep yourself hydrated. If you are transporting another person, have a couple of bottles of water available for them just in case.
    j. Gas. As much as possible, report to work with a full tank of gas. It is a good idea to not let your tank get below half full.
    k. Always carry a notepad and pen.

l. A **mileage log**. Some productions compensate cents per mile driven for a work run; others will reimburse gas receipts. If you are being paid per mile, you'll need to keep a log of your starting and ending miles *for each stop*. You'll be asked to write the to/from destination, as well as the reason for the run. An example of a mileage log can be found in the Appendix.

5. *Have a clean car* – You never know what kind of run might come up. You may need to take the director to set or a cast member across town. Always make sure at least the inside of your car is free of trash and doesn't smell of old feet. You are representing the show. If you have been assigned a production rental vehicle, it is still your responsibility to keep it clean. Also, it is never appropriate to have drugs or alcohol in your car or on your person while on the job.
6. *Reliability* – Your car must always be in safe and working condition.
7. *Logistics* – Do you know the size of what you are picking up or dropping off? Can you carry it? Will you need a cart? Will it fit in your car or on public transportation?
8. *Time frame* – Some runs are more time-sensitive than others. Be sure you know the level of urgency associated with the run. Will the vendor close soon? Do you need to be back by a certain time?
9. *Feeding yourself* – There are times when you may be asked to go on multiple runs that will take a few hours. Check with the PC or APC if you need to stop for lunch while out. No one wants you to starve, but make sure they know if stopping for lunch will be part of the run.

While on the run

1. Call or text the office.
    a. When you arrive at your destination.
       Information changes quickly. There may be updates that affect your run.
    b. When you depart your destination.
       Make sure the office knows when you are on your way back and that you successfully completed the run.
    c. If you have a question!
       Don't assume anything. The store doesn't have the right kind of tea? Call and ask what a suitable replacement might be. The item to be picked up isn't ready yet? Call and find out if you should wait.
    d. If you get lost.
       It happens, even in the age of GPS. Let the office know there will be a delay in the run. Ask for help if needed.
2. Personal runs or errands should never be done on Production Company time.
3. Do not text and drive. In many states it is against the law to handle your phone while driving. This includes sending text messages.

Before you return to the office

1. Make sure you get a receipt if you made a purchase.
   A receipt must include the name of the vendor, address, phone, date, itemized list of items purchased, and the total amount paid. Some smaller vendors may

have more generic receipts. In this instance, take a business card or menu to accompany the receipt. Gas receipts must show price per gallon and reflect every gallon you pumped.
2. Call or check in with the office to let them know you are on your way back; is there anything else they need while you're out?

Cast and VIP runs

1. When dropping an item at a cast member or Producer's house, check with the Coordinator where the item should be left, and if there are any specific instructions, such as to leave it with the doorman or not to knock on the door.
2. Make certain your vehicle has sufficient gas before driving a cast member. You wouldn't want to run out halfway to your destination and be stranded with an actor who is needed on set.
3. When driving a cast member or Producer, *do not speak unless spoken to.* Focus on the road and the safety of you and your passenger. The drive is not social hour. Cast may use this time to focus on their work.
4. Drive with caution and consistency. Avoid being an aggressive driver, and keep your driving pattern smooth. Practice safe driving habits. Constantly accelerating and braking or taking turns at high speeds is not only unprofessional and unsafe but can create anxiety for the person you are driving.

Once the run has been completed, make sure your supervisor and team know. If your show uses a "run board," be sure to remove the run from the list. Check, and done!

The law and insurance

Parking tickets and tickets due to traffic violations are your responsibility. Always obey the law. As a personal vehicle owner, you are required to have car insurance. The Production Company will also carry non-owned auto liability insurance to protect the company. In the case of an accident on the job, your personal car insurance will come into play first. If you are driving a production-rented vehicle, make sure you have a copy of the Production Company's insurance policy in the vehicle. More information on accidents and workers' compensation is in Section 7.

Set runs

"Set runs" are specific errands to make drop-offs and pickups to the film set. As we've stated, every office has a "to set" box where departments can send interoffice envelopes, packages, equipment, and materials to their crew members working on location. There is often a collaboration between the office and the Transportation department with regard to runs. Check with your Coordinator regarding what types of runs are appropriate to ask Transportation for help with. A lot of times the Transportation department will handle taking the bigger items to set (the extra camera package likely won't fit in your compact!), but whenever an Office PA goes to set, they should check the to set box for anything that needs to go with them. All day, every day, there will be items that need to get from the office to the set and from the set to the office.

Getting to location

The Locations department will provide maps for the cast and crew to get to each filming location, as shown in Graphic 4.18 and 4.19. This is the best tool to use for navigation. There may be specific directions you will need to follow that a traditional GPS will not provide, such as passenger vs. commercial routes, local back roads, or special access that has been granted to the Production Company. If you are filming on location in New York City, your map may also include subway directions and a city block layout.

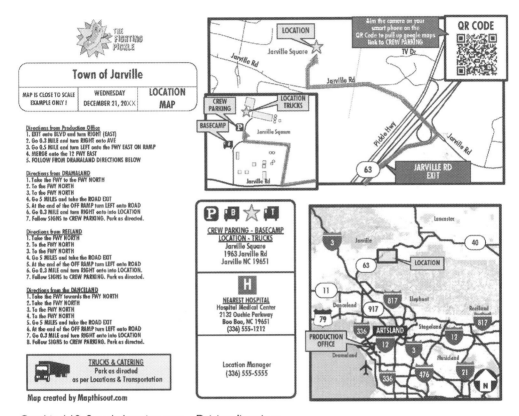

Graphic 4.18 Sample location map – Driving directions.

Navigating the set

The filming location is traditionally divided into five distinct areas.

1. The Set – Where the actual filming is taking place.
2. Basecamp – Where cast trailers, the hair, makeup, wardrobe, and other support trailers are parked, such as the production trailer or **honeywagon**.
3. Work trucks – Equipment trucks are parked closer to the film set for gear to get in and out quickly and efficiently.
4. Crew Parking – Where crew park their cars.
5. Holding/Catering – Where crew meals are served and/or background performers are held until needed on set. Sometimes this is the same area as basecamp.

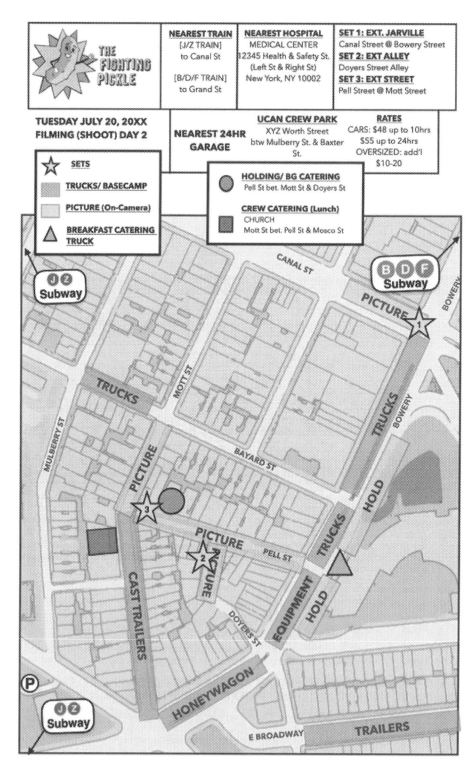

Graphic 4.19 Sample NYC Production Company footprint.

These areas can be spread out over a few miles or all within the same property. When you arrive on location, you will go to basecamp. The AD department will have a designated "production trailer" or a room in the honeywagon where you will drop off anything you've brought from the office. Make sure a member of the AD staff knows distro has been dropped off. The AD team will have assigned a Set PA to handle on-set distribution, who will then distribute it at the appropriate times to the appropriate people. There will be a "To Office" box in the production trailer where you can pick up materials that need to go with you back to the Production Office. This is production's own interoffice mail system.

Meetings, Greetings, and Scouts

The Production Office is relied upon to support the pre-production process. This includes preparing for meetings, location scouts, and assisting visitors (cast, crew, or otherwise) who may stop by the Production Office with a need.

A main component of pre-production for any feature film or television project includes meetings. Lots and lots...and lots of meetings. The good news is that for the most part they are generally the same type of meetings from show to show. On feature films, most meetings will happen during a dedicated pre-production period. In television, you are filming multiple episodes in a season and therefore will be continually holding meetings on a weekly basis, which are needed to prep each episode, all while still filming the current one. Meetings may be for a specific department or on a larger scale that include representatives from every department.

Location scouting is also a main aspect of pre-production. This is the process of seeking out practical filming locations and is managed by the Locations department. There will be a variety of scouts that happen that require the Director and creative department heads to travel to potential locations with the Location Manager. There are scouts to first find options for creative review, then to have the locations approved by the creatives, and finally to work out the logistics for filming, aka the **Tech Scout**. The Office PA is not responsible for scheduling meetings or scouts, nor will you be attending or directly participating in them. However, everything else associated with a meeting or scout you will be doing. This may include meeting setup and strike, preparing copies of any production paperwork needed, ordering food, preparing coolers, and notifying crew members about an upcoming meeting or scout.

It is common that every day in pre-production, a daily prep schedule will be issued listing the **prep meetings** and scouts happening for that day or week. Crew members are responsible for reading it and attending when requested. The Assistant Directors, in collaboration with the Production Coordinator, will generate the daily prep schedule. It is issued by the Production Office to the working crew. The 1st AD is responsible for running the meetings. Here are the most common types of pre-production meetings, and some of the people who attend these meetings. You need to be familiar with what they are for, and who generally attends.

Types of meetings

CASTING CONCEPTS

Purpose: Creative meeting to discuss cast of characters and what the Director is looking for in each role for the casting department to start the search.

Who attends: Director, Producers, UPM, Casting, the Writer, Showrunner (TV).

CASTING

Purpose: The process of casting the roles for the show.

On feature films, this process will likely be handled directly through the casting department, with the Director and Producers. However, in television, casting is an ongoing process for day players in each episode. Casting sessions might be held at the Production Office.

Who attends: Director, Producers, Showrunner (TV), and Writer-Producer (TV).

It can be argued that the casting process isn't specifically a "meeting." However, it will likely appear on the prep schedule and requires availability of key players.

SETS AND LOCATIONS MEETING

Purpose: Creative and logistical meeting to discuss what sets might need to be built vs. a practical filming location that needs to be found.

Who attends: Director, Producers, UPM, 1st Assistant Director, Production Designer, Location Manager, Showrunner (TV), sometimes the DP, and the Writer-Producer (TV).

PRE-PRODUCTION MEETING(S)

Purpose: Creative meeting. What are we trying to accomplish? This is the first big meeting and is an overview of the entire project, department by department. It aligns all departments on the show's vision and shapes the production plan.

Who attends: Director, Producers, UPM, 1st Assistant Director, Showrunner (TV), the Writer-Producer (TV), and department heads as available.

PRODUCTION MEETING

Purpose: Logistical meeting. This is where the 1st AD walks all department heads through how they are going to accomplish the show and discusses any production challenges. It is the last big meeting before filming begins and is a walkthrough of the entire project, script page by script page, element by element, department by department, in order to inform the departments of the production plan.

Who attends: Director, Producers, UPM, 1st Assistant Director, Showrunner (TV), the Writer-Producer (TV), all department heads, and any specialized departments.

SCRIPT TABLE READ

Purpose: A full read-through of the script with all invited cast.

Who attends: Director, Producers, Showrunner (TV), Writer-Producer (TV), Studio Representative, Network Representative, Production Company Representative, all invited cast members, sometimes UPM and 1st Assistant Director.

TONE MEETING

Purpose: Creative meeting to discuss the tone the show is trying to achieve, most often associated with episodic series.

Who attends: Director, Producers, 1st Assistant Director, Director of Photography, Editor, Writer-Producer (TV), Showrunner (TV).

LOCATION PHOTO SHOW AND TELL

Purpose: Creative meeting to present potential location options that have been scouted by the Locations department to determine if the look is in line with the show vision. Locations that are identified as possibilities will then be scouted in person.

Who attends: Director, Producers, UPM, 1st Assistant Director, Production Designer, Director of Photography, Location Manager, Showrunner (TV), Writer-Producer (TV).

COSTUME MEETING

Purpose: Creative meeting to discuss ideas for character costumes and looks.

Who attends: Director, Producers, 1st Assistant Director, Costume Designer, Production Designer, Director of Photography, Showrunner (TV), Writer-Producer (TV).

WARDROBE SHOW AND TELL

Purpose: A show and tell (yes, just like when you were in elementary school!) of the selected costume options and looks for specific characters, for final approval.

Who attends: Director, Producers, 1st Assistant Director, Costume Designer, Production Designer, Director of Photography, Showrunner (TV), Writer-Producer (TV).

PROP MEETING OR PROP SHOW AND TELL

Purpose: Creative discussion of any specific or unique props needed for the show. Can also be a "show and tell" of prop options selected by the Prop Master for final approval.

Who attends: Director, Producers, UPM, 1st Assistant Director, Production Designer, Prop Master, Showrunner (TV), Writer-Producer (TV).

STILLS/VIDEO MEETING

Purpose: Discussion of specific video playback needs, on-screen computer graphic builds, and still photos that need to be taken or acquired for use in the show.

Who attends: Director, Producers, UPM, 1st Assistant Director, Production Designer, Costume Designer, Set Decorator, Location Manager, Prop Master, Showrunner (TV), Writer-Producer (TV).

In addition to the most common meetings listed here, specialty meetings are also held as needed to discuss specific complicated sequences or events such as stunts, special effects, and visual effects.

Meeting setup

In some instances, it may be necessary to prep a conference room for a meeting. Meetings should be set up at least 15 minutes before the scheduled start time. Here are some factors to consider before setting up a meeting:

1. Is the room big enough to hold all attendees?
   Often the Production Coordinator will be responsible for securing the meeting room. It may be in a room at the Production Office or at an off-site location. Be

sure to ask what time it will be available for setup and by what time the meeting needs to be cleaned up. Someone may be using the space before and after you.

2. Are there enough chairs and table space for all attendees?
You may need to seek out additional tables and chairs in order for everyone invited to have a place to sit and a comfortable amount of space between them.

3. Is a speakerphone or video conference setup needed?
Does the room have existing technology, or do you need to track down a speakerphone or assist with setting up a video conferencing system? Some video conferencing systems require paid subscriptions. Check with your Production Coordinator if the company has an account.

4. Does there need to be food provided?
Some larger and longer meetings will have food provided. Including if it is a meeting being held during crew lunch with any "on" production crew members participating. Check with the Production Coordinator whether food will be needed. See the section on "That's lunch!" for specifics on placing an advance catering lunch order and meal setup procedure. Always make sure there are trash cans nearby. Water should always be available.

5. Is any production paperwork needed?
What type of meeting is it? Do extra scripts or schedules need to be copied? Check with the 1st AD regarding what they will need for the meeting.

6. Are any office supplies needed?
Have pens, notepads, and highlighters available.

Meeting strike

Once the meeting has finished and as soon as everyone has cleared out of the room, you can begin to restore it. Everything that does not belong in the room needs to be removed. Leave it cleaner than you found it.

Types of scouts

LOCATION SCOUT, AKA DIRECTOR SCOUT

Purpose: A creative scout. An in-person assessment of whether a practical location that has been preliminarily scouted by a member of the Locations department fits the creative look for the show. Often this is the result of the selections made in the location photo show and tell.

Who attends: Director, Producers, UPM, 1st Assistant Director, Location Manager, Production Designer, DP, maybe Showrunner (TV), Writer-Producer (TV), and VFX supervisor (if needed).

TECH SCOUT

Purpose: A logistical scout. The locations have been locked for filming. The 1st AD will walk through what will be filmed and address any final logistical needs. Each department assesses what they will need to do to support what will be filmed.

Who attends: Director, Producers, UPM, 1st Assistant Director, Director of Photography, Gaffer, Assistant Chief Lighting Technician (ACLT), Key Grip, Best Boy Grip, Production Designer, and select Art department reps, Location Manager, Assistant Location Manager, Set Decorator, Leadman, 2nd Assistant Director, Transportation Coordinator, Transportation Captain, Parking Coordinator. Sometimes also including the Showrunner (TV), Writer-Producer (TV), Sound Mixer, 2nd 2nd AD, and other crew members at the discretion of the 1st AD and UPM.

Requested attendance to meetings and scouts may vary from project to project. Consult with the Production Coordinator and 1st AD to confirm all anticipated attendees have been included.

Scout prep / Strike

Location and tech scouts are predominately coordinated between the Location Manager, 1st AD, and the Transportation department. Scouts can range from a couple of hours to an entire day to multiple days. It will be necessary to prepare snacks and drinks for the crew traveling in a vehicle from location to location. See later in this section under "Craft Services" for instructions on scout coolers. Coolers should be filled and loaded into vehicles ten minutes prior to departure. When the scout returns, coolers need to be emptied and cleaned for the next use.

Crew notification

In addition to the prep schedule, it may be necessary to call crew members regarding upcoming meetings/scouts or last-minute changes. A common phrase among crew is, "I didn't know about it." However, the Production Office is responsible for making sure every crew member requested to participate in a meeting or scout has been notified. You, as the Office PA, may be asked to make these calls. Here are tips when calling crew about a meeting or scout.

1. Always be clear about the TIME, PLACE, and what TYPE of meeting or scout is taking place.
2. If you leave a message, be sure to tell the person to call back and confirm they received the message. Make a note that you left them a message and whether or not they called back to confirm. You may want to keep a meeting call log. Don't forget to leave your callback number.
3. Make note if a person says they are unable to attend and inform the Production Coordinator.
4. Text notification is becoming more common. Confirmation that the message was received is still required, and always make sure the recipient knows who and/or what show the text is coming from.

Visitors to the office

At various times throughout production, visitors come to the Production Office, whether this is to attend a meeting, speak to a crew member, make a delivery, etc. They may be a member of the cast or crew, be expected or unexpected. Either way, they are there for a reason and you'll need to assist. Greeting those who visit the Production Office is also the best way to identify who should and shouldn't be there.

In the nicest way possible, greet everyone who walks in the door, and find a way to help direct them toward the purpose of their visit. If they are visiting a higher-up (a Producer, department head, etc.), then nicely ask the visitor to wait. Go to the person's office (or use the telephone intercom system if your office has one) and announce the visitor's presence. Confirm that they are available to meet with the visitor before bringing the visitor directly to their office.

If the visitor is a cast or crew member, see how you can help them get the information they need or escort them to the meeting room. If they are looking for another department's office, offer to walk them there rather than just giving verbal directions.

If the visitor is not there on production-related business, kindly find out why they have come. Is it to drop off a headshot or resume, are they trying to meet an actor, or are they making a personal delivery? Determine if you need to deflect or redirect them, or gently escort them out. Explain they should call to make an appointment with the appropriate person or email their headshot/resume. The office is a place where we don't like strangers hanging around. It's like the FBI; we have security issues and safety issues for our cast, crew, and the 400-pound safe in Accounting they might be planning to run off with (good luck to them!). It's important that we know who is walking in and what they want. If you're not sure what to do, ask the APC or PC.

In these instances, you are a crucial first line of defense, and how you handle the situation can have a huge impact. For example, an actor arrives for a table read and you nonchalantly tell them to go to the third floor and turn right for the meeting. They get lost and create a delay. Instead, take the time to walk them directly to the room, ask if they need a copy of the script, tell them where the bathroom is, and to help themselves to the available craft service you set up. You'd be surprised how grateful they can be by this simple assistance. In another instance, an unexpected visitor arrives at the PO looking for the Accounting department. Notify the department that they have a guest before you walk the person to the office only to find out it is a disgruntled crew member who immediately starts yelling at the staff and has been harassing the office for weeks. You now have to call security and have this person escorted off the property. A few procedural steps can save a lot of headaches.

That's Lunch!

When you are on a show, you often become immersed in the work. Your days are long, and the work is challenging, but you and the crew still have to eat! The Production department is there to help the crew get through the workday, and that means someone has to order lunch! This person will more often than not be the Office PA.

Lunch policies vary from production to production. Some shows will pay for department lunches during prep and wrap, some only during filming, some not at all and you will need to bring your own or go out. One philosophy behind the production-paid meals is that the "on" production crew is traditionally being provided a catered meal during filming, so those working in the Production Office should be fed as well. There are some shows that opt to give the crew on set a **"walk away"** lunch where a meal is not provided; however, a full hour of time is allotted for the crew to take a lunch break. In an effort to keep morale up, many producers recognize that food keeps the crew happy and working. It's needed to function, and everyone deserves a break to replenish their energies. Some departments will take care of meals internally. For instance, the Art PA may order lunches for the Art department. The on-set crew is provided lunch by the Catering department and therefore is not the responsibility of the Production Office. Check with your Production Coordinator to find out what the company policy is on lunches for the office staff. Is the production paying for it? Who is included? If production isn't paying for it, will the Production Office still be responsible for collecting, ordering, and delivering lunch orders? Everyone loves a "free lunch," so it is important to know the parameters so the UPM isn't surprised with an over-budget lunch receipt.

Lunch orders for the office will either be individual orders or a catered option from a restaurant. In either case, you may be responsible for selecting where to eat that day, placing the orders, and distributing meals once the food arrives. Having a collection of menus, also known as the "menu book," of nearby (reasonably priced) restaurants with different varieties of food types is common in offices. It's recommended to call the restaurant in advance to confirm they are open and taking orders ahead of circulating menus. To help you avoid grumbles that aren't coming from hungry tummies, below are the basic "how to's" when handling lunch duty.

Individual orders

1. Collecting orders – Check with your PC/APC if they have a preferred method.
    a. Scenario 1 – Make copies of the menu for everyone who is placing an order and hand them out at the start of the day. Make sure the crew knows that orders must be in by a certain time, that they should mark what they want on the menu, and be sure to write their name on the menu itself.
    b. Scenario 2 – One menu is passed around with a lunch order sheet with everyone's name listed that are approved to order. The lunch order sheet should have a column for the individual's name and a blank space for them to write in their order. Make sure you can read the order.
    c. Scenario 3 – Set up a digital order form such as a Google doc and email a menu link to those approved to place an order. They can then type in their name, order, and comments directly into the doc and send it back to you for the group order.

2. Payment – If production is paying, you'll need to get cash or a p-card from the Coordinator. If each individual is paying, you'll need to collect money from each person. Track how much they gave you and ensure they receive the right change. When Production is paying, there is likely a spending limit per individual order. Ask your PC what it is and make sure the limit is clear on the order form.

3. Order details – Double-check that all orders have included specifics such as sides, salad dressings, food allergies, etc. You will be asked for these details when placing the order. Rather than having to hunt someone down or guess, you'll already have the answer.

Ordering

1. Call the restaurant. Find out if emailing or placing an order online is possible. There is less room for error if they receive it in writing.
2. If calling in the order, make sure the person taking the order reads it back so you can confirm accuracy.

3. If ordering online, be sure to double-check each item as you make the selection and include any comments or preferences provided by the crew member.
4. Find out the total cost.
5. Ask when it will be ready for pickup.
6. Ask them to label each order with the individual's name, or a number that you can correspond to each persons' name. Sorting through food to figure out what is what and what belongs to whom is incredibly time consuming.

Picking up the order

1. <u>Always get an itemized receipt.</u> Make sure the name and address of the restaurant are on the receipt. Make sure the receipt is dated. If the name/address isn't printed on the receipt, get a menu and/or business card from the restaurant.
2. <u>Check that the order is complete.</u> Check the bag to confirm everything on the order is there *before leaving* the restaurant. Make sure there is plasticware, plates, and napkins.

Once you return to the office, hand out the orders hierarchically (meaning the boss eats first!), including plates, napkins, and plasticware, and return any change. If Production paid for the meal, write down everyone who placed an order on the back of the receipt or attach the lunch order form with all the names. Later in this section we will discuss the procedure for managing expenses.

If you are having the order delivered

There will be times when the Production Office is so busy that doing a run to pick up the order simply isn't possible, and you will have the order delivered. While this may seem like the "no brainer" solution, it isn't always the most efficient. Having control over when the food will arrive is preferred. Delivery drivers may get lost, delayed, arrive with an inaccurate order, or any other numerous problems that will ultimately be up to you to repair. If you are having the order delivered, ensure the delivery person knows exactly where you are located and how to find you in the office. Allow ample time for the delivery window. Check the order before they leave to ensure everything is correct.

Office-catered meals

If you are placing an order for a catered meal, Production will be the one to pay for it. The below applies to lunches, meetings, and other production-related instances where food is being provided. Be sure the restaurant you select will open early enough to prepare the meal for when you'll need it. When possible, order a day in advance.
   Questions to ask the PC or APC:

1. Are there any individuals with life-threatening dietary restrictions?
   It is a good idea for the office to keep a log of what cast and crew have dietary restrictions.
2. How many people will you need to feed?
   Most restaurant catering menus will indicate how many people an order of an item will feed. Use that as a good guide. Ask the restaurant if they feel the portions you've selected will feed X number of people.

3. Where will the meal be set up?
   You may need to clear space or set up a table for the meal to be served from.
4. What time does it need to be ready to serve?
   Those working in the office are more likely to keep hours that maximize the business day, rather than align with crew call. A good lunch window is usually from 12 p.m. to 2 p.m.
5. Do the meals need to be individually packed, or will they be served buffet-style?
   As a safeguard against the spread of germs, a production may opt for individually packaged meals rather than buffet style, which requires the handling of shared serving utensils.

Selecting the menu

Once you have chosen a restaurant, select a variety of food options. Be sure to include two to three options for a main dish with at least one being a vegetarian entrée. Select a variety of side items: vegetables, mac 'n' cheese, etc. Have a salad option or two as well as a starch or bread. If budget allows, a dessert can be added. Cookies are always a people pleaser!

Placing the order

1. Always be sure to have the order read back for accuracy.
2. Find out the total cost and confirm it is within the approved spending limit.
3. You will need to pick up the order or arrange delivery and have it set up and ready to serve at a certain time. Calculate backward to allow for setup and pickup time. This will help to determine what time the order will need to be ready for pickup at the restaurant or what time it needs to arrive at the office. Make sure the restaurant knows what time you'll need the order.
4. Ask them to include serving utensils, plates, napkins, and plasticware unless your office is providing their own.
5. Condiments and dressings should always come on the side.
6. If required, ensure that the restaurant can deliver the food in individually packaged single servings.

Meal setup

Presentation and accessibility are the goals. Individually packaged meals can be set up for grab and go. When setting up meals buffet style, here are some recommended guidelines;

1. The food will need to be set up in a way that looks pleasing and desirable. If you would want to eat it just by looking at it, others will too.
2. Remove lids and packaging used for transport.
3. Make sure each dish has a serving utensil.
4. Place plates at the front of the line and plasticware at the end.
5. Food should be easily accessible without needing to be reached over. When possible, have the food serviceable from two sides of the table.

6. Put hand sanitizer at the front of the line.
7. Label what the food items are.

Once the meal is set up and ready to serve, notify each department you've ordered for and let them know lunch is ready. Monitor the table as people come through, consolidating and tossing as containers are emptied. If approved by your PC, PAs can grab a plate first, but take an eating rotation shift so that someone is always monitoring the catering table.

Post meal

Meals should not sit out for more than one to two hours. Once everyone has been through, either wrap and store leftovers in the fridge or toss any food that will go bad and wipe down the table. Food waste can stink up an office quickly. If possible, have the trash removed sooner rather than later.

If the meal was paid for by petty cash or p-card from the APC or PC, turn the receipt in to them with any remaining change. Indicate on the receipt what it was for, i.e., "production lunch," "table read," etc. Make sure you take a minute to appreciate the joy that feeding people can bring.

Craft Services

Rather than a traditional corporate office breakroom filled with vending machines and possibly a place to sit and eat a meal, the Production Office space on a show may have an actual kitchen area. This space will have an assortment of free beverages and snacks, often referred to as "craft services," aka "crafty." On smaller productions, this may be as little as a coffeemaker and water dispenser. Larger productions may have a fully stocked kitchen. Managing craft services for the Production Office is a main responsibility of the Office PA. And it is a big job. The set will have its own craft services set up, but this will not be handled by the Office PA.

You'll need to consult with your Production Coordinator regarding the budget allowance for office craft services. This will give you an idea of the scope of snacks Production can provide (are you buying plain old pretzels or ones filled with peanut butter?!). Maintaining office craft services consists of three main tasks: purchasing, restocking, and cleanup.

Purchasing

You'll likely be doing a weekly shopping run for craft services. Some offices prefer to order through online grocery suppliers, but there will still be a need for an actual grocery run for items that aren't available online. Shopping at bulk food stores is recommended, as they carry larger quantities of items than a traditional grocery store. However, places like Trader Joe's and Whole Foods may have a specific item that the Producer requested to always have on hand. Crafty shopping will likely require a visit to multiple stores to fulfill the needs of your office. Make certain you have enough cash or a production p-card to make the purchases. Some basic items like coffee and milk must be on hand no matter what budget level you are working at; others will be at the discretion of the Production Coordinator. Always consult with your Coordinator on any item preferences. Table 4.20 is a sample general craft service purchase list.

Table 4.20 General Crafty List

GENERAL CRAFT SERVICE LIST

Sandwich Makings	Beverages
Selection of deli meat	*Coffee
Selection of deli cheese	*Assorted teas
*Selection of sliced sandwich bread	Assorted juices
*Peanut butter	*Bottled water
*Assorted Jam/Jelly	Soda - Coke/Pepsi, Diet Coke/Pepsi,
	Seltzer water
	*Milk (whole, 2%, skim, soy, almond)
Grab 'n Go snacks - cold	**Condiments**
Cottage cheese cups	*Salt/Pepper
*String cheese	Mayonnaise
Single serving yogurt	Mustard
Grab 'n Go snacks - nonperishable	Ketchup
Assorted individually packaged pretzels	Honey
Beef Jerky	Butter
*Assorted individually packaged chips	**Coffee Creamers, Sweeteners**
Assorted individually packaged crackers	*Coffee creamer
Individually packaged nuts - almonds, cashews, pistachios, etc.	*Sugar-regular, raw, sweet & low, splenda, equal, stevia
Assorted granola bars/protein bars	**Kitchen Supplies**
Individually packaged trail mix	*Large plates (paper or dishware)
*Assorted cereal	Small plates
Fruit/ Veggies	*Small bowls
Assorted fruit- bananas, apples, oranges...	Large Cold Cups
Dried fruit	*Large Hot Cups
Carrot/ Celery sticks	*Forks
Chocolate & Sweets	*Knives
Assorted cookie packages	*Spoons
Assorted mini chocolates	*Napkins/paper towels
Red vines licorice	Coffee Sleeves
	Coffee Lids

*the bare essentials

Restocking

Throughout the day you will be responsible for checking the craft service area. Does more coffee need to be made? Are the fruit snacks running low and need to be refilled? Is there enough Diet Coke in the refrigerator? Is the milk still fresh, or did it expire last week and should be tossed? Does a water cooler jug need replacing? Just as if you were working in a retail store, it is important to keep the shelves stocked. If you are out of something, start a list for the next shopping trip. Do not leave empty containers in cabinets or on shelves; it gives the impression the kitchen isn't being kept up with. If a bag is empty, toss it. Treat it better than your own kitchen.

Avoid restocking the kitchen toward the end of the day, on Fridays, or your last workday of the week. This avoids fresh foods going bad over the weekend.

Cleanup

You'll find that the kitchen area will be busier during certain times of day than others. This is usually first thing in the morning during the "coffee and bagel" rush, about an hour before lunch, and around 3 p.m. in the afternoon as people seek out snacks to get them through the rest of the day. These high-traffic times should be monitored. It is your responsibility to keep the kitchen clean and tidy. Do not let cream cheese sit out all day; mid-morning put it in the refrigerator. Someone left cracker bits on the counter? Wipe it down, so you don't attract bugs. Dishes left in the sink? Wash them. Consider occasionally using a cleaning wipe on high-traffic touch points like refrigerator doors, appliance buttons, and drawer knobs. Keeping the kitchen clean and sanitary will be a priority.

On the last workday of the week, the refrigerator should be purged of any leftover and old food from the week. If it hasn't been claimed, it is garbage. It is a good idea to post a sign on the refrigerator telling crew this is the policy so no one misses their old lunch.

Scout crafty coolers

In addition to stocking the kitchen area throughout the day, the Office PA will also be responsible for preparing snack coolers to accompany the crew on location scouts. When packing a scout cooler, it should be portable, easy to consume snacks, and have limited waste.

What you'll need:

One to two rolling coolers (it's easier to roll a cooler than carry it!)

Reusable plastic containers to hold snacks that may get crushed

Trash bags

Ice

Napkins or paper towels

Hand sanitizer

Individually packaged snacks from the list. Ensure there is a salty, sweet, and healthy option (such as easy-to-eat fruit like apples and bananas).

Pack a variety of beverages from the list provided. Be sure to include bottled water.

Once a scout has returned, the cooler will need to be collected, unpacked, and drained. And please, do not drain a cooler in the middle of a major walkway!

Research

A task that will be assigned to you often is research. Whether it is seeking out an obscure item for purchase, finding the nearest place to rent a canopy tent, or searching for an acupuncturist-yogi-hypnotist to come to set, you'll spend a good deal of time combing the Internet and making calls. Research is finding answers and navigating solutions. Ask yourself: would you order Thai food from a new restaurant without reading the Yelp reviews? Would you purchase a new phone before knowing the price? Ask all types of questions, so you can provide all the answers. The more you know about the research assignment requested of you, the better you'll be able to help the requestor make the most informed decision about what to do.

Before you start

Know the WHO, WHAT, WHERE, and WHEN for the information you are being asked to gather. Always start by knowing the urgency of the request. When do you need to provide the results? Are you looking for something needed on set that day? Or is it something for next week? This will allow you to prioritize.

<u>Who</u> needs to know the results? Is it the person who assigned the task to you, or is it to present to someone else?

Are you looking up information for your Coordinator or is the Coordinator having you do the research so they can give options to a cast member? While this doesn't change how thoroughly you do the work, it may affect the questions you ask.

<u>What</u> is the purpose of the item or service needed? What is being requested of you to ask?

Sometimes you'll be researching an item you have never heard of. Knowing the intended purpose of what the item will do and possibly how the item needs to function will help you find smarter answers.

<u>When</u> do you need the item or service?

You may find the item right away, but it might be out of stock. If the item is needed the next day, you'll need to find an alternate solution.

<u>Where</u> do you need the item or service?

If the service you are looking for only conducts business in their offices, would they make an exception to come to the Production Office or set, such as with a massage therapist or chiropractor?

The research should answer the following:

1. Is the item or service available for when you need it? How soon is it available? Can the item be put on hold for pickup? If not currently available, when will it be available?
2. Is it available locally, or will it need to be shipped? Can it be picked up?
3. What is the cost? Are there variations that affect the cost? Are tax and shipping included?
4. What forms of payment are accepted?
5. Are there any accessories, labor, or other add-ons associated that must be procured? Is there a cost for any of the add-ons?
6. What is the size of the item?
7. What are the specifications of the item or service? Will you need to explain how something works?
8. Is a photo of the item helpful?
9. Can the item be returned if needed?
10. How many other vendors provide this service or item? Do you need to compare with other vendors for supply and cost?

Doing research is a great opportunity for outside-the-box thinking. Don't be afraid to find a creative solution if you hit a stumbling block.

Ask these same questions of each new vendor. The research should be documented in an organized written manner and given to the requester. Always provide more than one option for securing the item or service (three is a good general rule of thumb).

Include the name of the vendor, contact info, and who you spoke with. Keep a copy of the research in case you should need to reference it again.

The AD Kit

The **AD kit** is the on-set Production Office toolkit and is used by the Assistant Director team. It is made up of files of Production and Accounting paperwork, such as scripts, schedules, and start paperwork, as well a variety of office supplies needed by the AD department. It is prepared before principal photography begins, usually by the Production Office at the request and specifications of the AD team. The AD kit lives in the AD trailer on set.

Most AD kits contain the following basic items; however, your 2nd AD will likely provide a list of the office supplies and paperwork they will need to have.

Table 4.21 AD Kit Office Supplies

Office Supplies	
2 × file tote bins	Stapler
Blank 10" × 13" clasp envelopes	Staple remover
Assorted click pens	Whiteout tape
Black fine point pens	Scotch tape
Red sharpies	1 × roll 1" white gaffers tape
Black sharpies	1 × roll 2" white gaffers tape
Assorted colored highlighters	Script brads
Legal-sized file folders	Medium binder clips
Legal hanging file folders (w/tabs)	Reams of blue legal paper
2 × legal-sized arch clipboards	Reams of white letter paper
Ink/toner for portable desktop copier	Reams of white legal paper
Push/Pull stamps	Reams of canary legal paper

Equipment (either purchased or rented):
    Desktop all-in-one copier/printer/scanner
    Portable Wi-Fi unit

Spare production paperwork:
    Scripts with revisions
    One liners with Day Out of Days
    Shooting schedules
    Crew lists
    Past days final/approved call sheets
    Past days final/approved production reports

Paperwork to gather:

Table 4.22 AD Kit Paperwork Lists

From Accounting	From the Office	AD's Will Provide
Box rental forms	Union and non-Union BG vouchers	SAG Exhibit G's
Timecards	Photo release	Walkie inventory
Start packets	Injury/accident report forms	BG breakdown sheets
I-9's	Loss and damage forms	
W-9's	Location maps	
W-4's	Safety checklists/forms	
Petty cash envelopes	Production safety manual	
Crew deal memos	Daily time sheets	
(Union and non-Union)		
Loan out paperwork		

What you'll need to do:
- Work with your APC to order the supplies and rent the equipment.
- Create hanging and internal files for all the spare paperwork listed and consolidate in the file bins.

SCRIPT REVISIONS AND SIDES

In addition to the departmental support tasks that will consume a majority of each day, there are responsibilities that fall on the Production Office to manage on an as-needed basis. This includes things like collating script revisions, creating the AD kit, pulling sides for the set, as well as general research.

Revisions

In an effort to ensure that everyone is working off of the most current information, the film and television industry maintains a relatively standard color-coding system when changes are made to production documents. Changes happen often throughout pre-production and principal photography, and the information must be disseminated quickly and efficiently. To this end, up to 12 different page colors may be used to indicate a document has been revised. The color-coding system applies to almost every production document distributed by the office: schedules, cast and crew contact lists, and scripts. You'll need to know this color order. It is generally the same for every Studio; however, be sure to check with the PC to confirm the revision color order preferred by your Studio or Production Company. Eventually, you will memorize this order, and it will be second nature. You'll always know what color paper to use for the next revision and to make sure the paper is always stocked in the office supply cabinet.

Standard color revision order

    WHITE – Production Draft/"locked script"/1st official approved version
    BLUE – 1st Revision
    PINK – 2nd Revision
    YELLOW – 3rd Revision
    GREEN – 4th Revision
    GOLDENROD – 5th Revision
    BUFF – 6th Revision
    SALMON – 7th Revision
    CHERRY – 8th Revision
    TAN – 9th Revision
    LAVENDER – 10th Revision
    GRAY – 11th Revision
    2ND WHITE – 12th Revision

Once you have gone through a complete color cycle, it will repeat. This time, being referred to as "2nd." 2nd White, 2nd Blue, etc. There also may be some instances where the Studio will shorten the cycle.

Script revisions

Script **revisions** are taken one step further as far as identifying changes. The white production draft script is also referred to as the **locked script**. Once the script is considered ready for wide publication, a production-designated representative (i.e., the Script Coordinator or 1st AD) will "lock" the script. This means that page numbers and **scene numbers** as of this draft will not change. This script "locking" system creates continuity and avoids confusion among departments who use scene and page numbers to prep. Continually changing the page and scene numbers creates havoc and endless additional work. As script changes are made, an additional scene or page number will be added.

    A script revision will use the following change indicators after a script is locked:

1. The cover page will maintain an ongoing list of the page revisions and the date they were issued. They will be listed in descending order.
2. Script page headers will include the name of the show, episode if applicable, revision color, and the date it is issued.
3. Changes in the script itself will be marked with an asterisk (*) on the right side of the page.
4. If a change to the script pushes dialogue or stage direction onto an additional page, this page acts as a continuation. It takes the previous page number and adds an alphabetical letter *after* the page number starting with "A," such as 32A if a page was added between pages 32 and 33. Page numbers are only located in the top right corner of the page.
5. If a change to the script creates an additional scene, the scene will use the next sequential scene number and add a capital alphabetical letter *before* the scene number starting with "A," such as A22, if a scene was added between scene 21 and 22 in a script. Scene numbers are located on both the right and left side of the page at the location of the scene header.

6. If a scene is cut from the script, the text will be removed and replaced with the word "OMIT," but the scene number will remain, so it is clear what was cut.

Refer to the sample cover page and script pages with revisions in the Appendix "Script Title Page" and "Script Revisions," to view examples. Understanding script revisions will be applicable when running script copies, collating scripts, and pulling sides.

Script Collating

When a script revision is generated, it becomes necessary for the updated pages to be collated into the existing script draft. This essentially is the process of replacing any page for which an update has been issued. Most of the time script pages will be distributed as a set of "revision pages" rather than handing out entirely new scripts each time. However, whether you are maintaining a sides binder (more on sides later) or making sure the cast, Director, and Producers all have a cohesive up-to-date draft, it will be necessary to know how to most efficiently collate a script. Many crew members today opt to receive their scripts digitally, in which case the digitally collated script will be emailed, because the collated version can be automatically generated in the scriptwriting program. However, there are still a number of key members – department heads and cast – who will request a hard copy of the script. As we discussed in "Revisions," the 1st production draft is distributed on white paper, and subsequent revisions will be printed in the next paper color order.

When Production receives script revisions, they may consist of only several pages of the script rather than a whole new draft. As a general rule, if a script revision has changes on more than 50% of the pages, your new script will be considered a "full" revision and be printed entirely in the next revision color. The header on the revised pages should indicate which color revision you're on. It will be accompanied by a new title page that adds this revision to the list of all the previous revision versions.

Quick and easy guide to COLLATING a script:

- Place both your current script pages and the new revised pages in two stacks in front of you.
- Take your first revised page and find the original in your current script by matching page numbers.
- Remove the original page from the current script and replace it with the new revised page. Replace page number for page number and ONLY remove the pages that have a revised page to replace it.
- Remember that sometimes a new revision will generate an additional "A" or "B" page. This gets inserted immediately following the revised page <u>without replacing</u> any other pages.
- If you are collating more than one revision color into a script, work backward. Insert the most recent revision color first. This will avoid continually replacing pages you just inserted. Follow the color revision order (i.e., remove the pink page for the new yellow page, remove the blue page for the new pink page, etc.).
- Once all pages have been collated, double-check that there are no missing pages. Do this by checking all page numbers throughout the full script. By the end of the show, you'll likely end up with a multicolor script that reflects all changes made over the course of the production.
- Insert a binding brad in the top and bottom page holes only.

You may want to keep a master white script copy that already has revised pages eliminated. For instance, you may have a copy of the white production draft with the blue and pink revision pages already removed, and you may have the blue revision pages that exclude the pink revision pages. This way you can save time and money (on paper) by only copying the pages you need, rather than making copies of pages that will just be tossed once you collate the revisions.

Sides

Production sides are a mini-version of the script pages scheduled to be filmed each day. They are used as a handy, quick reference on set by the cast, the director, AD's, and most department heads. The sides consist of the front of the call sheet and the script pages of the specific scenes scheduled. Paper sides are shrunk down to half the size of a regular sheet of 8.5" × 11" paper. Rather than carry around a cumbersome 60–110-page script, sides offer a more portable solution. Sometimes they are used via a tablet, phone, or other device to save paper. They are prepared by the office each night for filming the next day and can be generated digitally or by hand.

These sides are different from **casting sides**, which are only used and generated by the casting department. When you are pulling production sides, here are some things to consider if you are designated to create them.

Check with your Assistant Director on their sides preferences:

1. Should the scenes be compiled in call sheet order or script order? Shows rarely film a script in chronological order. Scenes will be listed on the call sheet in the order in which they will be filmed; however, the ADs may prefer the sides be arranged in script order.
2. Should you include full scenes when the call sheet indicates a "part (pt)" of a scene? This can save time and paper from copying portions of scenes that aren't needed, though some AD's and cast prefer to have the whole scene available in the sides for reference.
3. What quantity of sides are needed for set, and are any variations of the sizes needed? Often cast will request "large" size sides, which will be copied on full-sized 8.5" × 11" paper vs. the traditional half-size version.

Sides marking basics

Whether you are doing digital sides or hard copy, both require following specific steps: pulling, marking, and copying. In general, the entire process is commonly referred to as "pulling sides."

The marking process via either method includes:

1. Using the call sheet to identify the scenes that will be filmed.
2. Circling the scene numbers.
3. Crossing out or "X"-ing any scenes that are not being filmed that day.

Pulling sides digitally

There are a number of virtual Production Office systems we've touched on, and one component of these digital systems is the ability to create sides. This consists of importing the script and using the software to select scenes needed per the call sheet.

The system will then digitally generate the sides you need for each day. It's important to make certain you have the most current script revisions uploaded. You'll need to learn the software used by your Production Office to generate sides in this manner.

Additionally, you can also create digital sides using software such as Adobe Acrobat or Preview. Here is a step-by-step for this method:

1. Review the scene numbers on the call sheet. The sides must include the scenes listed. Sides can be pulled in advance off a **"preliminary" call sheet** during the day but must be checked against the final call sheet before being copied, as things may change.
2. Search your digital master script (the one with the most current revisions) for the corresponding scene numbers.
3. Drag and drop or "print to PDF" the script pages where those scenes appear and place them on your desktop. Double-check that you have pulled the entire scene.
4. From the "File" drop-down menu, select "Combine PDF" in Adobe Acrobat. In "Preview," drop the pulled script page files into the program and combine them in the order of your AD's preference (scene order per the call sheet or chronological script order).
5. Using the circle tool, circle the scheduled scene numbers on either side of the page.
6. Using the line tool, draw a line above the scene heading of the scene you have circled.
7. Use the line tool to draw a line at the end of the selected scene.
8. Use the line tool to create crossed lines (in the form of an X) on the scenes that appear on the page but are *not scheduled* to film per the call sheet. Be sure the "X" is across the entire scene, edge to edge of the page.
9. Repeat for all required scenes.
10. Print out the line-marked pages.
11. Double-check the scenes you have pulled against the call sheet. Do you have every scene that is listed? Do you have any extra scenes that need to be excluded? Have someone from the office staff review your sides once you have marked them.
12. Follow the copy instructions in this section!

In some instances, shows will opt to send a copy of the digital sides to the cast and AD department when the call sheet is emailed out each night. You'll want to save a digital copy of the pulled sides for this purpose and in case you need to print more.

Pulling sides by hand

Put together a "sides" three-ring binder. This should contain the most current version of the script, updated with revisions as they are generated. All pages should be on WHITE paper (the script header will indicate which revision color each individual page is).

Supplies:

- Ruler
- Black sharpie
- Correction tape (for mistakes….)
- White no-holed letter-size paper

84 Making it Happen, Behind the Scenes

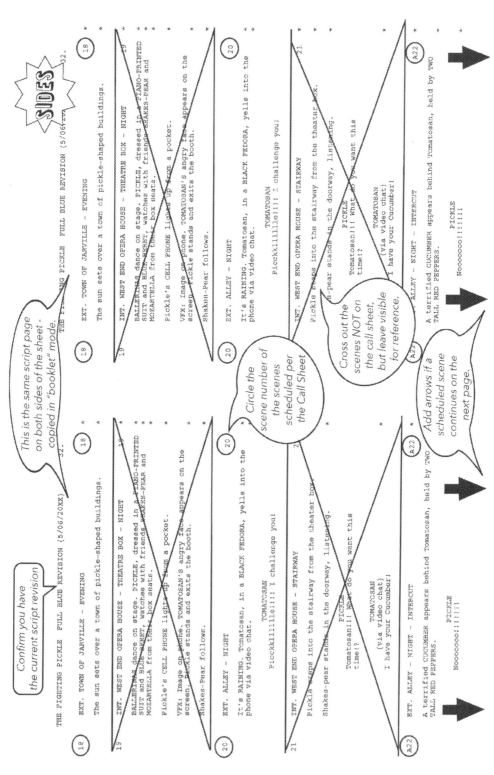

Graphic 4.23 Sample sides.

The steps:

1. Sides can be pulled in advance off a preliminary call sheet during the day but must be checked against the final call sheet before being copied as things may change.
2. Look for the scene numbers that are scheduled to be filmed per the call sheet.
3. Using the sides binder, pull out the script pages with the scene numbers on them. Be sure to look for scenes that continue onto additional pages. You do not want to be responsible for leaving a page out of the sides. The call sheet will list the **page count**, which you can use to reference the amount of pages you pull.
4. Make a copy on non-holed white letter paper of the pages you pulled from the sides binder. Be sure to keep all the pages in order and do not forget to return the original pages back to the binder. Do not mark the pages pulled directly from the binder.
5. Circle the scene numbers on both sides of the page that match the call sheet.
6. Take the black sharpie and the ruler and draw a horizontal line across the page above and below the scene.
7. Using the ruler, draw a diagonal "X" across any scene on the page *not* being filmed the next day. Be sure the "X" is across the entire scene, edge to edge of the paper.
8. Some AD's may want you to indicate when the scene continues onto the next page. In this instance, draw down arrows at the bottom of the first page where the scene continues. If a scene ends at the bottom of a page, you may consider drawing up arrows at the end of the page to indicate that the scene does not continue. This will also help avoid missing pages.
9. Have someone from the office staff review your sides once you have marked them.

Copying sides

Whether you have pulled sides digitally or by hand, the copying process is the same. This is sometimes referred to as "running" the sides.
   Supplies:

- A hard copy of the pulled and marked sides
- White no-holed letter paper
- Stapler
- Paper cutter
- Copy machine (ideally one that staples and has a booklet setting)
- Rubber band

The steps:

1. Sides must be run using the final approved call sheet as a top sheet.
2. Make a letter size copy of the final call sheet. You do not need to shrink it. It is generally acceptable to cut off the lower part of the call sheet when using it for sides, as this section is the advance and not applicable to the current day's filming. This will be your top page of the sides.

3. If you need to run any "large" sides, this is the time to do it.
4. For the small sides, make one copy of the pulled sides pages and call sheet cover on white no-holed letter paper.
5. Collate both sets of copies together (page one behind page one, page two behind page two etc.) so that you have two sets of each page collated together.
6. Select the "booklet" setting on the copier.* This will copy two pages onto one. Sometimes this is shown as "combine 2:1," indicating 2 pages to 1 page. By having a double set of pages, when you feed it into the machine, it will make identical stacks.
7. Select the corner staple feature.*
8. Run a test copy. Your output should have two copies of the same page on one page and a staple in the corner. Make sure all pages are there.
9. Once you have confirmed the settings are accurate, set your copy count and run them. Remember, your output count will be double. If the AD's have asked for 32 sets of sides, you'll only need to copy 16 sets, as you have duplicated the images on each page.
10. Once the sides are run, you will need to manually add an additional staple to the second set of sides in the middle of the page.
11. Using a paper cutter, cut them in half down the middle to separate them.
12. Rubber-band the sides together as a bundle and prep them to send to set, such as putting them in a labeled envelope.
13. Be sure to keep your master set of sides nearby in the sides binder in case more need to be run the next day.

You are done! Make sure the sides go directly into the "to set" box for distribution by the AD's on set.

If you pulled sides digitally, you may be able to print a half-size master that is already formatted 2:1, with two of the same pages on one sheet of paper. You'll need to print the call sheet in the same way, and then you can skip steps 4, 5, and 6. Go straight to copying, stapling, and cutting your sides.

Note: As a way to help save paper, some offices have adopted copying sides on the back of old script pages. This requires creating a collection system for crew members to drop their old scripts and the Office PA picking them up and sorting the paper. It is a tedious task; however, it can save an incredible amount of paper.

DAILY CHECKLIST

By this point, it should be very apparent how demanding and necessary the job of an Office PA is. It isn't rocket science, but the first time you do it, it might seem like it! Specific assignments will vary from office to office based on the preference of the Production Coordinator. In addition to the tasks mentioned thus far, Template 4.24 is a handy checklist to guide you through an average day.

---

* Copy machine functions may vary

OFFICE PA DAILY CHECKLIST
To be used as a general reference guide for day-to-day tasks

MORNING

Plan to arrive at work early and ready to work! Be prepared to jump right into the morning checklist and address any urgent matters.

<u>On your way in</u>
> Are you doing a run on your way into the office? Are you picking up a catered breakfast or an assortment of bagels? More orange juice?

<u>When you arrive to the office</u>
> Unlock the Production Office. Turn on all the lights. Unlock any other offices designated by the PC to be open in the AM.

<u>In the kitchen area</u>
> If you purchased breakfast, set it up (refer to *"That's Lunch"* for food set up guidance).
>
> Make coffee. Check that cream, sugar, cups, lids, sleeves, stir sticks are stocked.
>
> Make sure the kitchen is tidy.
>
> Check the water cooler, replace the bottle if needed.
>
> Restock the kitchen. Check food bins, refrigerator, paper products. Make note of anything that needs to be purchased.

<u>In the production office</u>
> Check the main voicemail and distribute messages.
>
> Office Machines: Turn on printers and copiers. Refill paper in machines. Does any copy paper need to be ordered?
>
> Distribute the morning paperwork from the "football."
>
> Check the production email account, forward any messages that need action taken.
>
> Check the general paperwork - Do more copies need to be made?
>
> Prep any coolers for scouts departing before 10AM.
>
> Is there any outstanding distribution that needs to be delivered?
>
> What pre-pro meetings are scheduled for the day? Do any photocopies need to be made or meeting rooms prepared?
>
> Is there any outgoing mail that needs to go to a mailbox?
>
> Make sure the production office is tidy.

<u>Pre-Lunch:</u> *The general window for lunchtime is between 12N-2PM.*
> Follow the procedures outlined in *"That's Lunch!"* for collecting and placing lunch orders.
>
> Clean up breakfast, tidy the kitchen, make space for lunch to arrive.
>
> Restock drinks in the refrigerator.

Template 4.24 The Office PA daily checklist.

THROUGHOUT THE DAY

Take initiative on these tasks as needed during the day.

Answering the phone is a 1st priority.

Check the "run" board to see if any runs need to be completed.

Check office machines to ensure they are stocked with paper, staples, toner.

Check the production email account, forward any messages, take action on tasks assigned to you.

Check the general paperwork - Do more copies need to be made?

Accept, log, and distribute all package shipments.

Outgoing mail should be taken to a mailbox, pick up mail from the mailbox (as applicable for your office).

Outgoing shipping deliveries should be taken to the nearest drop box.

When calls come in from the set updating their progress, shout them out and make sure the information is updated on the **progress board**. This includes: **1st shot, turning around, moving on/on the move,** lunch, **1st shot after lunch,** wrap. You'll also get a call from the 2nd AD or script supervisor with a lunch report. This does not need to be shouted out, but the information must be taken down and given to the APC or PC for distribution to the studio.

Restock the kitchen. Check food bins, refrigerator, paper products. Make note of anything that needs to be purchased.

Make sure the kitchen is clean and tidy. Wipe counters, clean up spills.

Collect and empty any scout coolers.

Clean up and reset any meeting rooms used.

Make sure the office is not a mess.

Organize office supplies. Does anything need to be purchased?

Don't let things pile up in the "to set" box. Check it every hour or so and take items to set (if the filming company and production office are on the same property) or arrange for them to be delivered to location (this may be you!).

If you don't have anything to do, ask.

WHEN YOU THINK THERE IS NOTHING TO DO

Wipe down the refrigerator.

Wipe out the kitchen cabinets.

Template 4.24 *(Continued)*

Making it Happen, Behind the Scenes 89

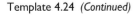

Collate scripts.

Do a sanitation pass of door handles and office machines with a cleaning wipe.

Fill staplers, empty 3-hole punches.

Does the First Aid kit need refilling?

Inventory crafty.

If you don't have anything to do, ask.

EVENING CHECKLIST

Pull sides for the next day.

In the kitchen area

Make sure the kitchen is not gross. Wipe counters, clean up spills.

Check that any "first thing in the morning" crafty is stocked. Milk, orange juice, coffee, creamer, paper goods. Does anything need to be purchased on the morning run?

If there is not a janitorial service, remove all trash.

Check the water cooler, replace the bottle if needed.

Make sure all dishes are clean and put away.

In the Production Office

Empty all trash from each desk and office.

Check office machines to ensure they are stocked with paper, staples, toner.

Outgoing shipping deliveries should be taken to the nearest drop box.

Outgoing mail should be taken to a mailbox (as applicable for your office).

Make sure the office _and your workspace_ are tidy.

Make meeting reminder/notification calls (when applicable).

Update Prep Schedule on white board (if your office does this).

Make sure any upcoming meetings the next day have been prepped (food ordered; copies made).

Prep coolers for any scouts leaving before 10AM the next morning (ice should be added the next day).

Make sure PO log is current for the day.

Make sure all items in the "to file" tray have been filed.

WHEN PRODUCTION WRAPS FILMING FOR THE DAY

Copy and distribute hard copies of call sheets throughout the office (as directed by your PC). (Call sheets do not fly before wrap!)

If you have been designated to do so, email the call sheet to the appropriate distribution lists.

Template 4.24 *(Continued)*

Run the sides.

Write next days' filming info on the production white board (if your office does this).

If you take the call with the daily wrap report information, distribute the information to the necessary parties per the APC or PC.

If other PA's are scheduled on a staggered call based around the crew call time, notify them if their morning call time changed from the preliminary call sheet, be sure the PC approves of their new time.

BEFORE YOU LEAVE

At the end of your shift, go over the status of any incomplete tasks you have been assigned, with the PC or APC.

Make sure everything in the "to set" box is straightened, in an envelope, and that the recipient is clearly labeled on the envelope.

Turn off office machines.

If based on a studio lot, confirm that your show's stages have been **Hot lock**ed, once any prep/wrap work has been completed on the stage for the day. The procedure for making sure the sound stages are locked every night will be dictated by your Production Coordinator.

Turn off lights and lock office doors.

NOTES & REMINDERS

_____
_____
_____
_____
_____
_____
_____
_____
_____
_____
_____
_____
_____

Template 4.24 *(Continued)*

BASIC ACCOUNTING

The Accounting department is responsible for tracking production spending, cash flow, and payments. The Production Office team generates P.O.'s and check requests, as well as tracks p-card and petty cash purchases in order to support Accounting. Completing daily office tasks requires you to have knowledge of basic company accounting procedures. How is an item being paid for? Once it's been paid for, how has the purchase been documented and reported to Accounting? All spending needs to be tracked, accounted for, and reported to the Studio or financing entity by the Accounting department. You are an indirect part of that process. A show may use a combination of some or all of the payment methods listed here. Accounting procedures will be relatively similar from office to office, and any specific preferences will be dictated by the production Accounting office and Production Coordinator.

Purchase Orders

A "**purchase order**," referred to as a "P.O.", is a document used to hold money in the budget for a purchase or rental for which production will receive an invoice at a later date. P.O.'s are money that is committed for payment. The show agrees to pay up to that amount for the goods and services rendered when invoiced. The Production Company will need to have set up a billing account with the vendor in order to use this method of payment. Traditionally, a P.O. is a hard copy document, sometimes on two-, three- or four-ply colored carbon paper, so that each page can be distributed separately. This is so that multiple departments can keep a record of their spending. In some offices, digital P.O.s are starting to be used, as was mentioned in "Digital Workflows," and require knowledge of web-based software. Refer to your Production Coordinator and/or Production Accountant for details if that is the case.

When making a purchase or rental, the vendor may ask you for the P.O. number. Once a quoted cost has been approved, you will either sign out a P.O., which you will complete with the details of the purchase or rental, or the Coordinator will provide you a P.O. number to give to the vendor to complete the transaction.

P.O. logs

The Accounting department assigns stacks of numbered purchase orders to each department. In the Production Office, there will be a P.O. logbook if you're working with hard copy P.O.'s. This binder will contain a sign-out sheet for each P.O., a copy of the completed P.O., and the "backup" or support documents showing the order detail and cost. The P.O. log is where you (and other office staff) will list each P.O. number as it is used. It will include the date, vendor name, description of the cost, and the amount. A P.O. log should be maintained whether your P.O.'s are digital or hard copy.

The P.O. log looks like this:

Table 4.26 Sample P.O. Log

			P.O. Log			
P.O. #	Date	Vendor	Purpose	Amount	Department	Signed Out or Completed By
10001	7/11/20XX	Dollies4Us	Dolly equipment rental	$3,001.99	Grip	B. Better
10002						

Making it Happen, Behind the Scenes

THE FIGHTING PICKLE
Pickles Main Street Films, Inc.
123 Avenue Q, Suite 456
New York, NY 00000
212-555-1111 phone
800-555-1112 efax

PURCHASE ORDER

Assigned PO Number

PURCHASE ORDER
30000
PO Number must appear on all invoices.

VENDOR: WHO we will have to pay?

Today's Date

Date _____

Vendor _____ Phone Number _____

Address _____ Fax Number _____

City, State, Zip _____ Contact _____

Are we renting or buying these items?

Dates of Rental

Federal ID or Social Security # _____ Corporation _____

(Choose One)   Purchase   OR   Rental   Rental Period _____ TO _____

(Circle One)   W9 form attached   W9 on File

All POs must be accompanied by a W9 form.

QTY	DESCRIPTION	ACCOUNT	UNIT	TOTAL
2.5 Months	SUV Rental - Producer Vehicle Start: June 12, 20XX Estimated End: August 30, 20XX		$1,199.99	$ -

How Many?

What items are we getting? For which department and what purpose or use?

This is for Accounting.

Unit: How much is EACH item?

TOTAL = QTY x UNIT

A "related party" is a crew member or crew member owned company who may rent or sell items to the production. It is important to notify the LP/UPM in the event the studio has specific guidelines.

Add Tax, Shipping and Fees here:

TAX	$ -
SHIPPING	$ -

By signing this Purchase Order I acknowledge that all related party transactions have been disclosed (if any) and were reviewed and approved by the Executive In Charge/Line Producer. If related parties exist, please disclose below:

GRAND TOTAL:	$ -

Total Amount should match the attached quote.

Approvals

Requested By: _____

Department: _____ UPM Approval: _____

Department Head Approval: _____ Line Producer Approval: _____

Production Finance Approval: _____ Production Accountant Approval: _____

White/Yellow Copies - Accounting   Pink Copy - Production   TRANSACTION #: _____

Document 4.27 Sample purchase order.

Completing a P.O.

Document 4.27 walks you through the information required when filling out a P.O. You will use the vendor quote as a reference and include the vendor name, description of the purchased or rented items, and the estimated costs.

Once you have completed filling out the P.O., it will need to be reviewed. Have the Production Secretary or APC check it for mistakes. The PC will sign off on it and pass it around for approvals to the Supervisor, UPM, and/or Line Producer. Every office has a different chain of approvals for P.O. processing, but the basics are the same.

Distributing a P.O.

Once a P.O. has been approved either by the PC, Supervisor, UPM, or some variation thereof, it will come back to you to distribute it appropriately so that the Accounting department can keep proper track of the spending. If you are using digital P.O. software, distribution will usually be internal. If an invoice comes in for payment and the Accounting office does not have a copy of the P.O., they will not know it is approved to be paid. Always confirm the P.O. is approved before sending a copy or scan to the vendors.

Step-by-step example for distributing a hard copy P.O.:

Step 1 – Make a copy and/or scan the P.O. and a copy of the backup (every P.O. should have "backup" attached; this is either a rental quote, rental agreement, or some sort of proof of the estimated cost associated with the purchase or rental – this can sometimes be an email chain.) This should not be the invoice.

Step 2 – Separate the three-ply or four-ply P.O. (sometimes: white, yellow, pink, goldenrod). The P.O. color coding will be determined by the Accounting department. Check with the Coordinator on the correct distribution. Each office is different; sometimes the white stays with Production and sometimes the white goes to Accounting. Find out the right way for your office. Again, if you are using digital P.O.'s, this does not apply.

Step 3 – Attach the original backup to whichever parts of the P.O. you are giving to Accounting with a *paper clip*. Multiple pages of the P.O. may need to go to Accounting (white and pink, pink and yellow, or yellow and goldenrod, etc.). This way Accounting has the original documentation or agreement as proof of the cost of the purchase or rental, and they will keep this in the master accounting files. If digital, you will upload or scan and email the backup to Accounting.

Step 4 – Attach the *copy* of the backup to whichever parts of the P.O. you are keeping in the office. Make sure this is stapled or paper-clipped (at PC discretion), three-hole punched, and filed alphabetically or in numerical order (at PC discretion) in the P.O. book or production files. If your office prefers to file all P.O.'s digitally, make sure you scan the P.O., including the backup, and label it correctly for your digital files. The PC will provide you with a digital label format so all P.O.'s are logged uniformly.

Step 5 – Deliver the P.O. and original backup to the Accounting office.

Petty Cash/Purchasing Cards (P-Card)

More often than not, you will be responsible for a small amount of **petty cash** ("P.C.") or a **p-card** (purchase card). This is a way for the office to make purchases instantly rather than waiting for a check to be cut in order to buy things like pens or pick up lunches. Often petty cash is typically used for purchases under $250. You are responsible for and will be held accountable for this money if you lose it or a receipt. It should go without saying, but any company-issued money is to be used for approved production expenses only and should never be used for personal spending.

Handling the cash or p-card

1. You will either be issued a personal **petty cash float** directly from Accounting, or you will be using cash from a float assigned to the PC or APC. Always write down who gave you petty cash, how much you received, and when you received it. It's a good idea to keep track of the petty cash you have been given by someone else and document when you received it, so you know how much money you must return to them in the form of receipts and change.
2. Use a zipper pouch or designated wallet to hold petty cash. Keep it separate from your personal cash.
3. When you are finished making a purchase, return the remaining P.C. or p-card and receipts to the person you received it from. Each receipt should be labeled with what the purchase was for and for whom it was purchased. If you have been assigned your own p-card or float, you do not need to immediately turn in a single receipt and change to Accounting.
4. P-cards are like credit cards, and your charges instantly appear online. Make sure you keep those receipts to match with the online statements.

Receipt management

1. Always get a good receipt. NO EXCEPTIONS. A good receipt includes the name and address of the vendor and the itemized total. (A menu or business card can be used when no address is printed on the receipt). Receipts should always be originals.
2. If you buy a meal, write down the names for whom you made the purchase on the back of the receipt or next to the receipt when it is taped up for tracking.
3. Keep all receipts in one place (such as the zipper pouch) so they can easily be gathered, taped up, and submitted each week when you do a P.C. or P-card reporting envelope.

Expense reporting

1. Every receipt will need to be taped to a sheet of paper and individually logged using a designated top sheet provided by the Accounting department.
2. Check with your Accounting department on their preference for turning in petty cash receipts. How often should they be turned in? What is the turnaround time? How do they prefer receipts to be sorted and labeled? This may also be outlined in the "accounting procedures" typically issued with your start paperwork. Sort receipts by date and then type (lunch/office supplies/crafty/taxis/etc.).
3. Gas receipts: These may need to have the make/model and license plate of the vehicle written on them as well as the name of the driver who filled the tank. Prepaid gas receipts will not be accepted ever. Make certain the receipts include the price per gallon.
4. On the back of clean or scrap 8 ½" × 11" paper, tape the top and bottom of each receipt vertically to the page. Make sure receipts aren't folded or hanging off the paper. If a receipt is too long for a single page, you may cut it and tape both halves to the page, but ensure no information is cut off!

5. When taping receipts, you can fill a page, rather than just one receipt per page. Just don't overlap receipts, and don't make them sloppy. Line them up left to right and top to bottom.
6. Receipts should never be stapled. Often petty cash envelopes are scanned. Tape will run through a scanner, and staples will jam the machine.
7. As much as possible, be sure the tape does not cover any important information on the receipt. Over time, the adhesive in the tape can cause the ink on the receipt to fade or disappear.
8. Only use standard, clear adhesive single-side tape (i.e., no masking tape or duct tape!)
9. Number each receipt (oldest to newest) exactly as they are laid out on the page.
10. Once all receipts have been taped down, you'll need to log each expense on a petty cash or p-card envelope top sheet (Document 4.28).
11. List each receipt next to the number you've assigned it.
12. Check the total cost of the receipts at least twice. The total for the receipts plus any remaining cash on hand should add up to the total amount you received. When logging p-card expenses, you will not have a cash-on-hand amount.
13. In the instance where you made a return, the original purchase and the return will need to be listed separately on a different line. The return will be indicated by a minus sign in the amount column. The return receipt should be included with the taped receipts.

Replenishing your petty cash float

Once an envelope has been completed, you will submit it to the Production Coordinator for approval. It will eventually make its approval rounds to Accounting. If you were assigned a petty cash float from Accounting, they will provide you with a replenished float for the amount documented on the envelope. This way your float total always remains the same original amount. You don't need to turn in your remaining cash with each envelope until the end of the show. If you were using cash from someone else's float, once you return the change and labeled receipt, the assignment is complete. For future purchases, you'll be given a new temporary float. It is a good habit to submit your float for reimbursement when you are down to about half the amount you were given. Turnaround is not instant, so in order to avoid running out of cash, stay on top of submitting your receipts.

Once your work has been completed on a show, you will be expected to turn in any remaining receipts and the cash/p-card before receiving your final paycheck.

Check Requests

A **check request** is a request for a check that needs to be cut in order to pay for a purchase at the time of service or pickup. Checks or sometimes wire transfers are primarily used when immediate payment is required.

A check request has all the same information that a P.O. does – vendor name, address, quantity, description, purpose, and most importantly, the *date* the check is needed. If you have been tasked with completing a check request, you will also need to include a **W-9 tax form** from the vendor. Accounting will require this before a check can be cut. Document 4.29 is a sample check request.

Making it Happen, Behind the Scenes

PETTY CASH/ P-CARD ENVELOPE

NAME:
POSITION:
DATE:

Envelope #:
Amount Reimbursed:
Recipient Signature:
Audited By:

PLEASE GROUP RECEIPTS IN ORDER OF TYPE (i.e. GAS/MEALS/OFFICE SUPPLIES, ETC.)

#	Date	Paid to - Vendor Name	Item(s) Purchased	Acct	Set	Amount	#
1	5/17/20XX	Gas Station	Gas - Vehicle Plate #			14.84	1
2	5/23/20XX	Gas Station	Gas - Vehicle Plate #			43.51	2
3	5/11/20XX	Market	Water for Location Scout			20.00	3
4	5/21/20XX	Market	Office Crafty			158.71	4
5	5/21/20XX	Market	Batteries			8.65	5
6	5/17/20XX	Hardware Store	9 Key Copies			16.75	6
7	5/17/20XX	Local Restaurant	Lunch - Office Staff - 7 people			91.66	7
8	5/18/20XX	Local Restaurant	Lunch - Office Staff - 7 people			76.54	8
9	5/08/20XX	Furniture Store	(2) Folding Tables			64.95	9
10	5/08/20XX	Supply Store	(3) Cases White Paper			113.97	10
11	5/08/20XX	Supply Store	Pens, Notepads, Blue Paper			37.89	11
12	5/09/20XX	Shop	Donuts for Pre-Pro Meeting			9.99	12
13	5/21/20XX		Cake for Producer Birthday			24.99	13
14	5/23/20XX	SpendandBuy	RETURN - Red Fedora			-12.99	14

Annotations:
- Name of vendor, company, person or place where purchase was made from.
- Items purchased, purpose and key details such as license plate numbers and number of people served should be included.
- For Accounting Use Only
- Amount of purchase, must match the corresponding receipt.
- Receipts get numbered separately to match the numbers listed here.
- **PC LOG** - This document may be used for both petty cash or P-card receipt tracking and submitting. Refer to your accounting department guidelines for specific instructions.
- Once the envelope is turned into accounting, it will be circulated for approvals before your float can be replenished or you reimbursed.
- If you were given a cash float, you account for it here and any money remaining or due.
- Total Amount of Receipts.

Approvals:
DEPT HEAD
ACCOUNTANT
LINE PRODUCER
UPM

Total Receipts: $ 669.46
Petty Cash Advanced:
Cash Enclosed:
Balance Due:

Document 4.28 Sample petty cash/P-card envelope.

Making it Happen, Behind the Scenes 97

Pickles Main Street Films, Inc.
CHECK REQUEST FORM

A Check Request <u>does not</u> take the place of an invoice. Pro Forma Estimates, Receipts, Invoices, Contracts, etc. <u>must</u> be provided as backup and turned in to Accounting. W-9 must be attached or On-File.

Date _____   Date Needed _____ (ASAP Is Not A Date)

Payable To: _____ (Name, Address, Contact Person or Vendor due Payment)
_____
_____
_____ Tel. _____

Contact: _____ Fax. _____
Federal ID / SS # **(REQUIRED)** _____ W-9 Attached: YES   ON-FILE

Acct.	Set	Description	Cost
(For Accounting tracking purposes.)		(Item(s) being purchased, or purpose of payment)	(Price of items)

(Purpose of check)
▶ **PURCHASE**
▶ **RENTAL:** _____ to _____
▶ **DEPOSIT**

(This total amount should match the attached invoice.)

Total Request: _____

Requested by _____   Dept. _____
Dept. Approval _____
Producer _____   (Approvals!)
Prod Manager _____
Accounting _____

(What should Accounting do when the check is cut?)

- **GIVE TO REQUESTER**
- **HOLD**
- **MAIL**

Document 4.29 Sample check request.

SUPPORTING CAST AND CREW TRAVEL

Although many cast and crew work locally in large production hubs like LA, New York, and Atlanta, it is relatively common on most projects to have some members of your cast and crew who will need to travel in order to work on the show. Even on a show with an entirely local crew, you may still need to travel cast, Producers, or Directors. Supporting travel needs will be ongoing throughout prep, principal photography, and wrap. When cast or crew are expected to travel to a location for filming, they are being asked to leave their home comfort zone, and things often become personal very quickly. You will be expected to stay sharp, calm, cool and collected. You may be asked to assist with airport pickups, housing accommodation setup, gift baskets, and welcome packets.

Cast and crew on a production are either considered to be a **"local"** or a **"distant"** hire. A local hire implies they live and work within a specific radius of the production location and can easily travel home at the end of a workday. The distant hires are being asked to work away from or outside of that radius and thus cannot return home easily at the end of a workday. The work radius is generally designated by the Union or Guild contract the production is working under and varies by location.

Most often an Office PA will be a local hire. In rare occasions, you may be asked to travel when a film is being produced outside of a production hub or in a more remote area. Either way you will need to have an understanding of what it means to have cast and crew traveling in and out for your show.

In an earlier section, we mentioned Travel Coordinators and their place in the Production Office staff. Not every show will have a designated, in-house Travel Coordinator, and travel arrangements for cast and crew may fall to the office staff, and sometimes with the assistance of a third-party travel agency. They will book flights, as well as arrange housing, rental cars, and other ground transportation for cast and crew as needed. Contractual travel specifics are usually outlined in a cast or **crew deal memo**. A **travel memo** will often be issued to inform key production personnel about the travel arrangements made for an individual. Although you may not be booking the travel, you should be aware of travel memos and how your particular office handles them. If you are included on the distribution of a travel memo, you likely are being tasked with an aspect of travel assistance for that person.

Airport transfers

On occasion you may be asked to assist with or arrange an airport transfer for a cast or crew member. Most often cast members will have car services arranged for them. There are a number of car service companies used nationwide. You should know what company your office uses most often and if there are any scheduled pickups each day. Knowing the arrival or departure schedule of a cast or crew member allows you to anticipate the support you'll need to offer.

Conversely, you personally may be asked to do an airport pickup or dropoff. In addition to following the guidelines outlined earlier in this section under "Runs," be sure you've done your homework on the following:

- Is the pickup vehicle clean and full of gas? Whether this is your personal vehicle or a production rental, it's important you're ready for the run!
- Which airport is the person traveling to/from?

- What time is their flight arriving or departing? Is it domestic or international? This will determine how early you must drop them off or how long after they land you can expect to pick them up.
- For a departure:
  - How long will it take to get to the airport before their flight? Depending on the time of day, you may need to allow for traffic. You may also want to find out how early the individual prefers to arrive, so you don't allow too much or too little time for them to get through the airport.
  - Make sure you know which airline you are dropping them off at.
  - Do they have luggage that needs to be checked and would require extra time in the airport?
- For an arrival:
  - What time are they expected to land? Can you track their flight online and get up-to-date arrival information? There are many useful apps that are extremely accurate at tracking flight status.
  - Does the person you are picking up have your contact information? Do you have theirs? Call or text them when you arrive so they know you are standing by and where to meet you.
  - Will they be passing through customs and need extra time?
  - Will they have a lot of luggage?
  - Where can you park to await their arrival?
  - Are they expecting to be picked up inside at baggage claim or curbside?
  - If you have been asked to meet the individual at baggage claim, do you have a sign identifying them (first initial, last name) or you (Pickle Main Street Films), so they can easily find you?
  - What is their destination once you leave the airport? Their housing accommodation? The Production Office? Wardrobe for a fitting?

Cast and crew accommodations

Distant location or not, some of your cast and crew may be provided living arrangements in a local hotel, corporate housing, or a furnished apartment such as an AirBnB. You may be asked to assist in getting these homes-away-from-home prepared for the guests. It will be important to familiarize yourself with each hotel or housing arrangement. You may need to deliver scripts, call sheets, gift baskets, etc.

Where is the property located? Is there a gate code or security information you will need to access the property? Are there certain times when you can access the property or hotel room to make a delivery?

You may be asked to make advance purchases and stock these homes to help keep the guests comfortable. The PC, APC, or Travel Coordinator will provide you with information to make purchases for each person, be it a Producer, cast member or department head.

If you're assigned these tasks, ask your PC for clarification about the following:

- Who will be staying there? A cast member? Crew member? Producer?
- How long will they be staying? Does it need to be stocked up for a month or just a few days?

- Does the property provide bedding? Towels? Cleaning Supplies?
- Is there a cleaning service on the property? Laundry in the building?
- Is there local dining information available to the guest? Room service? Local menus?
- Do you need to stock their fridge? If so, are there special items they have requested?
- What amenities does the hotel offer? Refrigerator and microwave in room?

Gift baskets

Studios and production companies know how important a good first impression is, and they may opt to send a welcome gift basket so their guest feels right at home upon their arrival. Sometimes Producer Assistants or Studio Executive Assistants will handle cast gift baskets, but it may be asked of the Production Office. We've already discussed the importance of research, and here it can come into play in a big way. Where can you purchase a fresh gift basket for your guests, and what kind of things should this include? Your PC or APC will provide insight and budget as to the size and type of gift basket, but you will need to research and present the best options.

Here are some questions to consider:

- Who is the recipient?
- Has their agent or assistant provided any tips on what the person might like?
- Do they prefer flowers over food?
- How long will they be staying?
- Are they new to this location? Would a basket of goods from local vendors be preferred over something more generic?
- What is the budget for gift baskets?
- Can they be placed in the guest's accommodations before their arrival? Do they need to be delivered to the cast member's trailer on set?

Be sure to gather as much information about the person and purpose of the gift basket as you can, so you can find the best fit in your research. Plan with the Production Coordinator as to how to pick up or deliver the gift basket to the recipient in a proper timeline prior to their arrival.

Welcome packets

When you have a guest from out of town, even if they have been to that town before, it is customary (and nice!) to provide basic local information they can use for their stay. Be it a Producer, cast member, or an entire crew living on location, a welcome packet of information is an extremely helpful resource and can hopefully avoid you being asked the same questions over and over by each new arrival! Your Production Coordinator may have a template, but you will be asked to compile the information that goes in it. Here are some basic things to include:

Location information:

- Where are they staying? Include the hotel/accommodation name, address, phone, and website, if available.

- Where is the Production Office in relation to the accommodation? Provide an address and a map showing the location and directions to the Production Office.
- Where are their accommodations in relation to the nearest big city?
- What resources and amenities does the accommodation offer?
    - Laundry service or laundry facilities.
    - Daily cleaning service.
    - Room service.
    - 24-hour doorman.
    - On-site fitness center.
    - On-site restaurants.
    - Parking.
- List emergency production contacts. Who should they call from production if they have a problem? What if it's after hours and the Production Office is closed?
- Emergency services. Where is the nearest hospital? Twenty-four-hour medical clinic?

Local Resources:

- Nearest laundromat and hours.
- Local pharmacy and hours.
- Local grocery store and hours.
- Coffee shops and bars.
- Four to five local restaurants with takeout and/or delivery (what are the local delivery services or apps available in that area?). Try to list a variety of food options.
- Nearest banks.
- Nearest US post office.

Entertainment and Attractions:

- Local museums or places of interest.
- Outdoor fitness areas such as parks or hiking trails.
- Indoor fitness centers/gyms.
- Music venues.
- Movie theaters.
- Retail and shopping areas.

Is there other information you have that may prove useful to the guest? Anything specific to the production that may be important for their stay? It's a professional courtesy to make your cast and crew feel as at-home as possible when working on location.

This section was meant to prepare you to be an expert on all aspects of working in the Production Office. You now have the knowledge needed to set up an office, file all the things, work digitally, distribute documents, and how to keep the office operating at its highest level of efficiency. The step-by-step processes may seem challenging, but once you put these words to action, it will be way easier than you think. You can use this guide on the job to collate scripts and run sides, set up meetings, and refill the office supplies. Refer to the graphics, lists, and sample documents provided to help do your craft services shopping, package distribution, paperwork logging, and turn in your petty cash receipts. Everything you need to do the job is here.

But there's still more.

KEYS TO SECTION 4

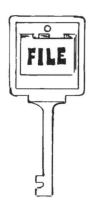

- By applying the "how tos" in this section you will be performing the role of an Office PA at a professional level.
- These guidelines should be adapted to the preferences of the office in which you are working.
- Ask the right questions. Do the research.
- Sometimes the best contribution you can make to a project is to ensure your cast, crew and Producers feel at home, whether on location or in the Production Office.
- Treat every assignment like a story; it should have a beginning, middle, and end. What do you need to do before starting the task, how do you perform the task, and what makes the task complete?

5 TURNING THE PAGE ON PRODUCTION PAPERWORK

Finally! You've reached the paperwork section we've talked so much about. Production paperwork is the backbone of production operations. It informs, records, and dictates every aspect of the show and contains information the cast and crew need to do their job. We will walk you through each type of document, what it is used for, and provide examples for you to best understand its purpose. These documents may be created and distributed in hard copy or as digital files. You will be responsible for helping to distribute all of them.

Production paperwork can be categorized into seven groups:

- CONTACT LISTS: *The Who's Who!* Used to collect and share contact information for cast, crew, locations, and production vendors.
- SCHEDULES: *When and where it all happens.* Schedules are used to organize the timelines for pre-production through post production and for each day of filming throughout principal photography.
- SCRIPTS: *What's the story?* The foundation of what is being filmed. The written action, sets, characters, and dialogue to be brought to life on camera.
- REPORTING: *Who? What? Where? Why? And How?* Paperwork containing information required to be reported to the Studio or producing entity regarding production costs and schedule progress.
- FINANCIAL: *Day 3 cost how !*$%^ much?!* Paperwork documenting work hours, pay rates, and costs associated with principal photography.
- POST PRODUCTION/EDITORIAL NEEDS: *How do the puzzle pieces go together?* These reports are crucial to the editorial team to ensure they have a detailed account of what was captured while filming and to assist them through the post production process.
- OTHER: *What else do we need to know?* Paperwork generated by the office and various other departments to provide information needed for others to do their job.

Many of the documents in these categories will undergo multiple revisions over the course a production. The revision colors outlined in Section 4 will apply. Much of this paperwork is generated in the pre-production phase for both feature films

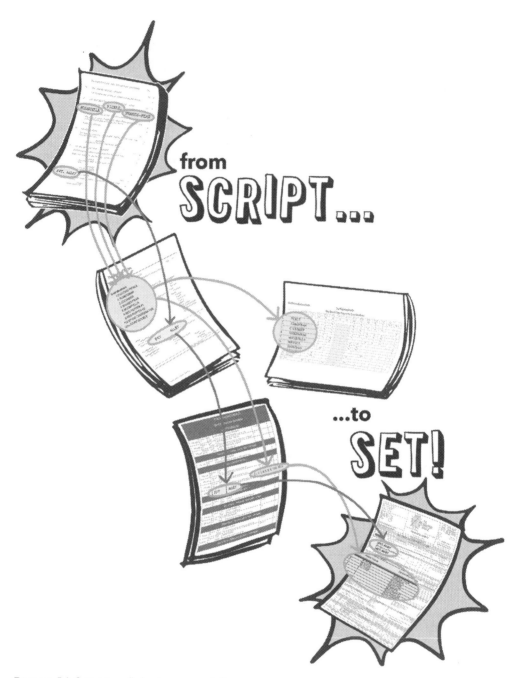

Diagram 5.1 Script to call sheet paperwork flow.

and television series. Paperwork distribution may be more demanding in television due to the repetitive production cycle where documents will be generated episode by episode. For example, a 15-episode season of a television show may issue two or three one line schedules per episode in pre-production and maybe one more during principal photography of that episode, if needed. This means you may be distributing up to 60 or more one line schedules in a single season! However, a feature film may issue five one line schedules in the pre-production period (white, blue, pink, yellow, green) and possibly a few more during principal photography as needed based on schedule changes. Being familiar with what these documents look like and how the information they provide is used will better prepare you to support the production.

FROM THE SCRIPT TO THE FILM SET (VIA PAPERWORK)

With incredible amounts of money on the line for every show, a little repetition is necessary to ensure information is properly tracked, shared, and managed. There are areas of redundancy within the various types of production paperwork that link one document to another. This is most apparent in the process of how the script gets translated into what will actually be filmed on that day, as in, "How do we go from a script page to what is captured on camera?" Diagram 5.1 illustrates the script-to-set process in a nutshell.

In pre-production, the script is broken down into elements that either appear or are heard on screen. This is called the **breakdown process** and is done by the Line Producer and/or UPM for the purpose of budgeting, and by the 1st AD for the purpose of scheduling. It is essentially pulling apart the script, scene by scene, and identifying departmental needs. The breakdown excludes dialogue. Once the script has been reduced to a skeleton, these lists of elements are organized into categories such as actors, costumes, props, locations, set dressing, special effects, stunts, etc., by scene. Each scene is compacted down into **strips** in order to build a "one line" schedule. This schedule will determine how many days the show should (or has to) be filmed in. The strips are relatively concise and include only the most crucial information, such as scene number, number of script pages, set, scene description, and cast members. Once the schedule has been built, its sister document, traditionally called the "shooting schedule," is born. This document will list all of those pulled-out script elements in full detail in one master reference document. It is essentially the script without stage direction and dialogue, which lists the elements within their categories. The one line schedule has another sibling, called the "Day Out of Days" (DOOD). This is a chart that lists what filming day a cast member or other element is working. The Day Out of Days speaks a slightly different language than its siblings. It uses coded terms to indicate what status the element is in on any particular day. This "status" code is also reiterated on the Exhibit G, call sheet, and **production report** for all cast members and stunt performers, and can also be applied to elements such as special effects, vehicles, animals, etc.

Day Out of Days code translation:

S = Start – The first workday for a character or element, often listed as SW (Start Work).
W = Work – The character or element is working.
H = Hold – The character or element is not working this day but is on standby should they be needed.
TR = Travel – The performer is traveling this day.
FT = Fitting – The performer is having a fitting this day.
F = Finish – This is the last workday for a character or element, usually accompanied by a "W" for WF (Work Finished).
R = Rehearsal – An actor or stunt activity is being rehearsed and may not appear on camera.
D = Drop – The character or element has a break in their work and are temporarily dropped from the schedule.
PU = Pick Up – The character or element is picking up their work and resuming their schedule.
SWF = Start, Work, Finish – The character or element is both starting work and finishing work on this day.

Once principal photography starts, information from the one line schedule, shooting schedule, and Day Out of Days are merged together into the daily call sheet. Each of these documents references the other. The call sheet is then used as the guide for what will be filmed that day. That's how a script makes its way to the set. The End.

Morning paperwork

Once you have the call sheet, a day of filming is ready to begin. Throughout the filming day, paperwork is generated on set to organize and track filming progress. These documents make up the daily paperwork and are filed in the "day files." At wrap during principal photography, the set will deliver an accordion file folder or "football" of paperwork generated that day. The morning Office PA is responsible for distributing the paperwork per the morning distro log and returning the empty file back to the AD's. This is processing the morning paperwork. The football gets passed back and forth within Production, hence earning its name "football." Many of these documents are now sent digitally between set and the office, but the review and distribution of these documents will still fall to the Production Office and as part of the Office PA's responsibilities. Morning paperwork documents will be highlighted throughout the categories in this section.

CONTACT LISTS

Crew list

A comprehensive list of phone numbers and email addresses of all crew, Studio, Network, and Production Company staff on a show. It will include cell phone numbers as well as office lines and extensions (if applicable). When you need to reach someone on the crew, this is what you will use. The contact information listed on the crew list is collected by the Production Office and is approved to be listed by the crew members themselves. The information they provide the PO is the preferred method of how they want to be reached. If someone has elected not to list a cell phone number, such as the Accounting Department or the Producer, they likely prefer you to contact them through their work number or email only. The crew list is generated by the Production Office and is distributed at the discretion of the Production Coordinator. An example crew list can be found in the Appendix.

Vendor list

A list of businesses and third-party vendors a production uses for things like housing, equipment rentals, services, expendables, and other purchases. It includes phone numbers, email addresses, and physical addresses, as well as a contact representative. If you are asked to call a vendor for research, to place an order, or to give them a P.O. number, this is the document you will use to contact them. The vendor list is generated by the Production Office and is distributed at the discretion of the Production Coordinator.

Cast list

A general list of all cast members and their roles for the show or episode. Commonly, only agent and manager contact information is listed along with the performer name and role. This version of the cast list excludes pay rates, Social Security numbers, and cast personal information such as home addresses, phone numbers, or email addresses. The cast list may be generated by the Casting department or the Production Office and is distributed at the discretion of the Production Coordinator.

Confidential cast list

A detailed contact list of all cast members and their roles for the show or episode. This list includes confidential information such as pay rates, select deal points, personal phone numbers, home addresses, and email addresses, as well as agent and manager contact info. This document may also include Social Security numbers and is deemed <u>highly confidential</u>. When a script needs to be delivered to a cast member's home, this is where you will find their address. The confidential cast list may be generated by the Casting department or Production Office and is distributed at the discretion of the Production Coordinator.

Location contact list

A list of all practical filming location addresses for the show or episode. This can vary in detail to also include direct contact information for the property representative and date of filming or be more general to simply list the address of each location and its set description. It is unlikely you will have a reason to reference the location contact list, as you will not be contacting locations directly and will use a location map when making runs to the set. The location contact list is generated by and distributed at the discretion of the Location Manager.

Phone extension list

This is a list of the phone and extension numbers assigned to crew working in the Production Office who have a designated landline phone. It includes the department, people's names and positions, and their extension numbers. This list is placed next to each office phone so crew can easily direct and transfer calls to one another.

SCHEDULES

One line schedule

The "one line" schedule, also referred to as the "strip board," breaks each scene in the script down into a brief description of WHO, WHAT, WHEN, and WHERE. This document will tell you when any scene in the script is scheduled to be filmed and is a good reference when you need to determine when the company will be at a specific set or location. One tip about reading the one line schedule: the scenes filming that day are located above the strip that identifies the filming day. As you read the document from top down, notice the strip indicating "end of day X." This is called a daybreak. The strips above that marker are the scheduled scenes. The one line schedule is generated by the 1st Assistant Director and distributed at the discretion of the UPM and 1st Assistant Director. Graphic 5.2 is an example of a one line schedule.

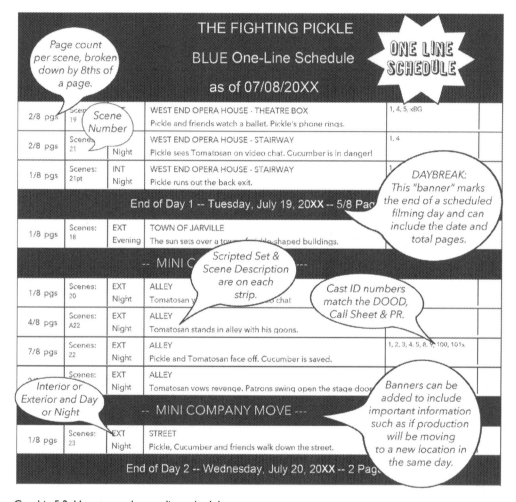

Graphic 5.2 How to read a one line schedule.

Day Out of Days (DOOD)

This document assigns each character in the script a number and is a chart of when they are scheduled to work based on the one line schedule. You are not responsible for notifying a cast member of when they will be working. However, the Day Out of Days can be used as a reference for cast schedules. For instance, if an actor has already completed their work on the project, they will no longer need to receive a script and can be removed from distribution. The DOOD is generated by the 1st AD and distributed at the discretion of the UPM and 1st AD. Graphic 5.3 is an example of a DOOD.

Turning the Page on Production Paperwork 109

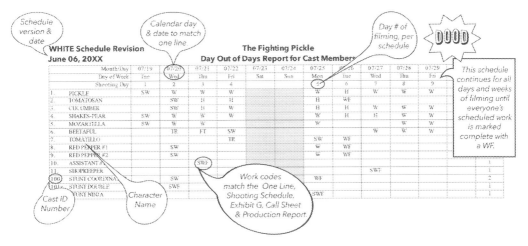

Graphic 5.3 How to read a Day Out of Days.

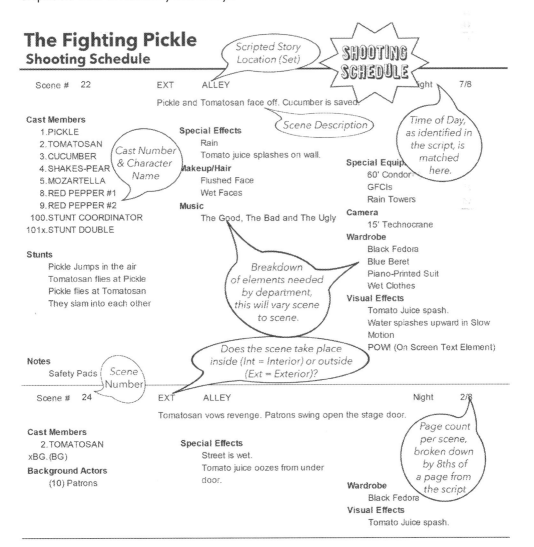

Graphic 5.4 How to read a shooting schedule.

Shooting schedule

The shooting (filming) schedule is a detailed list of all scripted and unscripted elements needed for filming, sometimes organized in filming order based on the one line schedule or chronologically by scene number. It includes a breakdown of everything that is a part of each scene, such as characters, props, set dressing, hair and make-up needs, special equipment, extras, costumes, animals needed, and pyrotechnics. This is another document you likely will not need to reference often. But you will need to know its purpose. The shooting schedule is generated by the 1st AD and distributed at the discretion of the UPM and 1st AD. Graphic 5.4 is an example of a shooting schedule.

Season production schedule

Typically, only seen on scripted television series, this document outlines the entire prep and principal photography schedule for the season. It will include episode numbers, episode titles, who is writing and directing each episode, as well as listing prep, filming, and air dates. Based on the air date of the first episode, the production schedule may determine when the entire season will need to begin production (more on this in a later section). The season schedule can be used to reference which Writer and Director have been assigned to a specific episode and to confirm that the episode's documents are distributed to the correct individuals. The season schedule is distributed at the discretion of the Producer or Showrunner. An example of a season production schedule can be found in Section 9.

Production calendar

Often seen primarily on feature films, this document outlines the prep, principal photography, wrap, and post production schedule for the film as a whole. This calendar may be shared with the Studio, Producers, Director, and department heads. It is a great document to see the full scope of the timeline from start to finish. The production calendar is generated by the UPM or Production Coordinator and distributed at the discretion of the UPM.

Prep schedule

This document lists all meetings and scouts required for preparation of the show. It includes the type of activity, time, location, and who is expected to attend. The type of activities mentioned in Section 4 under "Meetings, Greetings, and Scouts" will be listed here. The prep schedule is distributed daily during the pre-production period. The schedule is dictated by the 1st AD and the document is often generated by the PC or APC. It is updated daily and distributed to all parties involved in the activities listed, as well as others per the discretion of the Production Coordinator. Document 5.5 is an example of a prep schedule.

Turning the Page on Production Paperwork   111

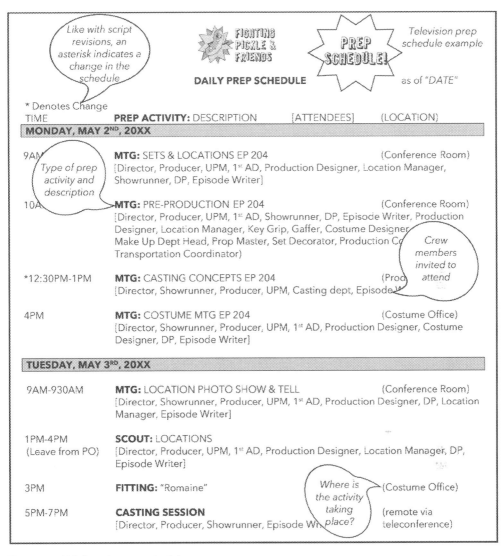

Document 5.5 Sample prep schedule.

Call sheet

This is the blueprint for each upcoming day of filming. It lists times for cast and crew members to report to work, what will be filming that day, any special departmental needs, equipment that will be used, and the location where filming will take place. As a general rule, everything on the front of the call sheet is what is happening in front of the camera, and everything on the back of the call sheet is what is happening behind the camera. The call sheet is generated by the 2nd AD and distributed at wrap every day of principal photography, once it has been approved by the 1st AD and UPM. Despite the document being called a "call sheet," cast and crew phone numbers are not part of this piece of paperwork other than on commercials. The call sheet should not be confused with the crew list. This is a document you will use often. It is needed when pulling sides, updating the progress board, confirming where filming is taking place, and determining who is working that day. The original call sheet (usually signed by the 1st AD and UPM) is filed as part of the morning paperwork distro. Document 5.6 is an example of a call sheet.

112 Turning the Page on Production Paperwork

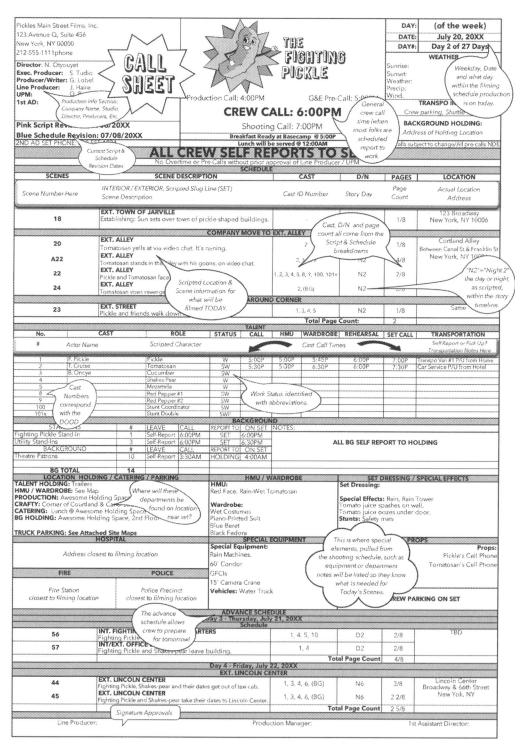

Document 5.6 How to read a call sheet.

CALL SHEET

CREW CALL: 6:00PM
THE FIGHTING PICKLE
Wednesday July 20, 20XX
Day # of # Days

#	TITLE	LV	CALL	NAME	#	TITLE	LV	CALL	NAME	#	TITLE	LV	CALL	NAME
	PRODUCTION					**COSTUMES/WARDROBE**					**PRODUCTION OFFICE**			
1	Director		6:00P	N. Otyouyet	1	Costume Designer	O/C		S.E. Crandell	1	Production Coordinator		O/C	H. Pilch
1	Producer/Writer		O/C	G. Lobel	1	Asst Costume Designer	O/C		C. Lothies	1	Asst Production Coordinator		O/C	T. Hartsfield
1	Line Producer		O/C	J. Haire	1	Wardrobe Supervisor	O/C		H. Bogart	1	Production Secretary		O/C	I. Bergman
1	UPM		6:00P	O. Brooks	1	Key Set Costumer	O/P		V. Corum	1	Office Production Ass't		O/C	YOU!!
1	1st Assistant Director		6:00P	S. Reed	1	Set Costumer	O/P		G. Debole	1	Office Production Ass't		O/C	A. Awesom
1	Key 2nd Asst Director		4:00P	P. Elizabeth	1	Set Costumer	O/P		W. Towear					
1	2nd 2nd Asst. Director		4:00P	L. Norma							**ACCOUNTING**			
1	DGA Trainee		4:00P	J. Rait	1	Costume Coordinator	O/C		T. Shirt	1	Production Accountant		O/C	P. Orli
					1	Costume PA	O/C		D. Ressme	1	1st Asst. Accountant		O/C	T. Holloman
1	Key Set Production Ass't		4:00P	R. Simone	1	Tailor	O/C		P. Lauren	1	2nd Asst Accountant		O/C	P. Nelson
1	Set Production Assistant		4:00P	U. Lockup						1	2nd Asst. Accountant		O/C	C. Ounts
1	Set Production Assistant		4:00P	B. Grus						1	Payroll Accountant		O/C	Y. Grogu
1	Set Production Assistant		4:00P	P. Isup		**MAKE UP**				1	Payroll Clerk		O/C	M. Oney
1	Add'l Set Production Ass't		4:00P	I. Lovemovies	1	Make Up Dept. Head		4:45P	S. Sebag					
1	Add'l Set Production Ass't		4:00P	C. Kane	1	Key Make Up		5:00P	R. Two	1	Accounting Clerk		O/C	A. Filer
					1	Make-Up Artist		5:30P	T. Hayden		**LOCATIONS**			
					1	Add'l Make Up Artist		5:30P	D. Sullivan	1	Location Manager		O/C	G. King
										1	Key Asst. Locations Manager		O/C	L. Skywalker
						HAIR				1	Asst Locations Manager		O/C	D. Decerbo
	CONTINUITY				1	Hair Dept. Head		4:45P	L. Park	1	Location Scout		O/C	M. Scorsese
1	Script Supervisor		6:00P	S. Evoy	1	Key Hair		5:00P	B. Sty	1	Locations Coordinator		O/C	L. Motive
					1	Hair Stylist		5:30P	I. Clip	1	Locations Assistant		O/C	P. Picasso
	CAMERA									1	Locations Assistant		O/C	F. Aplace
1	Dir. Of Photography		6:00P	P. Irma	1	Add'l Hair Stylist		5:30P	K. Koss	1	Unit PA		O/C	A. Shaker
1	A Camera Operator		6:00P	A. Arri		**ART DEPARTMENT**								
1	B Camera Operator		6:00P	C. Pany	1	Production Designer	O/C		R. McQaurrie	1	Parking Coordinator		O/C	C. Threepio
1	1st Assistant "A" Camera		5:45P	T.C.S	1	Art Director	O/C		N. Mate	1	Asst Parking Coordinator		O/C	M. Owens
1	1st Assistant "B" Camera		5:45P	Y. Cinemato	1	Ass't Art Director	O/C		SS. Berg		**CATERING**			
1	2nd Assistant "A" Camera		5:45P	BB Eight	1	Art Department Coordinator	O/C		M. O'Brien	1	Catering Chef		O/C	R. Toeat
1	2nd Assistant "B" Camera		5:45P	C. Lapper	1	Art PA	O/C		H. Solo	1	Sous Chef		Per RT	I. Cooks
1	Digital Image Tech		5:45P	A. Lut						3	Catering Assistant		Per RT	T. Helpers
1	Loader/Media Manager		6:45P	J. Nadelman		**CONSTRUCTION**					Early Breakfast rdy for		15 Crew @	5:00P
					1	Construction Coordinator	O/C		L. Builder		Crew Breakfast rdy for		80 Crew @	5:30P
					1	Key Carpenter	per LB		C. Nails				14 BG	5:30P
1	Still		6:00P	P. Forme	1	Construction	per LB		F. Wood		Crew Lunch rdy for		95 Crew @	11:30P
					1	Car	per LB		C. Bacca				14 BG	11:30P
	GRIP				1		per LB		C. Macchia					
1	Key Grip		5:00P	F. Lag	1		per LB		H. Levenstone		**POST PRODUCTION**			
1	Best Boy Grip		5:00P	C. Stand	1	BB	per LB		U. Wrench	1	Post Producer		O/C	B.
1	"A" Dolly Grip		5:00P	D. Pollock	1	Construction Grip	per LB		S. Bullock	1	Post Supervisor		O/C	8.
1	"B" Dolly Grip		5:00P	W. Sote	1	Shop Electrician	per LB		J. Bulbs	1	Post Coordinator		O/C	H. Jaxt
2	Grip		5:00P	C. Rane, O. Perator	1	Construction Shop PA	per LB		I. Hanrin	1	Editor		O/C	S. Jones
2			6:00P	H. Oldon, F. Life						1	Assistant Editor		O/C	P. Leia
1			O/C	C. Fortyseven	1	Greensperson	O/C		T. Plants	1	Post Production Ass't		O/C	H. Rylan
1	BB		Per CF	L. Anders Brown										
1	Rigging Grip		Per CF	R. McKee		**SCENIC**					**CASTING**			
1	Rigging Grip		Per CF	W. Maxwell	1	Charge Scenic	O/C		B. Ross	1	Casting Director		O/C	J. Faris
					1	Camera Scenic		6:00P	O. Screen	1	Casting Associate		O/C	E. Hornak
					1	Scenic Journeyman	per BR		M. Falcon					
	LIGHTING				1	Scenic Foreperson	per BR		P. Brusher					
1	Gaffer/Chief Lighting Technician		5:00P	M.P. Prisco Jr	1	Scenic Artist	per BR		C. Williams	1	BG Casting Director		O/C	D. Shahrir
1	Best Boy Electrician		5:00P	F. Lights	1	Scenic Artist	per BR		J. Goldman	1	BG Casting Associate		O/C	B. Ackground
1	Lighting Board Operator		5:00P	K. Miller		**PROPS**				1	BG Casting Assistant		O/C	C. Finder
2	Electrician/Lamp Operator		5:00P	L. Bulb, C. Ondor	1	Prop Master		6:00P	C. Red		**TRANSPORTATION**			
1	Electrician/Lighting Tech		5:00P	D. Johnston	1	Assistant Prop Master		6:00P	J. Peterson	1	Transportation Coordinator		O/C	D. River
					1	Add'l Props		6:00P	G. Haire	1	Transportation Captain		O/C	O. Mobile
					1	Add'l Props		6:00P	H. Ands	1	Transportation Co-Captain		O/C	T. Rucker
										1	DOT Coordinator			T. Yota
1	Basecamp Genny Op		5:00P	G. Otgas		**SET DECORATION**				1	Van 1			F. Ord
					1	Set Decorator	O/C		A. Blue	1	Van 2			C. Verolet
1	Key Rigging Gaffer		O/C	P. Relight	1	Ass't. Set Decorator	O/C		E. Lephant	1	Electric Truck			I. Niti
1	BB Rigging Electric		Per FR	R. Iggs	1	Set Dec Buyer	O/C		L. Toshop	1	Grip Truck			B. Truck
1	Rigging Electric		Per FR	M. Haire	1	Leadperson	O/C		B. Anactor	1	Camera Truck			T. Gears
1	Rigging Electric		Per FR	A. Crewmember	1	Foreperson	Per BA		T. Hanks	1	Set Dressing Truck			S. Wagon
										1	Rigging Grip Truck			B. Entley
	SOUND				1	On Set Dresser		6:00P	O. Set	1	Rigging Electric Truck			C. Adillac
1	Sound Mixer		6:00P	D. Uhearme						1	Wardrobe Trailer			A. Udi
1	Boom Operator		6:00P	M. Icra	1	Set Dresser	Per BA		I. Move	1	Hair/Make Up			J. Eep
1	Sound Utility		6:00P	P. Hone	1	Set Dresser	Per BA		B. Ontopofit	1	Honeywagon			L. Rover
					1	Set Dresser	Per BA		A. Dresser	1	Cast Camper			L. Incoln
	ADDITIONAL LABOR									1	2 Rm/Fuel			H. Yundai
1	Video Playback Operator		N/C	S. Alan		**SPECIAL EFFECTS**				1	2 Rm/Genny			D. Odge
1	VFX Supervisor		6:00P	G. Lucas	1	SPFX Supervisor	O/C		N. Lobel	1	3 Rm/Cable			J. Upiter
					1	SPFX Coordinator	O/C		B. Lowstuffup	1	Swing Truck			M. Oon
	HEALTH & SAFETY				1	SPFX Technician	O/C		M. Akerain					
1	Set Medic		5:00P	R. Youok		**CRAFT SERVICE**								
1	Health & Safety Officer		5:00P	F. Iredude	1	Key Craft Service	Ready @	6:00P	C. Snackle					
					1	Craft Service Ass't	Ready @	6:00P	S. Pop					

PRODUCTION NOTES: Bring RAIN GEAR (in case of bad weather) and a SMILE!

TRANSPORTATION NOTES: Vans leave from the corner of Someplace and Someplace else.

Document 5.6 (Continued)

Preliminary call sheet

The preliminary call sheet is a draft of the call sheet. Typically, only distributed to department heads, it is copied on yellow (canary) legal paper and stamped "PRELIM" so that no one can confuse it with the actual call sheet. In some circumstances, a final call sheet may need to be revised and a new call sheet distributed. Revisions will follow the same color structure as script revisions. Yellow is far enough down on the revision color order that it is *extremely* unlikely an official yellow revised call sheet would be distributed. The preliminary call sheet allows departments a chance to make changes or ask questions before the final call sheet is distributed. Often simply referred to as "the prelim," it is generated by the 2nd AD and distributed at lunch or midday every day of principal photography once approved by the 1st AD and UPM.

Extras breakdown

This is a pre-production document that identifies the quantity and type of background performers needed for each scene per filming day. Different from the **background breakdown** that comes in each night in the football, it mimics the one line or shooting schedule in format. It is generated by an AD and distributed at the discretion of the UPM. It will give you an idea of how many extras will be called in to work on a particular day. This information will also be listed on the shooting schedule.

SCRIPTS

Studio script outline

Primarily used only in television, this is an outline of a script draft that is being released to the Studio for notes. Distributed at the discretion of the Showrunner.

Network script outline

Primarily used only in television, this is an outline of a script draft that is being released to the Network for notes. Distributed at the discretion of the Showrunner.

Studio script draft

Primarily used only in television, this is a pre-production draft of the script that is being released to the Studio for notes. Distributed at the discretion of the Showrunner.

Network script draft

Primarily used only in television, this is a pre-production draft of the script that is being released to the Network for notes. Distributed at the discretion of the Showrunner.

Production script

The first official draft of the script. It will be on white paper and be the first script to lock scene numbers and pages. Distributed at the discretion of the Producer or Showrunner.

Some shows may have varying degrees of "pre-production" script drafts with specific distributions assigned to them, (such as a draft for department heads only). Every show has nuances.

Script revisions

Revised pages of the script. Revisions are marked with asterisks (*) on the side of the pages to indicate where a change was made. If there is an asterisk on the page, the page will be a different color than it was previously. See "Script Revisions" in Section 4 for a refresher of the details. Distributed at the discretion of the Producer or Showrunner.

REPORTING DOCUMENTS

Production report

The production report is the companion document to the call sheet and includes all information from a single day of filming. It is generated after filming wraps each day. This is where we record the cast and crew in (start) and out (end) times, scenes filmed, duration of screen time filmed, the number of background performers that worked, the amount of film rolls or camera cards used, and the amount of sound "rolls" or data recorded. Whereas the call sheet dictates what is intended to happen, the production report reflects what *actually* happened on that day. It will also list any delays, injuries, or damaged equipment that was reported. Commonly referred to as "the PR," it is often initially generated by the 2nd 2nd AD and cleaned up by the PC or APC before distribution.

The "preliminary" production report is the first distribution. It is likely missing a few bits of information but is distributed so that those needing information from it immediately (i.e., Accounting) can begin their review process. Accounting uses this document as a way to track spending, and the Studio and Producers use it to track progress, which can be indicative of potential cost overages. This will be distributed as part of the morning paperwork each day.

The "final" production report is approved and signed off on by the UPM for Studio approval and final distribution. This document is the official record of the completed day's work and is considered a legal document. The production report is distributed at the discretion of the UPM and Production Coordinator. Document 5.7 is an example of a preliminary production report.

Lunch report

The lunch report is a progress report of what has been filmed by lunchtime each day. Lunchtime occurs approximately six hours after crew call. The lunch report will include the scenes, number of pages, and estimated screen time that has been filmed up to this point, as recorded by the Script Supervisor. The information is called in

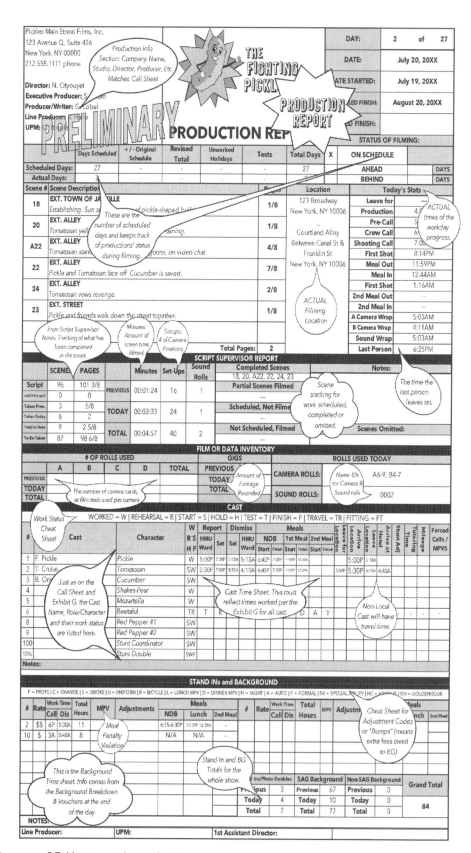

Document 5.7 How to read a production report.

PRODUCTION REPORT

CREW CALL: 6:00PM (18:00)   **THE FIGHTING PICKLE**   **CAMERA WRAP:** 5:03AM (29:03)   July 20, 20XX   Day # of # Days

PRELIMINARY

PRODUCTION

#	TITLE	NAME	IN	OUT	MPV
1	Director	N. Otyouyet	6:00P	5:03A	
1	Producer/ Writer	G. Lobel	O/C		
1	Line Producer	J. Haire	O/C		
1	UPM	O. Brooks	O/C		
1	1st Assistant Director	S. Reed	6:00P	5:03A	
1	Key 2nd Asst Director	R. Elizabeth	16:00	30:11	
1	2nd 2nd Asst. Director	L. Norma	16:00	30:31	
1	DGA Trainee	J. Rait	16:00	30:11	
1	Key Set Production Ass't	R. Simone	16:00	30:31	
1	Set Production Assistant	U. Lockup	16:00	30:31	
1	Set Production Assistant	B. Grus	16:00	30:31	
1	Set Production Assistant	P. Isup	16:00	29:03	
1	Set Production Assistant	R. Rolling	16:00	30:31	
1	Add'l Set Production Ass't	I. Lovemovies	16:00	30:31	
1	Add'l Set Production Ass't	C. Kane	16:00	30:31	

Crew Member Names & Positions

CONTINUITY

1	Script Supervisor	S. Evoy	6:00P	6:03A	

CAMERA

1	Dir. Of Photography	P. Irma	6:00P	5:03A	
1	A Camera Operator	A. Arri	6:00P	5:03A	
1	B Camera Operator		6:00P	4.11A	
1	1st Assistant "A" Cam		5:45P	6:11A	1L
1	1st Assistant "B" Cam		5:45P	4.45A	1L
1	2nd Assistant "A" Cam		5:45P	6:11A	1L
1	2nd Assistant "B" Cam		5:45P	4.45A	1L
1	Digital Image Tech		5:45P	6:11A	1L
1	Loader/ Media Manager	Edelman	5:45P	6:11A	1L

Other shows may stick with the 12hr clock and use AM / PM

1	Still Photographer	P. Forme	6:00P	5:03A	

GRIP

1	Key Grip	F. Lag	5:00P	5.54A	2L
1	Best Boy Grip	C. Stand	5:00P	5:54A	2L
1	"A" Dolly Grip	D. Pollock	5:00P	5:54A	2L
1	"B" Dolly Grip	W. Soto	5:00P	5:54A	2L
1	Grip	C. Rane	5:00P	5:54A	2L
1	Grip	H. Oldon	6:00P	5:54A	
1	Grip	O. Perator	6:00P	5:	
1	Grip	F. Life	6:00P	5:54A	
1	Key Rigging Grip	C. Fortyseven	O/C		
1	BB Rigging Grip	L. Anders Brown	Per CF		
1	Rigging Grip	R. McKee	Per CF		
1	Rigging Grip	W. Maxwell	Per CF		

LIGHTING

1	Gaffer /Chief Lighting Tech	M. P. Prisco Jr	5:00P	6:25A	2L
1	Best Boy Electrician	F. Lights	5:00P	6:25A	2L
1	Lighting Board Operator	K. Miller	5:00P	6:25A	2L
1	Electrician/ Lamp Operator	L. Bulb	5:00P	6:25A	2L
1	Electrician/ Lighting Tech	C. Ondor	5:00P	6:25A	2L
1	Electrician/ Lighting Tech	D. Johnston	5:00P	6:25A	2L
1	Basecamp Genny Op	G. Otgas	5:00P	5:54A	2L
1	Key Rigging Gaffer	P. Relight	O/C		
1	BB Rigging Electric	R. Iggs	Per PR		
1	Rigging Electric	M. Haire	Per PR		
1	Rigging Electric	A. Crewmember	Per PR		

SOUND

1	Sound Mixer	D. Uhearme	6:00P	5:24A	
1	Boom Operator	M. Icra	6:00P	5:24A	
1	Sound Utility	P. Hone	6:00P	5:24A	

ADDITIONAL LABOR

1	Video Playback Operator	S. Alan	N/C		
1	VFX Supervisor	G. Lucas	6:00P	5:03A	

HEALTH & SAFETY

1	Set Medic	R. Youok	5:00P	6:11A	
1	Health & Safety Officer	F. Iredude	5:00P	6:11A	

COSTUMES/ WARDROBE

#	TITLE	NAME	IN	OUT	MPV
1	Costume Designer	S.E. Crandell	O/C		
1	Asst Costume Designer	C. Lothes	O/C		
1	Wardrobe Supervisor	H. Rosarri	5:30P	5:54A	1L
1	Key Costumer				
1	Set Costumer	D. Dobble	5:30P	5:54A	1L
1	Set Costumer	W. Towear	5:30P	5:54A	1L
1	Costume Coordinator	T. Shirt	O/C		
1	Costume PA	D. Ressme	O/C		
1	Costume PA	R. Lauren	O/C		

Some shows will use military time/ the 24hr clock to reflect work hours

MAKE UP

1	Dept. Head	S. Sebag	4:45P	5:40A	4L
1	Make Up	R. Two	5:00P	5:40A	3L
1	Make Up Artist	T Hayden	5:30P	5:40A	2L
1	Add'l Make Up Artist	D. Sullivan	5:30P	4:24A	2L

HAIR

1	Hair Dept. Head	L. Paris	4:45P	5:40A	4L
1	Key Hair	B. Stylin	5:00P	5:40A	3L
1	Hair Stylist	I. Clip	5:30P	5:40A	2L
1	Add'l Hair Stylist	K. Koss	5:30P	4:24A	2L

ART DEPARTMENT

1	Production Designer	R. McQaurrie	O/C		
1	Art Director	N. Mate	O/C		
1	Ass't. Art Director	SS. Berg	O/C		
1	Art Department Coordinator	M. O'brien	O/C		
1	Art PA	H. Solo	O/C		

CONSTRUCTION

1	Construction Coordinator	L. Builder	O/C		
1	Key Carpenter	C. Nails	Per LB		
1	Construction Foreman	F. Wood	Per LB		
1	Carpenter	C. Bacca	Per LB		
1	Carpenter	C. Macchia	Per LB		
1	Key Construction Grip	H. Levenstone	Per LB		
1	BB Grip	U. Wrench	Per LB		
1	Construction Grip	S. Bullock	Per LB		
1	Shop Electrician	I. Bulbs	Per LB		
1	Construction Shop PA	I. Hannin	Per LB		

Call & Wrap times are listed for each individual who worked. They may vary, even within a single department.

SCENIC

1		Boss	O/C		
1		O. Screen	6:00P	5:24A	
1	Scenic Journeyman	M. Faicon	O/C		
1	Scenic Foreperson	P. Brusher	O/C		
1	Scenic Artist	C. Williams	O/C		
1	Scenic Artist	J. Goldman	O/C		

PROPS

1	Prop Master	C. Red	6:00P	5:24A	
1	Assistant Prop Master	J. Peterson	6:00P	5:24A	
1	Add'l Prop	G. Haire	6:00P	5:24A	
1	Add'l Props	H. Ands	6:00P	5:24A	

SET DECORATION

1	Set Decorator	A. Blue	O/C		
1	Ass't. Set Decorator	E. Lephant	O/C		
1	Set Dec Buyer	I. Toshop	O/C		
1	Leadperson	B. Anactor	O/C		
1	Foreperson	T. Hanks	Per BA		
1	On Set Dresser	O. Set	6:00P	5:24A	
1	Set Dresser	I. Move	Per BA		
1	Set Dresser	B. Ontopofit	Per BA		
1	Set Dresser	A. Dresser	Per BA		

SPECIAL EFFECTS

1	SPFX Coordinator	N. Lobel	O/C		
1	SPFX Assistant	B. Lowstuffup	O/C		
1	SPFX Technician	M. Akerain	O/C		

CRAFT SERVICE

1	Key Craft Service	C. Snackle	6:00P	5:54A	
1	Craft Service Ass't	S. Pop	6:00P	5:54A	

PRODUCTION OFFICE

#	TITLE	NAME	IN	OUT	MPV
1	Production Coordinator	H. Pilch	O/C		
1	Asst Production Coordinator	T. Hartsfield	O/C		
1	Production Secretary	I. Bergman	O/C		
1	Office Production Ass't	YOU!!	O/C		
1	Office Production Ass't	A. Awesome	O/C		

ACCOUNTING

1	Production Accountant	P. Orli	O/C		
1	1st Asst. Accountant	T. Holloman	O/C		
1	2nd Asst. Accountant	R. Nels	O/C		
1	2nd Asst. Accountant	C. O	O/C		
1		Y.	O/C		
1		M. O	O/C		
1					
1		A. Filer	O/C		

Meal Penalty Violations. "L" means crew member did not break for lunch on time or with company. "D" would indicate penalty at wrap when a 2nd meal (6hrs after lunch) would have been due. i.e. Dinner).

LOCATIONS

1		King	O/C		
1		Skywalker	O/C		
1		L. Decerbo	O/C		
1		M. Scorsese	O/C		
1		L. Motive	O/C		
1		P. Picasso	O/C		
1	Locations Assistant	F. Aplace	O/C		
1	Unit PA	A. Shaker	O/C		
1	Parking Coordinator	C. Threepio	O/C		
1	Ass't Parking Coordinator	M. Owens	O/C		

CATERING

1	Catering Chef	R. Toeat	16:00	28:46	
1	Sous Chef	I. Cooks	16:00	28:46	
3	Catering Assistant	T. Helpers			
	Breakfast Ordered		99		
	Breakfast Served		99		
	Lunches Ordered		109		
	Lunches Served		111		

POST PRODUCTION

1	Post Producer	C. McCrum	O/C		
1	Post Supervisor	B. Killian	O/C		
1	Post Coordinator	H. Jaxton	O/C		
1	Editor	S. Jones	O/C		
1	Assistant Editor	P. Leia	O/C		
1	Post Production Ass't	H. Ryian	O/C		

CASTING

1	Casting Director	J. Faris	O/C		
1	Casting Associate	E. Hornak	O/C		
1	BG Casting Director	D. Shahmir	O/C		
1	BG Casting Associate	B. Ackground	O/C		
1	BG Casting Assistant	C. Finder	O/C		

TRANSPORTATION

1	Transportation Coordinator	D. River	O/C		
1	Transportation Captain	O. Mobile	O/C		
1	Transportation Co-Captain	T. Rucker	O/C		
1	DOT Coordinator	T. Yota			
1	Van 1	F. Ord			
1	Van 2	C. Verolet			
1	Electric Truck	N. Nfiti			
1	Grip Truck	B. Truck			
1	Camera Truck	T. Gears			
1	Set Dressing Truck	S. Wagon			
1	Rigging Grip Truck	B. Entley			
1	Rigging Electric Truck	C. Adillac			
1	Wardrobe Trailer	A. Udi			
1	Hair / Make Up	J. Eep			
1	Honeywagon	L. Rover			
1	Cast Camper	L. Incoln			
1	2 Rm / Fuel	H. Yundai			
1	2 Rm / Genny	D. Odge			
1	3 Rm / Cable	J. Upiter			
1	Swing Truck	M. Oon			

PER CAPTAIN

NOTES! Here will be relevant production notes regarding the day such as injuries, loss & damage, weather delays, etc.

NOTES:
1 A Safety meeting was held at call by the 1st AD.
2 Sound Department reported a broken mic pack. A Loss & Damage report has been filed. Replacement value $TBD.
3 J. White (Background Performer) tripped and hurt their knee. They were seen by the medic and returned to work. Injury report has be
4 Hair and Make Up departments both broke for lunch late from 12:12A - 12:42A, thus incurring additional lunch meal penalties.

Document 5.7 *(Continued)*

to the office by the Script Supervisor, an AD, or a Set PA, then documented by the designated person in the Production Office and sent to the UPM, Studio, and/or Production Company each day. If you are the one to take this call, consult with the APC before sending the information to the Studio. Template 5.8 includes an example of a lunch report.

THE FIGHTING PICKLE

DATE: July 20, 20XX   DAY: 2 OF 22

LUNCH REPORT

CREW CALL:	6:00PM	SCENES SCHEDULED TODAY:	18, 20, A22, 22, 24, 23
SHOOTING CALL:	7:00PM	SCENES COMPLETED BY LUNCH:	18, 20, A22
FIRST SHOT:	8:14PM	SET UPS:	7
LUNCH:	11:59PM - 12:29AM	MINUTES:	0:54
		PAGES:	6/8

WRAP REPORT

FIRST SHOT AFTER:	1:16AM	SCENES COMPLETED TOTAL:	18, 20, A22, 22, 24, 23
CAMERA WRAP:	5:03AM	SCENES SCHEDULED, NOT COMPLETED:	
		SCENES FILMED, NOT SCHEDULED:	
		TOTAL SET UPS:	24
		TOTAL MINUTES:	4:57
		TOTAL PAGES:	2
NOTES:	What a great day!		

Template 5.8 Sample lunch and wrap report.

Wrap report

Similar to the lunch report, this document is a snapshot progress report for the entire day. It essentially answers the question "Did we make our day?" (aka "Did we finish filming everything that was scheduled on the call sheet?"). This way the Studio can track if a production is not on schedule. The wrap report will include the scenes, number of pages, and estimated screen time that was filmed that day as recorded by the Script Supervisor. The information is called in by the Script Supervisor, an AD, or a Set PA, documented by the designated person in the Production Office, and distributed daily. If you are the one to take this call, consult with the APC before sending the information to the Studio. Template 5.8 includes an example wrap report.

POST PRODUCTION/EDITORIAL NEEDS

Sound reports

A report of the sound rolls or data recorded each day by scene. It includes the duration of sound that was recorded as well as notes regarding good and bad takes. A copy of this document is sent to the **post house** and Editor. It is generated by the Sound Mixer and distributed as part of the morning paperwork.

Script supervisor report(s)

The Script Supervisor generates three documents during the course of a filming day. These may be generated in hard copy form or digitally using industry-specific software and shared with the Editorial department as part of the morning paperwork distribution.

The Daily Progress Report – A summary of the work completed that day. More detailed than the wrap report but with less information than the production report, it includes how many scenes and pages were filmed, how much estimated screen time was filmed, the amount of camera and sound rolls used, the times the first shot and first shot after lunch were taken, what time the company officially broke for lunch and camera wrapped, as well as any notes that may specifically affect editorial. It also tracks previously filmed and remaining work to be done. Most of the information from this document is used to compile the production report.

The Lined Script – Indicates exactly what dialogue or action each film take covered. Typically, it can look like script pages with squiggle lines on it.

The Editor's Log – Distributed to the Editor, it will indicate exactly what was filmed, how it was marked on the **slate**, and often can include notes about the type of lens used and what film takes the Director preferred of each particular shot. The editor's log will be given to the Post Production department for further editorial team distribution.

Camera reports

The camera reports are generated for each camera card (or film magazine) used by the camera. They include details such as the scene and take numbers filmed on it, how each take was labeled, lenses or filters used, and it may also indicate if a shot was "G" (good) or "NG" (no good). When shows film on film stock, this report will also be a detailed inventory of the amount of feet per stock that was used as well as any **"short ends"** remaining. This information is documented by the 2nd Assistant Camera person and will be distributed as part of the morning paperwork.

DIT log

The DIT log or "digital imaging tech" data report is similar to the camera report. It tracks the amount of data recorded that day. Often, this report will include stills or screen shots of each take for the colorist to match visual data in post. Generated by the DIT, it is distributed as part of the morning paperwork.

FINANCIAL

Exhibit G

This is a SAG-AFTRA (Screen Actors Guild) document required to be completed by productions employing Guild performers. It is a daily timesheet for all cast members, including stunt performers. This document will contain original signatures of cast members as approval of their work hours and should be handled with care and never marked up. The exhibit G, sometimes just referred to as "the G," is completed on set by the AD team and distributed at the discretion of the Production Coordinator as part of the morning paperwork.

Purchase orders

Discussed in detail in "Basic Accounting" in Section 4, this is a document for accounting. P.O.'s are used like money and are budget "placeholders" for approved costs that allow future expenses to be tracked. Each department will have its own way to distribute and log purchase orders. Refer to Document 4.27 to review.

Catering report

On days where the company has hired a caterer, the caterer will provide a report of how many meals they served. This helps Accounting track the daily cost of meals. The count can also be compared to the amount that was requested to be served in order to catch any discrepancies. The catering report will be distributed as part of the morning paperwork.

Extras vouchers

Payment vouchers are distributed to the background performers working on set each day. This is their timecard and includes their start, lunch, and end time as well as any special compensation adjustments. These will be distributed as part of the morning paperwork.

Skins

The skins come from the extras casting company and are a list of the background performers scheduled to work that day. It will list their names and reporting times. This may or may not come through the Production Office. It may go directly to the AD's from the extras casting company.

Background breakdown

The background breakdown is a summary of the background performers that actually reported to work that day. It groups them by quantity per work hours, times they broke for lunch, and indicates any pay adjustments. It is completed by the AD department on set and comes in the football for distribution with the morning paperwork. The AD's will supply a copy of the background breakdown with the extras vouchers for checks and balances to determine if the correct number of vouchers for extras worked has been received.

Daily time sheets

Completed by each department daily at their wrap, these documents will list all the crew members who reported to work and their work hours. This is then recorded onto the production report and cross referenced by the payroll department. The on set crew Daily Time Sheets will be distributed as part of the morning paperwork.

OTHER

Cast deal memos

This document contains production-related individual deal points for each cast member. It includes the actor name, contact info, pay rate, and any contractual information that has been negotiated between the Agent, Casting Department, and the Producer. Similar to the cast list, content might vary that distinguishes a "confidential" vs. a "non-confidential" cast deal memo. Either way, this is a highly confidential document and is distributed at the discretion of the UPM or the Production Coordinator.

Cast contracts

This document is highly confidential and must be treated as such. This is the signed original employment contract from the cast member. It includes all of the points in the cast deal memo drafted into a legal contract. Generally, these are signed by cast members on set before they appear on camera and then immediately shuttled to the Production Office. Long-form contracts are generated by the Studio Business Affairs or Legal department. Most of the time, short-form or SAG-AFTRA contracts will be generated by the PC. They will be countersigned by the Producer or UPM and selectively distributed to departments like Accounting and Legal at the discretion of the Production Coordinator.

Still photo breakdown

Some shows require still photos for on-camera use and may need a separate filming unit to be hired to create these props or set dressing items. This breakdown will detail exactly what is needed as indicated in the script. The still photo breakdown is usually distributed at the discretion of the Production Coordinator.

Standards and practices

This is a document that comes from the Network and is a detailed list of what is or is not acceptable to be aired on their Network based on what is scripted. This ensures something isn't filmed that might be too offensive for their viewers or goes against the Network's brand. Standards and Practices is generated by the Network for almost every script revision and is distributed to department heads.

Clearance report

This is a document typically generated by the Studio, or an independent script clearance company, based on the current script draft and revisions. The report is a detailed list of names, locations, addresses, artwork, trademarks, brands, etc. that can or cannot be used on screen without clearance or permission to do so. This can include character names or even names on buildings and signs. The clearance report is distributed at the discretion of the Production Coordinator.

Set lists and directors' plans

The set list is generated by the Art department and is a list of all the scripted sets for each show or episode. It indicates which sets are to be built on stage and which will be practical on-location sets. The directors' plans are overhead floor plans of the sets, which assist the Director and DP in their shot selection and design. This is distributed at the discretion of the Art Department Coordinator.

Most production paperwork is relatively self-explanatory and easy to comprehend based on what it is called. Some of these documents are written in "movie speak" and require a little bit of translation in order to decipher. Knowing how to properly read these documents will help you be a more effective Office PA. The sample documents provided should help you through a typical day working in the Production Office.

There are a handful of other common documents used on every production, such as the **show budget** or the script supervisor breakdown. However, they are not listed here, as it is unlikely you will be expected to handle those documents.

Look at the progress you've made! At this point in the book, you now have all of the information you need to do the job of an Office PA. You know production paperwork, office operations, and the skills needed to perform the job. But there is so much more to any job than just the ability to do it. How do you maximize your performance? It's learning what falls between the work and you that can play a large role in your success. Decisions and actions that affect getting and keeping a job, why you might consider taking one job over another, and sometimes simply looking out for number one (you!) are what can help you make the most out of the work experience. The information in the next chapters offers valuable companion information to help you maintain your path in the industry. Being able to navigate the intricacies of how the work comes together will take time and experience. This book alone cannot do the work for you, but it will guide you on that journey as you figure out how to piece it all together.

KEYS TO SECTION 5

- Production paperwork can be broken down into seven category types: contact lists, schedules, scripts, reporting documents, Post Production/Editorial needs, financial, and other.
- Most document types are industry standard and are the same from show to show.
- There are documents that provide information of what is "planned" to be filmed and final reports of what was "actually" filmed. All are essential to tracking the completion of the work.
- Each document has a specific purpose, and this paperwork plays an important role in bringing a script to life on the set.

6 MASTERING THE ART OF WORKPLACE PERFORMANCE

What separates the professionals from the amateurs? It's not only knowing what to do, but also knowing how to perform in the workplace. How well do you work with others? Do you take ownership and pride in the job? Are you actively engaged in each task? How open are you to continually trying to learn new things on a daily basis? This section recommends ways to be effective in your job performance, and the bonus is that much of it can also be applied to life in general. Some of this may seem like common sense and obvious, but reiterating it here will hopefully sharpen your instincts. The combination of skill and performance is key.

IMPRESSIONS AND PERCEPTIONS

The Production Office is a professional place of business. Cast, crew, Producers, and Executives know that it is the central point of communication for the production. How the Production Office performs their responsibilities gives an impression of their functionality so others will perceive them to be efficient. Whether it is ensuring every visitor is greeted, answering the phone on the first ring, or responding to a crisis calmly, it all creates the perception that the office can and does handle anything.

The saying goes, "fake it 'til you make it," but the truth is – you can't fake what you don't know. In production, sometimes things change so quickly it is impossible to be on top of everything all the time. Production is notorious for "hurry up and wait." Either things happen all at once and there are many layers of work that need to be done simultaneously, or you are on standby waiting for that one thing that needs to happen that will trigger everything else. The job of the office is to help all the other departments run smoothly and efficiently. Sometimes that means creating the *impression* that we have everything under control even when we might still have a few things that need to be worked out. There are a number of ways to demonstrate the office is operating at its best.

There is no reason to panic

Many industry professionals started by learning on the job. You will have to learn how to do a lot of tasks, both quickly and accurately. It is natural to get overwhelmed working a new job, especially on something like a movie or television show. Tasks become urgent at the drop of a hat, and you'll have to react. Over time a trust will build among the office staff, and you are part of that. That trust includes the expectation that you will execute a task to the best of your ability and that you won't panic

DOI: 10.4324/9781003252825-6

under pressure. Being able to keep a calm, cool head in the midst of a flurry of activity reinforces this trust. After all, we aren't saving lives, we're making entertainment!

Third drawer from the left

How organized an office is, is also part of the impression it gives. If a document or supply cannot be found with little fuss, the office may be perceived as unorganized and messy and not operating most efficiently.

Keep your shirt on

We'll discuss dress code later in this section; however, it is important to know that you represent the production at all times. This includes having a professional, work-appropriate appearance. If the impression you give is frumpy or impractical, it will be a reflection on the Production Office as a whole.

Who's holding on line 2?

Ever tried calling your Internet provider only to be put on hold forever? The longer you wait, the more frustrated you get. All you want to do is speak with someone, but a robot keeps telling you to wait. The same philosophy can be applied to the Production Office. When a call is not answered within the first couple of rings or a caller is put on hold for too long, they will become frustrated and start to question the effectiveness of the Production Office. The impression is that the office is too busy to handle a simple phone call. You are responsible for promptly managing the phones.

"No Problem, I'm Right on Top of It!"

Attitude creates an impression. When you respond to a task or a request in a manner that exudes competency, you give the impression that you will complete the task, and you'll happily do it as part of the job you've been hired to do. If your response is to argue or to reply with "fine" or "sure, whatever," it sends the message that you may not be up for the task and can be perceived negatively. Unless you are being asked to do something that causes harm to you or someone else, or do something illegal, your response should never be, "no." An acceptable response to a request would be, "yes, absolutely!" or "got it, let me find out and get back to you!" Oh, and no complaining. When the assignment seems rudimentary or a waste of your expensive education or talent, remember that it is not your place to question why the assignment needs to be done. The answer is simple, because it *needs* to get done. These assignments are exactly what you've been hired for. There is no "someone else" to do it. That makes you pretty important in the grand moviemaking scheme.

ASK QUESTIONS. TAKE NOTES.

Do not be afraid to ask a question. Before you start any task, be sure you understand what it is you are being asked to do. If you need clarification, ask, and ask in that moment, rather than guessing. By asking a question you are taking ownership of the assignment and demonstrating you want to do it right. You should feel empowered to ask questions so you can perform to the best of your ability.

It is much better to ask how to do something right the first time than to find out afterward that you did something wrong and don't know how to fix it. Mistakes happen, but an assignment that needs to be redone is a waste of valuable time and can be avoided.

When asking questions, do not forget the hierarchy. The higher up the person is on the Production pyramid, the less inclined you should be to approach them first. Start with their assistant, or the department's second in command before going to the top unless otherwise instructed. Most of your assignments will be from other Production Office staff, and chances are many of them worked their way up in the Production Office and have done the work you are doing. Your best resource might even be with your fellow PAs.

Many questions can be answered simply by knowing where to look. Always try and find out answers to the simple questions before asking your superior. Use existing resources – check emails, files, prep schedules, notes, etc. If the master crew list isn't in the hard copy or digital files and you need to make copies, ask the other PA or the Production Secretary for the most recently approved draft (then make a new master and put it in the files)!

Always carry a notepad and pen. No one expects you to remember everything, even if you think you can. Writing down instructions or the answer to a question indicates you are taking the information seriously and actively listening. This gives the impression that you are ready for an assignment, ready to learn, and ready to deliver an accurate result. You care enough about doing a good job to write the details down. You always want to present this side of yourself to your team, that you are always prepared to do your job.

LISTENING AND COMMUNICATING

Listening and hearing

Much of the information that fuels your day comes from what isn't being said directly to you. This bears reiterating: just because information wasn't delivered to you personally does not mean you should tune it out. This is one place where eavesdropping is sort of okay. If you are alert, paying attention, and listening to the people around you, you will be prepared for whatever comes your way. Then, when a related task is assigned, you'll be ahead of the game because you've been paying attention. Practice listening as well as hearing and comprehending. If you aren't hearing what is being said, then how can you constructively communicate within your team?

Information you overhear in passing should be considered preliminary and not intended to be shared with anyone outside of the Production Office. It can be used as a tool for you to anticipate a need, but not widely shared until confirmed or instructed. This is a quick way for misinformation to spread and can potentially cause a chain reaction of unnecessary work.

Active listening

Be an active listener when being spoken to directly. Pay attention to the person speaking to you, whether they are asking you a question or providing you with instruction. Show that person you are paying attention with eye contact, note taking, or nods of understanding; texting and looking at your phone during a conversation implies you're distracted, unengaged, and is considered disrespectful. Concentrate and remember what is being said and the tone in which it's being said. Then actively respond. If they are asking you a question, perhaps repeat it to them to confirm you understand and are going to find the appropriate answer. If you are being given instructions for a task, a run, or an assignment, reiterate the instructions back to the person to make sure you didn't miss any steps and express to them the action you intend to take. These actions show you were paying attention, you heard and comprehend what is being said to you, and you intend to do the job correctly.

Communicating

The single biggest problem in communication is the illusion that it has taken place.
– George Bernard Shaw

The Production Office is responsible for communication and notifying the crew about numerous production-related information, and you may be the one doing the relaying. First, find out exactly who needs the information; consider that the recipient does not know the information unless you have personally told them. Meeting times and locations change, a run needs to be delayed, whatever it is, if you have been tasked with making notifications, it is important to confirm with each person involved, even if someone says, "I've already told so and so." You should not skip that person without verification from them that they have received the most accurate information. Circumstances could have changed in the time it took you to notify crew of the previous message.

Know what information you are authorized to share. For instance, other than general crew call for each day, the Production Office does not give out individual call times. Phone calls that come in from a cast or crew member asking for their call time must always be directed to the 2nd AD. This is an instance where the Production Office might not have the most up-to-date information, even if you are looking directly at the call sheet with a time next to the person's name!

Assumptions

As the saying goes, "Don't assume or you'll make an Ass out of U and Me." Everyone knows not to do it, yet everyone still does it, and it can create havoc in the Production Office or on the film set. Things change so rapidly in film and television that one cannot afford to assume they have the most current information at any given time. Before you offer an answer to a question or respond to a request, consider if you have been told the information directly, and how long ago you received it. It is never okay to give out information you've heard in passing, as it could be interpreted as the official "Production Office response," even though it may be hearsay. Cast and crew rely on the Production Office to deliver accurate information. Maintaining this trust is vital. If you do not have an answer or think the information you have may be outdated, tell the person asking, "I'll find out and get right back to you." Then, go *ask*. Sometimes you might *think* you know something, but you might not be sure…so always ask and be certain before you give out any information (to anyone!).

Information sharing

As has been expressed repeatedly, the office is constantly receiving and disseminating information. Some of that may come to you in a variety of ways. Imagine, it finally happened, and the Showrunner came into the office and spoke directly to you! Never mind the fact that you were the first person they saw, and they may have referred to you as "hey there" because they can't remember your name, and the person they needed to talk to was not around. The point is, they are talking to you! "We need to push the production meeting to 2 p.m." or "My mom is coming by later; can you make sure she can get onto the lot?" Whatever the information is, make sure it gets passed on to the Production Coordinator *before* taking any action. A meeting push causes a chain reaction: notifications, space availability, catering adjustments, etc. Your information sharing starts with your immediate supervisor. If you receive information, make sure to share it with others in your department (meaning the Production Office staff) so they are not caught off guard. Never put the Production Office in a position of not knowing a piece of information that the UPM or Producer may ask about. The Production Office is the main communication hub for the entire show. You're a team, and information sharing keeps everyone in the office on the same page.

This reporting hierarchy practice also applies to your interactions with other departments. Refer to the crew organizational structure from Section 1 when interacting with the Producers and other crew and departments. How you communicate information, when, and to whom are equally important. Knowing how to communicate this new information increases the efficiency of the Production Office workflow.

There will be times when a cast or crew member approaches you with a task. Not everyone will follow hierarchy protocol. They may skip asking your APC or PC for help and come to you first, such as when the Costume Designer asks for your help with a run or needs a tedious task to be done because their staff is too busy. Of course, the office will assist in any way they can, but you'll need to clear it with the PC first. Your assignments come from the PC and APC, and you should not accept tasks from others without ensuring your boss has approved it. The PC and APC will know what the general needs are for the day and can make an informed decision before prioritizing a task for another crew member or department.

Confidentiality

Working in the Production Office, you will be responsible for distributing highly confidential information. This could be a document with a cast member's phone number or the Producer's address. This information should *never* be used for any purposes other than for the production. When taking a job as an Office PA, you are being entrusted to keep private information *private*. Names of cast and crew members should not be given out to unauthorized callers or visitors. Always ask permission from your PC regarding what information you are permitted to share. Some productions may have you sign a **non-disclosure agreement (NDA)** in which you are agreeing not to speak about the project to any third party. That includes sharing information socially or publicly on social media.

INITIATIVE AND FOLLOW THROUGH

Production gets busy! You may be given a single task or ten at once to complete. When you are given multiple assignments, ask the priority level of each one. Which tasks need to be completed within the hour? The day? The week? Yesterday? It is your responsibility to communicate what assignment you are currently working on, when you have completed it, and that you are able to take on the next round of work. If a task was unable to be completed or there is a delay, make sure the Coordinator knows this and why. They may have you pick it back up the next time you report to work, or it may get handed off. Follow through is vital; the Coordinator may think a task has been completed unless you've told them otherwise. At the end of the day, they are responsible for ensuring the work has been done.

Taking initiative

In general, taking initiative is a good thing. However, in the Production Office your initiative should be focused on the responsibilities within the purview of the Office PA. It will be up to you to inform your office team when it's time for a crafty run or the copy paper is low. You should bring these needs to the attention of your immediate supervisor and offer solutions for completing them. However, it would not be acceptable to call a vendor directly and place an order for more copy paper without first receiving approval. Do not problem-solve without communicating with your team.

Anticipating

If this, then that. By mastering your active listening skills and the office "how to's" outlined in Section 4, you'll soon start to know what needs to happen *before* it happens. You'll check the prep schedule and see a location scout for tomorrow morning, so you will need to prep a cooler and crafty for the scout. Many of your day-to-day tasks will become second nature. There will also be circumstances that perhaps you haven't been looped into. If you were actively listening to conversations within your team, maybe you heard that a blue schedule will be ready for distro later, so you make certain the office has blue paper. This goes hand in hand with knowing when and how to take initiative in your office. You want to anticipate the need and be prepared to act; this way you aren't scrambling later. At the same time, remember to communicate with your PC or APC regarding staff work assignments and find the balance between anticipating a need and stepping on a coworkers' toes. Some Production Offices have multiple PAs and the work may be split among them. Once you have completed work that has been assigned to you, perhaps you see a task that has been assigned to a fellow PA is still in progress. It is okay to offer to help, but if it isn't a communal office task (such as handing out distro), check with the PA or your APC first before just jumping in. Again, be cautious of overstepping someone else's assignment to avoid double-duty, miscommunication, or hurt feelings, which wastes time and resources. No one wants to be made to feel like they aren't doing their job.

Offering suggestions

A way to demonstrate pride in your workplace and show that you respect the job is when you can offer suggestions or improvements that promote efficiency. When you have been tasked with an assignment, it may come with very specific instructions.

In this case, follow them. You may think of an alternative or more efficient way of performing the task and are encouraged to brainstorm in this way. However, do not execute a task in a manner other than how you have been instructed without first consulting with the PC or APC. Determine when a good time would be to discuss an alternative way for a task to be completed. The PC or APC may have a reason for why the assignment needs to be completed in a specific manner. This happens all the time and for reasons that may or may not make sense. That's life in the movie biz! The same applies to general suggestions. Find the right time to discuss your idea.

If you overhear a conversation about a problem, consider who is talking before jumping in to offer a solution – you may not know all of the context and thus could cause confusion or frustration. If you think you might have information or a solution relevant to a specific situation, speak to your APC or PC first and determine how best to present it to the involved parties.

Always be working

There is always work to be done, and in the extremely rare instance where you are in the "waiting" period of a 'hurry up and wait', and you have caught up on all the work; *look busy and/or find something to do*. Online shopping, texting and playing video games *does not* constitute looking busy, and if the Producer witnesses this, they may think there isn't enough work to be done and your job could be eliminated. The PA who takes the initiative to organize the office supply cabinet is demonstrating they can accomplish a task without supervision and may then be rewarded with more responsibility and a chance to learn something new.

Urgency and complacency

Within reason, every task you are assigned should be treated with a sense of urgency. Double urgency if someone is in a holding pattern waiting for the result. The sooner you complete a task the sooner you can move on to the next or be available should an emergency arise. During principal photography, production moves very quickly. You should never find yourself complacent or bored. There is always a task to be done, or a reason to be on standby ready for your next assignment.

If you find yourself consistently becoming complacent or bored working in the Production Office, perhaps it's time to consider another department or another field. There is so much to do and so much happening all around you on a film or TV show that complacency may be a sign it is not the right place for you, and that's okay.

BEING ONE STEP AHEAD

Be a local expert

When working in a **non-production city**, most of the cast and crew will be traveled in from out of town. This means they are not familiar with any aspect of living and working in the city. One of the most beneficial ways to earn your place on the production team is to be a local expert. It is presumably your hometown, so it should be easy! You know that the production will need to set up a Production Office. They will need space, furniture, office machines, coffee, snacks, etc. They will want to dine at local restaurants, need to do laundry, or want to visit the sights on the weekends.

The Production Coordinator will come to you to find the nearest and least expensive place to buy office supplies or help to create a "welcome packet" of local resources and services available that the cast and crew can use. Every one of these things and so many more will be asked of the Production Office. Being able to provide answers makes you invaluable.

Be resourceful

What if you're not native to the city where the show will be filming? What if you're on location yourself? The Production Office will be expected to creatively problem-solve, and so will you. Out-of-the-box thinking could be just the answer to saving the day. Being resourceful means finding solutions to challenges by being proactive, open-minded, and persistent, and using your imagination helps too!

How to be resourceful:

1. IDENTIFY the need or task. What needs to be solved or completed?
   Example: The Production Office needs a copy machine. The rental is for the next three months, and the machine needs to be there in two days.
2. CONFIRM the purpose of the need or task. Why is there a need?
   To make copies! The production needs 24/7 access to a machine that can make multiple copies of 120-page scripts and double-sided schedules, be able to reduce an image to create sides, copy on multiple paper sizes, and ideally print some images in color. Thus, a dedicated copy machine is needed at the office full time.
3. EVALUATE solutions. Does a solution immediately come to mind? Is the task straightforward? Or is further investigation required?
   Production could rent a machine from a local vendor. You've made some calls, searched on the Internet, and learned that the closest place to rent a copy machine is in the next town, and they don't have a machine available for another week.
4. DECIDE if the solution is viable. Does it fit the parameters of the need?
   You've spoken to the PC, and waiting a week for the copier is acceptable. However, if it isn't and production can't wait, then…
5. SEARCH for another solution. What are some other ways this can be solved? What other businesses or who else might also have this type of need?
   On a basic level, the Production Office has the same needs of any other office and therefore is adaptable to out-of-the-box solutions. Does a neighboring business have a machine you can borrow? Yes, but only before 5 p.m. Monday through Friday.

   The local church has a machine you can use, but they are ten minutes down the road. Too far to drive every time you need to make a photocopy.

   You could buy a desktop machine for a relatively low cost; however, bulk printing will be incredibly slow, and you'd go through toner very quickly.

   Hmmm, but it's summer. School is out and there is a high school nearby. You reach out to them and discover they have a machine in the teacher's lounge that doesn't get used often. They agree to loan it to you for the rest of the summer in exchange for a "special thanks" in the film credits!

   Hooray! You found another solution! Present it to the PC for approval, and it's on to the next mission.

By applying these steps to every need, you will eventually find a resolution that fits. The answer will always be "no" if you don't ask, so get creative.

Striving to be better

Constructive criticism comes with the job just as improving is part of the job. Expectations are high. There will be times where you may have misunderstood an assignment and are asked to redo it. You thought you delivered exactly what was asked only to be told the work is incomplete. You'll learn as you go. Everyone makes mistakes. Own them, fix them, do better next time. The important takeaway is to recognize what needed to be done differently. Don't take this criticism personally. When you make an effort to perform better, it will be reflected in your work. The Japanese call this philosophy Kaizen (ky-zen): always strive for continuous improvement.

Incorporating these practices with the office "how to's" makes you a professional Office PA that will be in high demand. Your exceptional performance confirms you were the right hire for the job. However, while knowing how to do the job and the way you are expected to do it is essential, there is still one more component, professional etiquette.

OFFICE ETIQUETTE

There is a standard of human behavior that is sometimes forgotten in the Wild West of filmmaking. We're not talking about proper leg crossing or lifting pinkies for tea, but a level of decorum and dignity in the office is greatly appreciated as it would be anywhere in your life. Whether or not you've worked an office job in the past, if you are reading this book you've likely never worked in one as an Office PA. As with everything discussed in this book, there is a specific way you are expected to perform the job, and how you handle yourself in the office environment is part of it. Here are some common sense guidelines when working in an office environment.

- *The Production Office is not your house*
    Be respectful of the shared space.
    Hang up your coat.
    Don't leave your bags on the floor for someone to trip over.
    Clean up after yourself.
    Don't leave food out. Food trash should be thrown away in the kitchen, never in the office wastebasket. No one likes a stinky office.
    Pick up trash whenever you see it. If a trashcan is full, take the bag out. Replace the bag.
    If you use the last of something, make sure it gets replaced.
    Put things away. Don't leave clutter lying around.
- *You're not at the bar*
    Don't yell.
    Avoid cursing. Don't drop f-bombs and other foul language in the workplace.
    Conversations about inappropriate subjects such as getting wasted, getting stoned, your sex life, etc., are not acceptable in the office. Additionally, getting stoned, getting wasted, or having sex in the office are *also* not acceptable!
    It is absolutely never appropriate to show up to work intoxicated or to sneak booze into your desk.

The Production Office is not social hour. Avoid extensive chitchat. There is work to be done.

Listening to music may or may not be appropriate in your office. Ask your PC before blasting tunes or wearing earphones around the office while you do your work. You need to be able to hear and hold conversations without distraction.

- *Treat everyone with equal respect*

  Be nice.

  The old adage "treat others how you would like to be treated" always applies. No matter where on the hierarchy someone falls, they and you are equally important to the completion of this show.

  Speak to everyone in a professional manner.

- *Common courtesy counts*

  There are loads of people that come into the Production Office every day – the FedEx guy, the 3rd Grip, the building landlord, the Producer, maybe Brad Pitt – You never know who will walk in! Salutations are not overused or outdated, and no one should be ignored. All the lessons from childhood about how to treat others still come into play here and every day. Respect, kindness, courtesy, these are all important in life and our workplace. A "good morning" goes a long way, even if you're personally having a bad day. Say it. This definitely applies to your fellow office staff, but also to every person that walks into the office. This lets them know that the office is a welcoming place and is there to assist. Someone who has never been to the office before might not know whom to approach. Help them out with a "hello."

  When someone looks like they are struggling, offer to help.

  Personal workspace is just that, personal, someone else's, as in *not yours*. Never take up residence at a co-worker's desk. If you borrow something put it back. No one wants to be on the hunt for a stapler in a stapling emergency (it could happen…!). Unless computers are designated to be communal, an individual's computer should be considered off limits. Respect your coworkers' privacy. It's simply not your workspace, and both out of respect and the health of others you should not invade someone else's space. The same philosophy also applies in reverse. Don't leave anything of yours on someone else's desk or workspace. No one wants to come back from the bathroom to find your fountain drink leaving condensation all over their desk. And don't get us started about taking someone's favorite pen….

  Also, use "please" and "thank you," because why not?

- *Interrupting*

  In general, yes, it is rude to interrupt someone mid-conversation. However, "excuse me" is appropriate, and there may be times where it is necessary, such as when an expected return phone call comes in or there is an emergency on set. If you are interrupting someone, approach them, but maintain distance within their eyeline. Hopefully, they will acknowledge you and beckon you for the information. If you need to interrupt someone who is on a call, perhaps slipping them a note with the caller's name on it will get you a quick "yes," they will take the call, or "no," they will call them back. If you have to interrupt a conversation between people, it is never appropriate to just butt into the conversation. Find a natural lull and again, try to catch their eye line. Most people can sense when you are near. However, do not hover. If a minute has passed and you haven't been acknowledged, stand down and walk away until the conversation is finished and then reapproach the person. You may get a quick glance, but if it isn't followed by a signal indicating "yes" or "wait," then "not now" is your answer.

Consider if there is someone else one step above or below them on the pyramid whom the information can be relayed to or who can answer the question or take the call. In some instances, it may not be necessary to approach the specific individual being requested. Check with your PC regarding how they would like these types of situations handled.

PHONE ETIQUETTE

Answering the phone will likely be the task that you do the most. It's always ringing and needs to be given first priority. *How* you answer the phone and handle communication with callers is an important part of the impression the office gives to everyone outside of it. You will be expected to answer the phone within the first one or two rings. Know how to work the phone and how your supervisors, PC, UPM, and Producer, prefer calls for them to be handled. Do they want a handwritten message? A text? An email? A voicemail? All four? You'll also need to be able to recognize when a VIP call comes in.

Here we'll walk you through the proper etiquette to familiarize yourself with the most common types of calls that will come in and how to appropriately handle them. You can practice some of these calls by using the examples in the Appendix "Answering common calls that come into the Production Office."

The Basics

- The Office PA is the "first line of defense" for calls that come into the PO. How you manage calls can greatly impact production operations.
- Always answer the phone within two rings! Do not assume someone else will answer the phone. Make an effort to hustle.
- Know the greeting preferred by your Coordinator. How do they want you to answer the phone?
- Know how your phone system works. Keep a list of all extensions near your phone for easy reference and learn how to transfer a call.

Depending on the scope of the project, each office may be set up a little different. Some may have one main office number where all calls come in; some may only operate off of cell phones. Assess your office situation and discuss protocol with your supervisor. In general, most of the rules presented here will still apply.

When you answer a call, you'll need to determine the following:

WHO is calling? What do they DO or where are they FROM?
Is the person an actor's agent? A rental manager from a vendor?
Get the person's name, title, and where they are calling from before transferring or announcing the call.

Who are they calling FOR? What does that person DO?
Did they ask for a specific person or department? Are they calling for your boss? Is the person expecting their call? If you do not recognize the name of whom the caller is requesting to speak with, ask what the person does for your show so you can narrow it down to a department.

WHY is this person calling?
   You don't need to get the ten-minute back story, but a simple one- or two-sentence reason for why the person is calling will suffice in order for you to give the information to the recipient.

WHO should take this call?
   There are times when a caller may not know who they need to speak with to get their question answered. Do they need a call time? Are they looking for a job? Do they need a check reissued? Check with your immediate supervisor to confirm who the call should be sent to if you aren't clear.

Is who they are calling for *AVAILABLE* to take the call?
   Whether the person they are requesting to speak to is in the office, on the phone, or simply not available, you'll need to navigate the response to the caller appropriately. Sometimes Producers or Production Managers won't want to speak to someone. Maybe you've had to continually deflect a persistent caller. It is not for you to understand their reasons why. Do your best to reassure the caller that their call will be returned, that you have passed the message on, and have no other information at this time. It can feel awkward, but it may happen ten times a day. If the person is truly not available for the call, you'll need to take a message.

Is there *SOMEONE ELSE* who can take the call?
   Can the call be transferred to an assistant or another department representative?

Do you need to gather more *DETAILS* before passing the call on?
   Sometimes you'll need to get a little more information beyond just the reason for the call before you can direct them to the right person.

How *URGENT* is this call? Is this a VIP caller?
   VIP callers include Studio and Network Executives, Producers, the Director, cast, and your bosses!

Do you have *AUTHORITY* to give out the information being requested?
   Never give out the name or location of the production or names of any cast or crew members without permission from your supervisors.

How to Give Good Phone

Ways to greet the caller

"Production, good morning (or good afternoon, good evening…)! How may I help you?" or "Production, this is [insert your name here]."
   You can use a combination of the above. Unless you've been given permission to do so, do not identify your production by name. Treat every caller as though you are happy to hear from them. Your voice can give you away. A curt greeting can be off-putting to a caller. It can be interpreted that you don't want to be there or there is a situation at hand in the office. Keep your greetings light and cheery, even in the most stressful times.

Don't be afraid

When you are first starting out, answering the phone can be intimidating. You'll only get better with practice. Do not be afraid to put a call on hold and ask an office mate how to proceed. Worst case, you accidentally hang up on somebody. While obviously not ideal, it happens, and the person usually calls back.

Sometimes the PC will assign a PA to stay and answer the phones while the staff manages a separate task away from the office. In this instance, you'll need to be able to handle multiple calls that come in at once. Never let a line keep ringing. If you have to put someone on hold to answer another line, then do so. Even though it can be a minor annoyance, most callers will be understanding.

Always be polite

You don't know to whom you might be speaking to when you answer the phone. It is better not to take a chance that it's the Producer or head of the Studio when you answer the phone with, "What's up?" That would be bad. Never mind the fact that you have just dropped a huge pile of script revisions on the floor and there is multicolor paper scattered across the hallway, someone just spilled juice all over the kitchen, and you sprinted across the office to reach the phone. Answer in a cheerful and calm manner. Make it sound like you have everything under control. For the record, it is never appropriate to answer the phone with "what's up?", "yo dawg," or "holla at me."

Answer, inquire, connect, repeat

It is not necessary for you, as an Office PA, to try and decipher what the caller needs or to solve their problem. Get enough information to transfer the call to the appropriate person. There may be some instances where you may be able to assist the caller yourself, as demonstrated in the examples in the Appendix "Answering common calls that come into the Production Office."

Seek out

Always try to find the person being requested by the caller. This may mean poking your head into their office, checking the kitchen, stepping into a meeting (with permission to do so), or calling their cell phone. Do not assume they are unavailable just because they aren't in your field of vision. Make a concerted effort to locate the person before taking the message. However, do not leave a caller on hold for more than two minutes. Alternatively, you can ask the caller if they would like to hold for a short while in case the individual is located or becomes available. Then if they can't be found, take a message.

VIP calls

Prioritize learning the names of the Producers, Studio/Network Production Executives, cast, and your supervisors to easily identify these "very important people" when they call into the office.

Let's practice taking a call!

RING! RING!

You: Production, good morning. This is (Your Name Here). How may I help you?
Caller: Can I speak to Accounting?
You: Of course, May I ask who is calling?
Caller: This is Pablo. (WHO)
You: May I ask where you are calling from and what this is regarding?
Pablo: I'm calling from AplaceYouBuyThings (FROM), and it's about an invoice (WHY). Can I just have Accounting?

You: Just a second, please. I will transfer you to Cameron in Accounting, who is handling invoices.

You need all of this information *before* transferring the call to the right person. In this case, you know that Cameron in Accounting is handling invoices because the Production Secretary has told you this in the past. Or you might put Pablo on hold to ask and find out whom the call goes to; that's okay. Once you know all this information, you can transfer the call to Cameron.

When you transfer a call, be sure to announce the call so the crew member (Cameron) knows who will be on the other end. This way no one is caught off guard or they can deflect the call if necessary – maybe they are busy and need you to take a message.

You: Hi Cameron, I have Pablo from AplaceYouBuyThings about an invoice for you.
Cameron: I am on the other line; can you take a message?
You: Of course, no problem.
Your Response to Pablo:
You: I'm sorry, I think Cameron is taking a break. (WRONG!)
You: I'm sorry, Cameron is not available right now. May I take a message? (RIGHT!)

When taking calls from individuals who are not directly part of the cast and crew, it is not the caller's business to know why the person they are trying to reach isn't available. Telling a caller that the person they need to speak with is not there, in the bathroom, or trapped under something heavy is not recommended. Either way, the fact that they are not in the office is not information the caller needs. Be careful not to overshare information.

Taking a message

When taking a message, it should include the WHO, FROM, and WHY information you have already gathered from the first part of the call. Write all of this down on a piece of paper so you don't forget. Then politely ask for the caller's phone number. Repeat the phone number back to the caller to make sure you wrote it down correctly.

If you are taking a message and don't understand what someone says – their name, where they are calling from, what they want – ask again! Have them repeat the information or ask them to spell a particular word or name. Write it down. Everyone understands the need to be precise, so there is nothing wrong with asking again if you don't understand. Better to get it right.

You: Hi Pablo, Cameron isn't available right now. May I take a message?
Pablo: Sure, have them call me back.
You: May I have your number please?
Pablo: They have it.
You: May I have it just in case?

If it is standard protocol for your office, email the message to the appropriate person from the Production email account (this way there will always be a record that you passed the message). The email should include all pertinent information regarding the phone call – the same things reviewed earlier – the WHO, FROM, WHY, and PHONE NUMBER. Messages should be sent right away. Always include the date and time of the call. Include your name in the message. If the recipient has any questions, they know whom to follow up with. Some individuals may prefer a handwritten message. In this case, messages can be taken on carbon-copy phone message logs, a bit old school but still useful and available at most office supply stores. These are pre-printed message pads and therefore easier to make sure you have not forgotten a piece of information regarding the call. The top sheet is given to the recipient, and the carbon copy will remain in your log for future reference. It is crucial that your handwriting is clear and legible when taking a handwritten message. Rewrite it if you need to.

Depending on the recipient, you may also need to text the message to the person. Graphic 6.1 is an example of an emailed phone message.

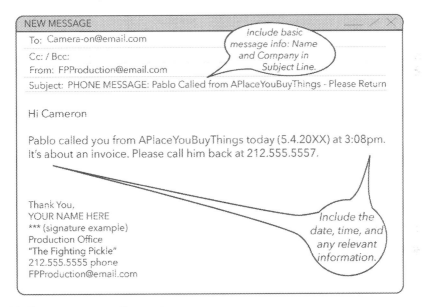

Graphic 6.1 Phone message email example.

Remember:
DO NOT give out confidential information unless authorized and you are speaking to a known cast or crew member that is part of your show. This includes addresses to the set or Production Office, the name and contact info of the Production Company, Studio, Producer or any cast or crew names.

DO NOT give out call times to cast or crew. The AD department is responsible for this.

Voicemail

Messages left on an office voicemail line should be documented and delivered to the recipients as described in "Taking a message."

When leaving a voicemail message, follow the instructions described in Section 4 under "Crew notification." Make sure you identify yourself, where you are calling from, your contact number, a brief reason for the call, as well as any instructions they need, such as, "Call me back to confirm" or "Call the vendor regarding an equipment question." A good habit is to repeat your contact number again at the end of the message.

Cell Phones and Texting

A quick note about cell phone etiquette. These days, having a cell phone is a requirement of the job. You need to be reachable at all times during work hours. This doesn't give you permission to take long personal calls or sit around texting or scrolling social media during the workday. Your cell phone is a means of communication and should not be a distraction from the work you need to perform. Be sure it functions properly, you have it charged during work hours, and that your voicemail box is set up and identifies you so callers know they've reached the right person if you don't answer. Check your messages and confirm that your voicemail is not full and can receive messages. When you receive a work-related call via your cell phone, be sure to apply the same professionalism you would when answering an office phone.

Text messaging is now an extremely common method of communication. When you are outside of the office and on a run, your PC or APC may text you to add items to your to-do list or check on your time estimate for completing a task. Additionally, if the PC or APC deem it appropriate, you may text them to provide updates when you're out instead of calling the office – this varies from show to show. It is not appropriate to discuss confidential matters via text. Remember, don't text and drive!

Many cast and crew members may prefer texting rather than a phone call when a short, specific piece of information needs to be relayed. It could be as simple as asking someone to call the Producer when they get a moment or a notification for a meeting. Confirmation that the information has been received is required, just as if you were leaving a voicemail. PC's, APC's, and AD's may elect to utilize text message chains for updates from set. Always check with your PC for appropriate texting protocols.

APPROPRIATE VS. NOT APPROPRIATE

Common sense dictates that in the work environment, interactions should remain professional and work related. Table 6.2 offers a few reminders of what is considered appropriate and expected interaction with departments vs. what never to do.

Table 6.2 Appropriate vs. Not Appropriate

Appropriate	Not Appropriate
It is appropriate to take an Office PA job to work in the Production Office.	It is *not* appropriate to take an Office PA job as a way to hang out on set.
It is appropriate to own up to a mistake.	It is *not* appropriate to lie and blame others.
It is appropriate to notify a member of the office staff if you need to step away.	It is *not* appropriate to wander off.
It is appropriate to introduce yourself to the crew.	It is *not* appropriate to wear a nametag that reads "Hi my name is Office Yoda" (but it is funny).
When asked, it is appropriate to make your career aspirations clear.	It is *not* appropriate to tell anyone who will listen, "I'm only working here till I sell my screenplay."

Continued

Table 6.2 Appropriate vs. Not Appropriate (Continued)

Appropriate	Not Appropriate
As much as possible, it is appropriate to leave work at work.	It is *not* appropriate to bring your personal life to the office.
It is appropriate to treat co-workers with respect and keep conversations work-related.	It is *not* appropriate to gossip and spread rumors.
It is appropriate to keep profane language reserved for when it is really needed. Use fewer F-bombs. It's not professional.	F*^B! this s%&).
It is appropriate to take a disagreement away from a public place.	It is *not* appropriate to shout and throw staplers across the office.
If asked, it is appropriate to get a list of expendables needed by the Sound department.	It is *not* appropriate to stand under the boom mic and shout, "Can you hear me now?"
It is appropriate to notify the AD team when you have brought distro to set.	It is *not* appropriate to do a quick drive-by of basecamp, tossing envelopes out the car window and shouting, "Fetch!"
If asked, it is appropriate to bring the director their storyboards left in the office.	It is *not* appropriate to ask the director to watch the short film you wrote and directed last weekend.
It is appropriate to let a personal call go to voicemail so you can call them back when you are off of work.	It is *not* appropriate to answer a personal call and engage in a full conversation, loudly, wandering the halls, while on the clock.
It is appropriate to try to get someone's attention by standing in their eyeline for a short time, until they acknowledge you.	It is *not* appropriate to walk up to a person and continually poke their arm to get their attention.
It is appropriate to be on time to work.	It is *not* appropriate to be late to work.
There is no appropriate situation for you to approach a cast member if not instructed to for a particular purpose.	It is *not* appropriate to stand outside a cast member's trailer, camera in hand, ready to pounce for a selfie.
It is appropriate to ask the producer for their lunch order.	It is *not* appropriate to toss a package of fruit snacks on the Producer's desk, mumbling about how cheap the show is.
It is appropriate to ask the DP if they are available to attend a scout per the AD department.	It is *not* appropriate to ask the DP about the questionable artistic choices they made filming their last project.
It is appropriate to help research vendors that rent a specific piece of lighting equipment.	It is *not* appropriate to tell the Assistant Chief Lighting Technician you shot your short film with a flashlight and to "make it work."
It is appropriate to confirm the name and contact info of the Special Effects Technician working the next day.	It is *not* appropriate to ask if they can set your ex's car on fire.
It is appropriate to check the name of a hair supply vendor with the Hair department head.	It is *not* appropriate to ask if they can do your hair for your date on Thursday.
It is appropriate to confirm where the costume show and tell will take place.	It is *not* appropriate to ask if they will make you a Halloween costume.
It is appropriate to check that the Art department office machines are in working order.	It is *not* appropriate to put a sign on their printer that reads, "Out of order. Deal with it."
It is appropriate to find out how many people from the Set Decorating department will attend the production meeting.	It is *not* appropriate to ask if you can have the orange couch when production wraps.
If a special treat is put out at crafty, it is appropriate to allow the set crew to filter through first.	It is *not* appropriate to rush in from the office, cut in line, and shout, "Oooh sandwiches!"

Continued

Table 6.2 Appropriate vs. Not Appropriate   (Continued)

Appropriate	Not Appropriate
It is appropriate to confirm who receives what paperwork in Accounting.	It is *not* appropriate to toss your petty cash in the air and shout, "Can I get it all in one's?"
It is appropriate to find out if the Transportation department has a run going to set before you do one.	It is *not* appropriate to tell the Transportation department you are sick of doing runs and they should do them all. "It's in the name."
It is appropriate to check with the Locations department on what time the scout will be leaving.	It is *not* appropriate to ask to throw a party in the mansion location.

PROFESSIONAL CODE OF CONDUCT

There is no "official" industry-wide code of conduct, but almost every Studio and Production Company will have guidelines for how you should conduct yourself while under their employment. These will usually be outlined on a page (or five!), in the **start work packet** and include information on Studio protocols for professional behavior, as well as anti-harassment guidelines. It will also outline the consequences for unprofessional actions. Remember, you represent the show at all times.

Here are some recommended guidelines for you to present the best, most professional version of yourself.

Work with Integrity

Your choice to work in the Production Office can be a defining moment on your career path in film and television. In all aspects, you want to put your best foot forward. A good way to demonstrate integrity is through your work. A strong work ethic and your personal standard to continually give 110% are ways to show professionalism. Respect yourself and the work you are doing. It's important to be honest, to be kind, and to treat others with respect. Know your own moral compass and use it as a guide in how you approach your work and your workplace each day.

1. *Be on Time.*
   The first rule of professionalism no matter the industry: don't be late.
   Sh*t happens, and circumstances may be out of your control (or you need a new alarm clock). So, if you are going to be late, take responsibility for it, and call the office. Notify the Production Coordinator as soon as you know you'll be late. Your tardiness may trigger a chain reaction. When you get into the office, get right to work. Don't make a habit of being late.
   When using public transportation such as the subway, if the train is late and you're stuck underground and can't get a signal, call the office as soon as you surface.
   Traffic, weather, and accidents are the biggest causes for delay when you are self-driving. If you are delayed, call. Many states require the use of a hands-free device. Be safe and pull over to make the call if you need to. And if you absolutely could not call sooner, call when you park the car and say: "I'm coming up, was stuck in traffic! SORRY!" Don't dwell on the cause of the lateness or its effects on the office. Get to work and move on!
   On the opposite end, remember that you are expected to work your full shift until you are released. Asking to go home early is insulting and disrespectful. Who will pick up the work if you go home early? Your boss? Your co-workers?

Other than for an illness or extreme emergency, sending you home early is up to the discretion of the PC; don't count on it happening often. Respect the job you are doing, arrive a little early, stay a little later. It matters and is noticed.

2. *Wardrobe that Works*
The film industry isn't as shiny and glamourous as television and movies lead you to believe. However, that doesn't mean you can show up looking like you just rolled out of bed. Appearance does matter. Though the industry doesn't have a dress code, nor are suit and tie required, your attire should be clean and practical. Footwear should allow you to be safe and move quickly, open-toed shoes can be a safety issue, and high heels are discouraged. Clothing that is unclean or contains rude, offensive images or foul language should not be worn. It is never appropriate for your undergarments (or what they cover!) to be visible. It is possible to look professional wearing jeans and a T-shirt. Make the effort.

DON'T come to the office wearing:

Your PJs, sweats, or gym shorts.
A shirt with boobs or penises or offensive language on it.
Your favorite jeans with holes in the ass.
Your bra or boxers hanging out of your clothing.

Your appearance reflects your attitude about your job. Dress in a way that makes your parents proud when you meet Tom Hanks.

3. *Be Ready to Work.*
Everyone has "off" days – and this doesn't refer to vacation days (there are no vacation days in Production!) – but there are days when you wake up on the wrong side of the bed. You feel tired and slow, unmotivated…it is okay. But bringing your personal life to work is not professional, and you still have to show up and do the work. The great thing is that your job is to help make a movie or a TV show – and that is SO cool! It's awesome and amazing to work in an industry you love, so reflect your love into the work you do. Remind yourself of that to get through the rough days.

You are an integral part of the office team; avoid making personal appointments during work hours as much as possible. Things happen and exceptions can be made, but be sure to request advance approval from your Production Coordinator, and know that sometimes they might say no.

4. *Hygiene and Illness*
The Production Office is the first face of the show. It's important that the staff look clean, healthy, and put-together. If you are unwell, do not come to work. If you have symptoms of a contagious illness, stay home. No one wants to interact with someone who clearly looks like they should be in bed recovering. Call the PC as soon as you realize you are unwell. Sickness can spread very quickly in our tight working environment, and you risk making others in the cast or crew sick. It is just as important to take care of your own health as it is your co-workers. If you come to work displaying symptoms of illness, you will be sent home.

5. *Ego and Attitude*
Don't act like you know everything. You don't, and that's okay. An Office PA who is excited to show up to work every day and learn will likely be given more opportunities than a PA who is clearly just there for the paycheck. It's also important to recognize that not everyone who enters the industry at the PA level will

have the same background or experience. Maybe you went to film school or maybe you are making a career change later in life. Do not pass judgement on the past of your coworkers or compare their life and experiences to your own. All experience is valuable, and entitlement has no place in the Production Office.

When you've had some experience on other shows, you'll notice that there will be nuances from show to show in how the same assignments are to be completed. Repeatedly vocalizing how something was done on your last show is not always productive. How the PC wants a task to be performed on your current show may be different from how the PC liked it done on your previous show. Respect their preferences; they are the boss and the one who hires you.

Having and maintaining a good, positive attitude and being supportive of your team will go a long way to the success of your office operations. Working together is key, and you are not above anyone else. Nor should you look for praise after every task you complete. Your professional performance in the office is not reward-based, it is what is expected. If your work needs to be recognized as a singularly fantastic job done by you, it probably will be. However, if you are really motivated for self-improvement, find an appropriate time to speak with your PC about ways you can improve your performance. The Production Coordinator may appreciate that you want to be better, but you should also prepare for the constructive criticism you may receive.

6. *General Conduct*

   The Producers are not your buddies. The cast members are not your friends. Interaction with them should be strictly professional and directly show-related. Over time, if you're on a long job, it will be easy to get comfortable with your fellow crew members both in the office and on set, but it's your responsibility to maintain a professional attitude in the workplace.

   - Never gossip. Long hours and close working conditions almost always lead to some sort of gossip creeping up. It is not appropriate to participate in the spread of gossip. Just stay out of it.
   - Handling conflicts. Don't talk trash about your fellow crew or publicly vent if you are having issues with a co-worker. If you are faced with a problem with another crew member in the workplace, take the conversation outside, or take it to a supervisor to help mediate the situation. If that doesn't work, then call Human Resources for guidance. It is important to identify someone you feel safe speaking to on your team. The Production Office is not a place for negative confrontations. Everyone wants to work together peacefully as much as possible. Treat one another respectfully, and it will be easier to work out your differences professionally to keep your workplace safe.
   - Don't complain. Everyone in production has likely started somewhere at the bottom of the pyramid and knows the work you are being asked to do. You are part of the support team. Embrace it and strive to do a good job. There is no room for complaining.
   - Don't burn bridges. Someone always knows someone who knows someone who knows your roommate's dog groomer's lover, who knows your old boss. Personalities sometimes clash, but always strive to keep a solid professional working relationship with everyone you work with. You never know when you will need their assistance or will need to work with them again.

- Don't taunt, tease, or harass. With the long hours and high stress of production, it can be nice to keep things light, but be cautious of making jokes or comments that can be misinterpreted and that don't belong in the workplace. We'll discuss harassment in a later section, but comments about someone's personal hygiene, sexual preference, wardrobe, or even their desk decor can cause conflicts between you and other crew members. This may lead to someone feeling uncomfortable or unsafe in the workplace, which affects the Production Office functions.
- Sharing production information, including photos on social media, is not okay. You might be asked to sign a non-disclosure agreement or a **no-social media agreement**. Your workday should not be shared online. This is for the respect and safety of you, the production, cast, and crew.
- It is also not okay to invite personal guests to the Production Office or to visit the set. Your personal life, family, and friends need to stay separate from your day-to-day and don't belong roaming the halls of your workplace. This can be a distraction, a confidentiality issue, and a discomfort to other crew members.

Being a good Office PA isn't just about knowing what to do when given assignments. It's also about how you behave, how you handle tough situations, and how you rise up to those challenges. With practice, patience, and attention to detail, you will learn to be more confident in the day-to-day. Confidence is a step closer to becoming a professional, because it has a foundation in experience. On your first job, it is natural to be apprehensive and unsure. You're meeting new people, learning where things are, and the work is unfolding exponentially at what seems to be all at the same time. After a while though, you get the hang of things, and before you know it, you will have a schedule being copied, are stocking the refrigerator, answering the phone, and directing the On-Set Dresser to Accounting without raising an eyebrow. You got this.

KEYS TO SECTION 6

- Integrity is the best policy.
- The way the work is performed is just as important as how the tasks are completed.
- Excelling as an Office PA requires the same basic principles applicable to most any job. Take ownership of the work and it will show in your performance.
- Being a professional in the workplace is mostly common sense. However, being a professional Office PA requires an extra layer of attention.
- You are not the decision-maker. Don't overthink things.
- Applying a professional code of conduct will keep you on the right track in work and in life.
- Problem-solving takes practice and creativity.

7 REEL LIFE, UNHINGED

Congrats! You got the job! Your call time on Monday is 7 a.m. Now what? Other than making sure you know where the office is and how to get there on time, what else can you expect on your first job? Yes, you know what work you'll be asked to do and how it will need to be done, but what is it really going to be like? What can you expect on Day 1? When, how often, and how much do you get paid? What happens if you are injured on the job or lose your phone? What do you do when the job is over? The time between jobs is just as important as when you are on a job. When do you file for unemployment and how? What are your career path options? How do you make it to the top by working as an Office PA? What is a Union? These are all things to consider when you start any job. However, working freelance in the film industry comes with its own unique way of approaching the answers. Having a real life understanding of how to navigate this type of employment and the way it influences your life can help better prepare you for whichever path you choose.

TO FREELANCE OR NOT TO FREELANCE

Most jobs in the entertainment industry are on a per project basis and are considered freelance work. This essentially means you'll have multiple jobs and employers each year, unlike the average corporate salaried employee. You are not tying yourself to one company via a long-term contract and are free to select different companies and job opportunities that best fit your career aspirations. However, when a show ends, so does your employment on it. Production job lengths will vary from a few weeks to a few months or more. This constant variety may be exciting but also leads to income instability. When you're working freelance, the terms of your employment can vary. Occasionally you may **"day-play"** and only be hired to work one or two days on a job and then never again for that company. Some people thrive in this type of work; others have a harder time adapting to the uncertainty.

Alternatively, there are jobs in the industry that offer more stable work. Traditionally these jobs are considered "in house," where your employment is for a company that likely oversees multiple projects, such as working for a corporate conglomerate like a motion picture Studio, a large Production Company, or an agency. You are part of the staff and paid an annual salary. The work hours are likely more consistent, and your standard shift may be 9 a.m.–5 p.m. rather than 8 a.m.–8 p.m.

Many Hollywood hopefuls have started down their entertainment industry career path only to discover that this type of freelance employment affects the lifestyle they want to have, regardless of the opportunities it may bring. You may decide it's

DOI: 10.4324/9781003252825-7

not a good fit, but there is certainly no harm in giving it a try. Maybe you'll surprise yourself at how well you adapt to the pace and thrive, or maybe it helps you discover other avenues for your skill set. Either way, at least you have given it a chance and practiced applying the skills taught in this book, many of which apply to other lines of work. Then, when you are old and gray, you can tell your grandkids about that time you met Zac Efron while delivering a script. As long as you are making an informed decision about your future, it will be the right decision.

GETTING PAID

Payroll or independent contractor?

There are two ways you may be paid for your work on a show. The first and most common is through a payroll company. When you begin a job, you will complete a start work packet, and at the end of each week you'll be required to complete a timecard to report the hours you worked that week.

When you are paid through a payroll company, federal, state, and other associated taxes are removed from your paycheck each time it is issued. You get less of your compensation up front, but hopefully come tax season you don't owe anything, and you may even be eligible for a refund. At the end of each year, each of your employers will issue a **W-2 tax form** showing your entire earnings while under their employment. Many shows will use one of a handful of the same industry payroll companies. You may have pay stubs from multiple shows but receive only one W2 form at the end of the year if by chance all your projects used the same payroll company. When you are paid through a payroll company, your employer is required to pay into unemployment insurance and workers' compensation insurance for you. We'll talk more about this.

The other way you might be compensated is as an "independent contractor." Generally, this occurs on low-budget or very short-term projects and essentially treats you as a vendor rather than an employee. Hiring production crew members as independent contractors is becoming less common due to tax laws governing Production Companies and employees. However, there are also business and liability reasons why some employers make the decision to hire crew as independent contractors. In this instance, you generate an invoice for your work, which outlines the days and hours worked, and submit it for payment with a W-9 tax form. In the independent contractor model, the employer is not deducting any federal or state taxes, nor are they paying into any unemployment or workers' compensation insurance for you. At the end of the year, the employer will issue you a 1099 tax form, and you will likely owe state and federal taxes on any compensation since nothing was taken out at the time of payment.

PA Pay Rates

The job of an Office Production Assistant is considered entry-level. In light of that, the compensation often offered for this position can be low. By law, under the Fair Labor Standards Act, employers cannot pay you less than the federal minimum wage. Anything over 40 hours in one week is considered overtime, which is a federal standard workweek. Any time worked beyond 40 hours is calculated at 1.5 × (time and a half) or 2 × (double time) your base hourly rate. Whether this is calculated by the day or by the week depends on the payroll laws in your state of employment. Traditionally, film and television employers will hire you to work a 60-hour work week, at 12-hour days. Working a 12-hour day at a base hourly rate of $7.25, the current federal minimum wage, depending on how the state overtime is calculated, averages to about $101.50 per day, before taxes. As of 2020, some cities and states have raised minimum wage to $15.00 per hour, making the average 12-hour workday approximately $210 per day. Generally, a PA day rate will fall in the range of $150–$210/day, making your hourly rate between $10.71–$15.00. This does not mean negotiating a higher wage isn't possible. However, this is the current industry standard as of this publication.

If your employment can be classified as independent contractor work, your rate might be a little more flexible; however, make sure to discuss in advance what this rate will be and how it will be calculated. You will be invoicing for "services rendered" for the day(s) or week(s) you work, and it may not be as easily identifiable as an hourly rate. Know what you are committing to when agreeing to a rate and how the employer expects you to reflect the work on your invoice. Do the math to protect yourself and ensure you are making at least the minimum wage of your work state. It is also advisable to discuss your decisions to work as an independent contractor with your personal accountant, as it may have other tax or legal implications.

Holidays

Unions have designated specific annual holidays where, depending on a crew member's employment type, their members working on the show must be paid additional compensation or "holiday pay," whether the day is a workday or not. Due to this, Studios will avoid having crews work on holidays. As a non-Union Office PA, you should not expect to be paid for the day off.

Some good news: for the most part no one is a career production assistant. The job is a stepping-stone on your way up the pyramid. You won't be making this rate forever, but you will need to live on it while working as a PA.

Start Paperwork

When you start a new job, one of the first things you'll need to do before you begin your employment is your payroll and compliance paperwork, essentially referred to as your "start work." Your start paperwork packet comes from the Accounting department, and the contents will vary slightly from show to show.

A lot of companies are moving towards digital start paperwork. Do not be surprised if you receive the packet digitally or are asked to complete it through a web-based platform provided by the payroll company rather than being handed a packet of forms. There have been a lot of advances with industry payroll companies to "go green" and to find ways to expedite paperwork processing. It is a good idea to keep a copy of your start paperwork for your records in the event any issues arise in the future.

A basic start packet consists of the following:

Employer Documents:

1. <u>Crew Deal Memo</u> – This will list all of the deal points for your employment and serves as your employment contract. Basic deal points include your pay

rate, term of employment with a start date, as well as the position you are being hired for. The deal memo will likely also include contract language, such as your conditions of employment and other employer legal policies like a confidentiality clause, code of conduct, an **appearance release** clause, terms for dismissal, and **screen credit**. Most of these are relatively boilerplate, but don't be surprised when this greets you on day one.

2. Accounting Policies and Procedures – A lot of production companies will issue accounting policies with the start packet. It will confirm your employer of record (the business entity issuing your paycheck), the day you will be paid each week, and details your responsibility to the production regarding any money matters. This way, when you are processing your petty cash or p-card receipts (as outlined in Section 4), you'll know the nuances for how this particular show needs them done.

3. The employer may also include:
   a. Emergency Contact Form – In case someone needs to be notified if you are seriously injured or become ill on the job and need medical care.
   b. Production Company Policies and the Production Safety Plan – This outlines the policies that govern the Production Company and includes your participation in workplace safety and company conduct.
   c. Anti-Harassment Policy – This outlines the Studio or Production Company's harassment policy, including disciplinary action that will be taken and how to report an incident.
   d. **Box Rental Form** – In the instance you are compensated for using your personal computer for the job, you may be given a weekly "box" rental fee. This document is approved each week for payment and submitted with your timecard.

Payroll and Government Documents:

1. Payroll Company Start Form – This provides the payroll company the information they need in order to pay you. You'll complete most of the form yourself and will need to provide your name, address, phone, date of birth, etc. Some may have your rate and position pre-filled in. If not, it will be completed by the Accounting department as outlined in your crew deal memo.

2. **Form I-9** – Attached to the start form is a US Department of Justice Immigration and Naturalization Service document. This is used to identify your citizenship status in the United States and is a requirement for any US job. You will be asked to provide documents that establish identity and employment eligibility, such as your passport. Your driver's license would also prove identity, paired with your Social Security card, which would establish employment eligibility. A list of acceptable documents can be found on page 3 of the I-9 form available online via irs.gov.

3. Form W-4 – This form will let the employer know what tax deductions to withhold from your pay. If this is your very first job, you might want to check with your personal accountant or a family member on the best way to complete this form.

4. Direct Deposit Form – Many employers are now able to deposit your paycheck directly into your bank account. You will complete this form with your banking

information and turn it in along with a blank voided check or a bank direct deposit form that can be printed from your bank website. This is a great convenience versus having to deposit a paper check weekly.

5. <u>W-9 form</u> – This document is used to verify your Social Security number or tax ID number so an employer can legally report earnings paid to you. You will submit this document with an invoice when working as an independent contractor. It may also be required for you to receive a petty cash float.

Timecards

Each week you will be required to complete a timecard for the hours you worked. It is a good idea to keep track of your start and end times each day, rather than guessing on Friday what hours you think you worked.

Check with your Production Coordinator for the preferred way they would like your timecard to be completed. Often shows will have you deduct your 30-minute lunch period and then add 30 minutes to the end of your day so that your timecard reflects a full 12 hours worked. Some shows will need you to be very specific with in and out times, and on others you may be on a flat 12-hour guarantee. A guarantee means you are paid for that full amount of time even if you worked less. But if you worked more, then be sure to include any hours worked beyond the guarantee. On some occasions, your PC may want your timecard completed using "production time," meaning in **military time** and using tenths of an hour. While it is less commonly used in the office, crew working on set may follow this model. Using the 24-hour clock allows less room for error when the payroll department is calculating your work hours, instead of having to determine a.m. versus p.m. For example, if you got off work at 5:35 p.m., your timecard might read 17.6 (17 is military time for 5 p.m., 35 = 6/10ths, or "clicks" into the hour). Chart 7.1 shows how tenths of an hour are applied. Document 7.2 is an example of a completed timecard.

FILM & TELEVISION TIME

Time Example:	17.1	17.2	17.3	17.4	17.5	17.6	17.7	17.8	17.9	18.0
"Click"	0.1	0.2	0.3	0.4	0.5	0.6	0.7	0.8	0.9	0.0
Minutes Past the Hour	1-6	7-12	13-18	19-24	25-30	31-36	37-42	43-48	49-54	55-0

Brackets: 5:01P-5:06P (17.1), 5:25P-5:30P (17.5), 5:55P-6P (17.9)

24 Hour	1	2	3	4	5	6	7	8	9	10	11	12
12 Hour	1AM	2AM	3AM	4AM	5AM	6AM	7AM	8AM	9AM	10AM	11AM	12PM

24 Hour	13	14	15	16	17	18	19	20	21	22	23	24
12 Hour	1PM	2PM	3PM	4PM	5PM	6PM	7PM	8PM	9PM	10PM	11PM	12AM

24 Hour	25	26	27	(if production wraps past midnight, the 24hr clock continues counting into the next day)
12 Hour	1AM	2AM	3AM	

Chart 7.1 Tenths and 24-hour clock.

Reel Life, Unhinged 149

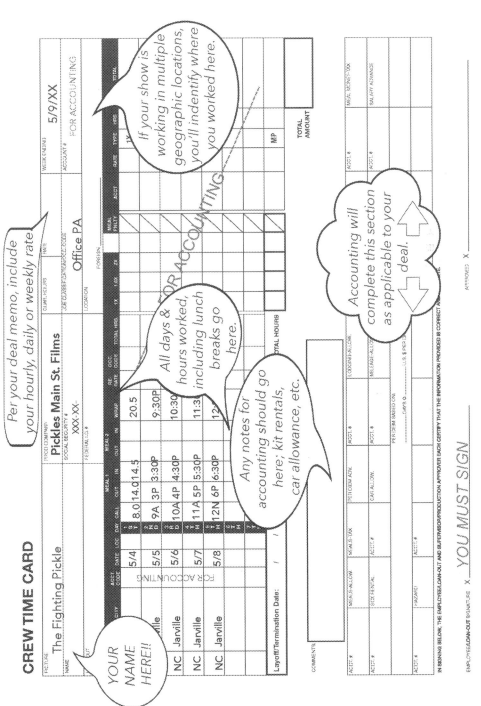

Document 7.2 Sample completed timecard.

UNEMPLOYMENT

Now that you've just started the job, let's talk about unemployment.

Unemployment insurance

In Section 3, we talked about how to determine the length of employment you might have on one show. It is both a positive and negative to know when your first and last days of work are. On the one hand, you know you'll have money coming in regularly for a certain period of time, but on the other hand, you know exactly when the money stops too. This is where unemployment insurance comes in, when one job ends but before the next one begins. When you work for an employer and are paid through a payroll company, the employer is responsible for paying into state unemployment insurance on your behalf. This is not something you'll see reduced on your paycheck, as it isn't a tax deduction. This is a cost of doing business for the employer. However, that is not the case if you are employed as an independent contractor. You will only be eligible for unemployment if your employer has paid into the state unemployment insurance program via the payroll company.

Unemployment insurance is exactly what it sounds like, insurance for when you are unemployed. It can be helpful in making sure you can get from job to job without losing the roof over your head. However, unemployment insurance doesn't just magically start appearing when you complete a job. It will require you to complete forms, either hard copy or online, via your state's unemployment website. You'll need to know your employment history for the past 18 months and have information on hand, like your first and last day of work for each employer, your hourly rate on each job, as well as the name, address, and phone number for each employer. Sometimes, your employer of record is not the actual Production Company you worked for but the payroll company itself. If not listed in the accounting policies, some pay stubs will have a box indicating what entity to use when filing for unemployment. You can also call the payroll company and ask if it's unclear. This may sound simple, but what if you've worked ten different jobs this year and it's November? You'll need to keep good records. This is why keeping a copy of your deal memo, saving your pay stubs, and documenting your first and last day of work will be crucial and save you headaches when trying to file for unemployment.

The compensation isn't a lot, and there is a waiting period and approval process before you will start receiving any money. You'll get a weekly amount that is based on the rate you were making on your jobs. *It will not be the rate you were receiving on the job.* Payment schedules vary per state, and there is a finite amount of money you are eligible to receive.

When receiving unemployment insurance, you will be required to show proof that you are looking for work and must report any work you do while collecting unemployment. They will factor in any earnings you report and withhold any insurance benefits for the week(s) you are employed. By doing this, it is possible to take temporary short-term gigs (i.e., a day or a week) while on unemployment. A word of caution, though, do not forget to report any earnings! You could find yourself in a serious pickle with the state for not doing so and potentially make yourself ineligible to receive future benefits. As soon as you start your next full-time job, end your unemployment insurance claim. Do not let a claim week overlap with your first week of paid employment.

Each state will have a different application system and eligibility requirements. It is your responsibility to figure out the process and you may or may not choose to claim it. Unemployment insurance is not intended to be your primary source of income, but knowing it is there if you need it may allow you to look for the next job that's the best fit for you and your career.

Unemployment is work

Let's be clear, just because you don't have a job and are unemployed doesn't mean unemployment itself isn't work. It is. Unemployment does not equal vacation. No employer is going to find you when you are sitting on your couch playing video games. Unless you are independently wealthy, most of us need income to feed, clothe, and house ourselves. Hence, the need for a job.

Looking for your next gig is ongoing. Who you know is still one of the best ways to find work. Everyone you meet on a project could help you land your next job. That's actually the beauty of being a PA; good ones are in high demand and can be recommended by almost anyone. As a show starts to wind down, the small talk eventually turns into, "What's next for you?" Some people may be jumping right onto another show, some may be taking some down time, but this is your chance to let them know you are available and looking, so if they "hear of anything," perhaps they can let you know or pass your name and number on.

If you haven't lined up a new job before you've wrapped, then you'll need to put effort into finding the next gig. Put feelers out as soon as you know your last day on your current job. There are many ways to job search, which we expand on in Section 10. You'll need to be consistent in your efforts, persistent but not annoying, target the right people, and follow up. Another good thing about looking for Office PA work is that employers don't expect you to have a ton of experience. Some is better than none, sure, and you have this book in your back pocket! But timing, attitude, and availability can also get you the job.

ON THE JOB

Beyond doing the job itself, there are aspects to learn that aren't specifically related to the work. What about the things that aren't task- or assignment-based, such as taking care of yourself and navigating your first day on the job? There are other considerations with being a responsible employee that allow you to perform better in the workplace. They can have a significant impact to you both on and off the job. It would be impossible to give examples of every single situation that you might encounter working as an Office PA, because so many are directly related to a specific set of circumstances. Some lessons in life can be taught, and some must be experienced.

Safeguards

Take care of you. With any job, you should always strive to perform at your best and to deliver on every task you are assigned. Many times, when you are on a show, you can become so entrenched in the job and in the production "bubble" that all of your attention and waking hours are devoted to work. Sometimes this is the perceived expectation of the job. Things like personal health, remembering to cash your paycheck, getting your cell phone repaired from when you dropped it on Day 2 while on a run, or getting that tweak in your back looked at after carrying paper boxes tend to get put off for another time. There is no magic time portal that can add hours in the day (we'd just use them to film more anyhow!). However, it is important to know your limits and look for ways the job can potentially offer helpful solutions to ensure you're taking care of yourself and not just the job.

Personal health

Don't be afraid to speak up for yourself when it comes to your health and safety. Production hours are long, and workdays can be stressful. You will need to take care of your own well-being, to sustain the course of the show. Get sleep, hydrate, and eat well. If you are ill, stay home. There is currently no federal standard sick leave for a freelance employee, though some states have sick leave guidelines that may apply to you on a long-running show. The responsible choice when you are feeling unwell is to prevent the spread of infection. Let your supervisor know as soon as possible and stay home to get well. Yes, the Production Office will experience some inconvenience in your absence (you are invaluable!), but there is no task that can't be reassigned. Always communicate with your Production Coordinator about your need for a day off for illness or to see a doctor regarding a pressing concern. Don't take risks with your health.

Some work may require lifting boxes or moving office furniture. Work smarter, not harder, when working with heavy loads. Be cautious to not hurt yourself or others. Do not take on physical responsibilities if you don't feel capable of doing so. If you are injured on the job, report it to the PC immediately. If you are injured on the weekend or outside of the job and the injury affects your ability to perform certain tasks, be sure to inform the PC so that duties can be reassigned until you are healed.

Workers' compensation

Workers' compensation is a type of insurance coverage that applies to all cast and crew members on payroll for a show. This is a protection for if you are injured while working, whether it be in the office, on set, or on a run during work hours. In the event you are injured, you must report it immediately to the PC so it can be reported to the insurance and/or payroll company. You'll be asked to complete an injury report detailing the date and time of the injury, a description of the injury, what you were doing when you were injured, if any equipment was being used, and how the injury occurred. If necessary, you will be provided documents to take to the doctor or hospital, so they know to bill the coverage as a workers' compensation claim and you won't be responsible for the payments.

If you have been hired as an independent contractor and are not paid via a payroll company, workers' compensation insurance isn't automatically paid into by the employer. You will need to ask if the shows' production insurance has coverage for independent contractors. Some shows might, some might not. Know this before starting a job, because if you are injured on the job, your medical costs will likely be out of pocket. Make sure you are protected in the workplace.

Personal property

In certain circumstances, you may be asked to use your personal vehicle or equipment to perform the job. As an Office PA you'll likely be required to bring your own computer and cell phone for working in the Production Office. They are tools of the trade. They need to function properly, and you need to be ready to use them for work.

If your equipment, such as a computer or cell phone, is stolen or damaged while on the job, notify your Coordinator. In some cases, this loss can be covered by the production's insurance. In other instances, the production may be able to help offset the cost of repair or replacement. However, often it may be your responsibility to repair or replace the lost or damaged items. If your company is providing you with a box rental fee, you may have signed an agreement that states it is your responsibility for providing and maintaining these items, not the production's, so it's important to take care of your personal items.

Do not assume your personal property is covered by the production, but make sure your Coordinator knows of any incident before assuming the burden will fall wholly on you.

Driving

Some productions may ask you to drive your personal vehicle for work purposes; other shows may rent a production vehicle to be shared by the office staff for runs. Make sure you discuss with your Coordinator regarding whether the vehicle you are driving will be covered under production insurance or your personal policy.

If you are driving your personal vehicle, be sure it has current auto insurance and that the Production Company is aware of your coverage. It will be your responsibility to keep your car in safe working condition. Before you start a new show, perhaps get a tune-up and check all your car's functions to make sure it's safe to operate. Keep a mileage log handy to track your work-specific runs throughout the day or ask production if a **car allowance** is being provided. Additionally, think about keeping an emergency kit in your car with jumper cables, flares, a first aid kit, a bottle of water, an ice scraper, etc., just in case.

If production has provided you with use of a rental car, be sure you understand how to operate the vehicle and that you feel comfortable driving it. You may be asked to drive a car, passenger van, or even a small truck. If you are not comfortable getting behind the wheel and navigating the vehicle through traffic, let your Coordinator know. There is no harm in admitting you are uncomfortable with driving a certain type of vehicle; however, the sooner the Coordinator knows what types of vehicles you *are* willing and able to drive the better. Make sure to keep a copy of the Production Company insurance certificate and accident report forms in the vehicle at all times. Your PC or APC can provide this paperwork. If you are driving and an alarm or dashboard alert comes on, or you notice the vehicle is having issues while driving, be sure to report them right away and have the rental company notified so the vehicle can be properly serviced.

In the event of a vehicle accident, be it in a personal vehicle or rental car, the most important thing to do first is make sure YOU and any passengers are okay! Call the police department so a police report can be filed and call the Production Office to notify them of the incident. Your Coordinator will provide you with all the insurance and reporting paperwork. You will be asked to provide as many details as you can about the accident. Document and photograph everything.

At any time if you discover that any vehicle – yours or the production vehicle – has incurred physical damage, you will need to document it and report it the same way you would in the case of an accident, even if you're unsure how the damage occurred. Together with your Coordinator, you can determine how best to handle any vehicle damage whether it's to swap a production vehicle rental with the vendor or send your personal vehicle in for repair.

Drowsy driving is a serious hazard that should not be ignored. If you are being asked to drive and feel fatigued, be sure to inform your supervisor; maybe someone else can do the run. Driving is one of the most common duties assigned to an Office PA. Make smart decisions to get enough sleep each night.

Don't text and drive.

Payday

One thing to mention that can potentially get overlooked in the excitement of being in a new job is remembering that you are not working for free. When you are just starting out and accepting a job as a PA, trust your instincts and protect yourself. If the employer doesn't invoke trust, don't take the job. Always know when payday is. Typically, in production you'll get a check once a week. Your paycheck will always be for the previous week you worked. If there is ever an instance where you have not received a check in more than a week or two, notify your immediate supervisor. Maybe it is an accounting error, maybe a wrong address, but do not wait until two months have passed before you realize you haven't been paid for your work. It sucks to say this, but some employers will take advantage. "The money is on its way," or "we're just waiting for this or that." A legitimate Production Company will not give you the runaround and will communicate upfront if there are any unforeseen payroll delays. If you and the employer have made a deal for compensation for your work, make sure you are getting it. It is as much your responsibility as it is theirs to ensure your paperwork is properly completed and filed, timecards are submitted, and payments are made/received in a timely manner.

"The show is over budget"

This may be a phrase you'll hear in passing conversations. Maybe it's true, maybe it is a dramatic assumption. Either way, at no time does this mean you should spend your personal money on a production expense. The show doesn't need your money, you need your money.

Harassment and abuse

This will be discussed more in the next section; however, you should never have to tolerate abuse or a hostile work environment. Get out and move on.

Day 1 / Your First Day

Your first day on the job can be intimidating. Meeting new people, figuring out what is expected of you, hoping you don't mess up your first assignment, etc. The good news is you've already put yourself at an advantage by reading this handbook! Whether it's your first day on your first professional job or your first day on a new show, here are some ways to help you further succeed:

1. <u>Take a tour</u> – If you were not responsible for the initial office setup, take a walk around and get a lay of the land. Learn where each department office is, the kitchen, bathrooms, light switches, and if on a Studio lot, where the company will be filming and the location of buildings that hold support services.
2. <u>Office Access</u> – Check with the PC regarding whether you will be assigned keys to the office. Test the keys and practice making sure you know how to lock and unlock the office. Is there an alarm system? Do you have the codes to activate and deactivate it? How many access doors are there to the building? Don't wait until the end of the day to figure it out.
3. <u>Get a crew list</u> – Start learning who comprises the production team so you can recognize names and departments when you hear them. Make it a point to meet anyone who has already started working. Introduce yourself!
4. <u>Learn the Production Office address and phone number</u> – You'll likely need to recall it from memory.
5. <u>Learn how to use the landline phones</u> – Practice putting people on hold, connecting a conference call, transferring calls, etc.
6. <u>Learn how the coffee machine works and how to make coffee!</u>

7. <u>Write things down</u> – A lot of new information will be thrown at you quickly. Carry a notepad and a pen.
8. <u>Go through the checklist and job assignments</u> – (discussed earlier in this book) with the PC or APC. Ask if they have any specific preferences or expectations of how they would like the work performed.
9. <u>Get a copy of the script and read it</u> – Know what you are making.
10. <u>Have fun</u> – It's your first day! Learn new things and remember you are contributing to the magic of filmmaking!

Lessons Learned on the Job

Some lessons can't be taught in a book. You may follow every step we've outlined, but we are all human and mistakes will happen. You will absolutely make them. It's part of the learning process, and there can be no success without failures and mistakes. The key is to learn from the mistakes and make sure they are not repeated. Here are some mistakes PA's have made and the lessons they learned.

The one with the mail drop

Once upon a time, an Office PA was going on a run to deliver an envelope to the payroll company. The outgoing mail was piling up in the office. Since they were leaving for the run, they figured they might as well drop the mail in the mailbox on the way. Payroll envelope and mail in hand, they headed out on the two runs. Walking down the street, they took the stack of mail and dropped it in the nearest post office box, but as soon as they released the handle, they realized they no longer had the payroll envelope in their hand!! They had dropped the unmarked envelope for payroll, containing a $500,000 check, in the post office box with the mail!

In a fit of panic, the PA tried to stick their arm inside the box to retrieve it – impossible. Then they thought, "I'll call the Postal Service and have them come open the box!" – no go. They flagged down a mail carrier, but they don't have the key to that mailbox. How were they going to fix this?!

In the end, the PA called the office and confessed to mistakenly dropping the unmarked envelope in the mailbox with the regular outgoing mail. The Coordinator understood, these things happen, and notified the Accounting department, which was able to send a wire transfer to the payroll company instead and void the check.

Lesson learned: Treat each run or assignment individually and think them through. Double check your actions as you execute each assignment. It also helps to make sure your deliveries are distinctly labeled. Be honest when you make a mistake. Most mistakes can be fixed, even if you think you've thought of all the solutions.

The one with the disgruntled GPS

In a faraway city, there was a PA who was filling in for just a few days on a TV series. Late one night, the writers issued script changes that would affect tomorrow's work, and the PC asked the PA to deliver the new highly confidential script to the show's lead actress. It had been a long day, and the PA was tired and wanted to go home, but her shift wasn't yet over. The Coordinator decided to let her leave early for the day so she could drop the script off on her way home. She took the script and plugged the address into her GPS.

The PA followed the GPS to the actress's neighborhood but in the middle of the block, the GPS suddenly said, "You have reached your destination." The PA couldn't tell which house belonged to the actress. It was dark and the house numbers weren't easy to see, so she went to the nearest house where the GPS identified and rang the doorbell – no answer. She looked through the window and didn't see anyone. The GPS led her here, so this must be it, right? She dropped the script on the front porch and left for home.

On her way home, the PA received a call from the Coordinator.

"Where is the script? Did you drop it off? The actress says she hasn't gotten it."

"I left it on the porch."

"What porch? The actress doesn't have a porch!" the Coordinator cried. "Did you check the address?"

"The GPS said I made it, so I figured it was her house."

"Did you knock on the door?"

"Yeah, no answer"

"Why didn't you call me?"

"The GPS said…."

"Please go back to the address, pick up the script, and call me. Then I will notify the actress and she can meet you outside her front door."

"Okay…."

Lesson learned: If you are making a delivery of important documents such as a script, be certain to confirm the address and get any details about the location that could be helpful. Do they have a porch? Is there a large flower pot out front? Is it an apartment? Follow the instructions you're given for delivery. If you are uncertain of an address, double check with the Coordinator, who can then call the cast member if necessary. As part of standard run protocol, always call the office once you've completed your task. GPS can have off days too, especially in remote or extremely dense locations.

The one where no one got hurt

A long time ago, a PA was out for a run in the production rental car. It was a busy day, picking up a new phone for the Producer, groceries for craft service, and toner for the copy machine. In between the grocery store and the office supply store, the PA was backing out of a parking spot and hit another car. Thankfully, no one was injured!

The PA got out of their car to speak to the other driver. This person was pretty mad. The production car wasn't badly damaged, but the front light of the other car was cracked. The driver asks for the PA's insurance information, and they hand over the production insurance form. Neither person calls the police, and in the PA's frazzled state, they don't get any information regarding the other driver. The other driver takes the papers from the PA and drives off. The PA heads back to the office feeling stressed and sad.

When they get there, they realize they forgot to pick up the toner! Now the other Office PA takes the car and heads to the office supply store. When they get to the car, they call the PC and report some damage to the back bumper that wasn't there before. The PC looks at the PA in the office, who hangs their head in shame, thinking they are about to get fired.

"What happened? It's okay, you can tell me," the PC says. The PA explains.

"So, you didn't get any information from the other driver?" the PC asks.

"No."
"And you didn't think to call the office when it happened?"
"I was embarrassed," the PA admits.
"It's okay, you weren't hurt, and the car is insured, but you must always remember to call. Please complete an accident report with any information you do remember. In case the other driver calls our insurance company for a claim, we can have a record."
The PA completes a report.

Lessons learned: It's okay to make a mistake. However, damage to any property must always be reported. Whether an accident or unknown incident has occurred, you must report the details so proper action can be taken.

The one with the key to the Production Office

Midtown Manhattan, New York City. It was the Office PA's first day and their first time working in NYC. They were determined to impress their new bosses with their diligence and hard work. The PC had given them a copy of the key to the front door of the office building earlier in the day. This door directly accessed the street. The day went on and they continued to work; there was lots to do! Before they knew it, it got to be late, and the office staff was packing up to go home. Still immersed in a project, the PA asked to stay a little longer. The PC agreed, reminding them to lock up when they leave. Finally, the PA decided to call it quits for the day. They packed up their things, turned off the lights, and headed out the door. The street was busy. Sliding the key into the lock the PA attempted to turn the key. But something was wrong. The door wasn't locking! They tried opening the door, turning the lock, and closing the door. They tried pulling the door tight while turning the key, jiggling the key in the lock, everything they could think of. The door would not lock! By now, it was nearing 10 p.m. In a panic they called the PC to get help. Unfortunately, he lived over an hour away. Here they were alone, their first day on the job, standing on a busy New York City street at night, in front of an office filled with electronics, furniture, personal belongings, and surely cash in a safe, and A DOOR THAT WON'T LOCK! Any random stranger who tries the door can just walk in and take things! The PC called the PA back and informed them that the only person with a key within a reasonable distance was the Producer. The Producer!? Surely this was grounds for firing. The PC calls the Producer and lets them know the PA is on their way. They would have to leave the door unlocked and make it across town to get the new key from the producer. This was a horrifying first impression. It was late and the subway lines were slow, with a long wait. The PA didn't have money for a taxi. The longer it took to get to the producer's home and back, the more at risk the Production Office was for someone to break in. Eventually, they made it to the Producer's home, embarrassed, apologetically got the new key, and headed back to the office. Thankfully the key worked, and it seemed no one had been the wiser to the unlocked door.

Lessons learned: Don't try to do all of the work in one day. Make reasonable choices regarding what is able to be accomplished within the workday. If your boss says it's time to go home, it's time to go home. Always test any key you are given at the time it is given to you.

The one with the sides redux

It was three weeks into principal photography and the Office PA had been on a roll: feeling good about their work, collaborating with the office team, and knocking the nightly sides out of the park. One afternoon the PA pulled the sides early, just after lunch, to get a jump start on the evening work and set them aside to run at wrap. Later that same afternoon, it starts snowing! The weather stations call for a snowstorm to hit overnight and production is supposed to film outside the next day. The UPM and AD's decide it's better to film on the stage instead of outside, since the scene won't match in the snow and most of the cast and crew are local and safe to report to work. Production wraps early to allow the crew to get home before the storm, and the PA runs the sides they pulled earlier so they too can go home. The next morning, the AD's call the office early in a panic! The sides they received were for the preliminary call sheet and not the final call sheet that reflected the scene changes for the **cover set**. They would need new sides ASAP! Both of the Office PA's rush to pull the correct sides and run them, taking turns copying, stapling, and cutting them. They call a Teamster to standby and then rush the new sides to the film set, hoping production isn't too delayed.

Lessons learned: Check the final call sheet before running the sides each night! Things might change throughout the day – sometimes due to weather but also due to a number of other schedule changes. Check your work.

CLIMBING THE PYRAMID

While it may be hard to see your path from the base of the pyramid, that is also what makes starting out so exciting. Look at all the steps you will climb, all the things you will learn, all the people you will meet along the way! This pyramid is your career path to success. Whether you pursue a straightforward approach to the top or take a few tangents along the way is up to you.

PA advancement

There is no one way or right way to advance your career, but working as an Office PA is a good start. A job in the Production Office is usually for a longer duration than just working on set during principal photography. You'll learn more of the production process as a whole because you are part of the pre-production, filming, and wrap periods. Plus, you are able to interact with crew and department heads during this time and see their role and how they function internally. It may provide opportunities and puts you in close proximity to almost every department on the show. When you are just starting out, this is a great way to get a taste of the many directions you can take to find your passion.

Everyone understands that no one intends to be a career PA and that every Production Assistant will move on or up. Jobs can become available within a moment's notice, and for all kinds of reasons. For instance, the person currently in the job needs to leave for personal reasons or got a promotion on another show, or an opening was created because the workload became too much for the current staff size. Whatever the situation, keep your ears open. It is okay to let the people you are working with know what career path you want to be on. Once you've mastered being an Office PA, it's time to take the next step.

Graphic 7.3 represents potential PA advancement opportunities that explore step by step department paths. It is by no means exhaustive or singularly representative

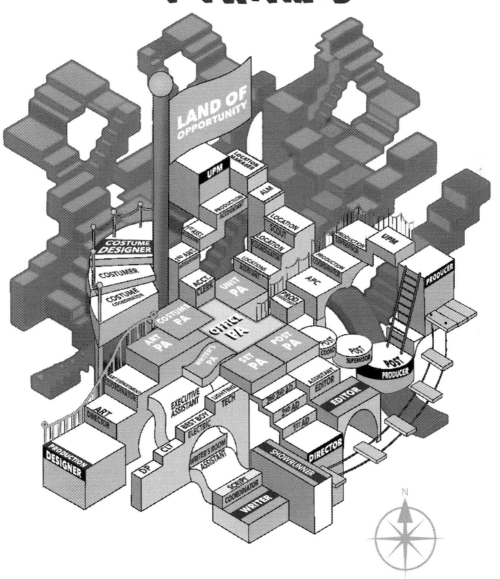

Graphic 7.3 PA advancement opportunities.

of the avenues you can take that could lead you on your career journey. No matter which direction you chose, the only way is up!

Some of the most common ambitions are in the creative realm, such as Writers, Directors, and Producers. Here are some of the ways you get there from being an Office PA.

Aspiring Writers: Seek out Writer's PA, Showrunner Executive Assistant, Writer's Room Assistant, and Script Coordinator opportunities.

Aspiring Directors: Seek out jobs as a Director's Assistant, Showrunner and/or Producer Executive Assistant, as well as any opportunities in Post Production, such as a Post Production PA. It is not unheard of for Script Supervisors, 1st AD's, Directors of Photography, and Post Production Producers to become Directors.

Aspiring Producers: You may find that you have a love for the Production Office and the more managerial aspects of filmmaking. Perhaps you want to work your way up to be a UPM or Line Producer. Following the career path in the Production Office is one way to get there. If the creative side is your passion, aspiring Producers should seek out jobs for a Producer Assistant, Executive Assistant, or opportunities in Post Production.

Not sure about your aspirations? That's okay! Working in the Production Office allows you to become familiar with all the other departments that comprise a film and TV crew. For example, maybe you find that being in the middle of the action on set is where you want to be and discover an interest in the Camera department. When the Camera Assistant or Loader calls the office to place an order, you'll become familiar with camera equipment and camera expendables. Maybe you catch the 2nd AC at wrap while on a set run, pick their brain about how to transition into working in the Camera department, and discuss the path to become a Director of Photography. Perhaps you've always loved fashion and creating looks and styles, and think you might want to be a Costume Designer. As an Office PA, you'll get to know what it takes to support that department and can then apply to be a Costumes PA on the next job. The examples provided here can apply to almost any department. That's the beauty of the Production Office; you'll have access and work-related interaction with any other avenues in production that your heart desires!

If you put in the time and dedicate yourself to earning your place on the office team, advancement will be quicker than you think. And because the staffing structure could vary from show to show, you could find yourself with a new title on your very next project.

Have fun and learn

Expand your knowledge base and vary your experience. Consider a show where you can work in the Accounting department. Take a job or two as a Set PA or with the Locations team. Give yourself a chance to learn about as many departments as you can. The best time to do this is when you are starting out.

One of the great things about being a PA are the opportunities you will have to learn and the access to those that want to teach you. Asking questions is a great way to demonstrate your enthusiasm and expand your knowledge, provided the timing of when you are asking the question is right (i.e., lunch or before or after the filming day). You'll often find many crew members are more than happy to offer up information about what they know and do. People like to talk about themselves, especially if they feel like their experiences can be beneficial to others.

Plus, they know just as well that the PA they are working with today could be in a position to hire them at some point in the future, so every relationship is potentially advantageous.

Once you've been in a job for a while, demonstrate your willingness to learn and know more. Can you assist with a task that is normally assigned to a supervisor? Would it be okay for you to sit in on the production meeting after it is set up? If you have proven yourself to be hardworking and diligent, these requests will more than likely be granted.

It really is about who you know and who knows you

At the end of the day, every effort to advance your career will center around meeting new people and establishing yourself as an invaluable asset. You'll need the right opportunity to get in the door and to work your ass off to stay inside.

Inspirational Stories

There might be stories out there about a PA who worked one job and then became the head of the Studio... actually, no there aren't, because that doesn't happen. The more experience you gain on your way up the pyramid, the better you will be able to perform. Knowing the expectations and demands of each job position creates better managers. Everyone needs experience, and that experience is what eventually leads them to the career of their dreams.

Here are some true stories about PAs who reached their goals!

The way of the staff writer

There once was an intern on the first season of a new Network TV show. The intern got the job via their college film program post-graduation and was very excited to work in the Production Office three days a week. The intern watched how the office worked and learned from the Production team. When the intern discovered that one of the Office PA's was leaving the show, the intern immediately applied for the full-time PA job. Having already proven themselves as a hardworking and passionate intern, and knowing how the Production Office operated, the Coordinator hired them right away.

The intern-turned-PA continued to work hard in their new position and got to know the team better. At the end of season one, the PA mentioned to the Unit Production Manager they wanted to be a writer. The UPM recommended the PA share some of their writing, and perhaps they could arrange a meeting with the Showrunner so the PA could learn about the job of writing in television.

The PA met with the Showrunner and asked them questions about writing in TV and what it means to be a Showrunner. They also shared a **spec script** for the TV show they were working on. The Showrunner was really impressed with the PA's passion and hardworking reputation from the office and asked if the PA was open to moving to Los Angeles, where the writer's room was based. The PA was open to the change if there was an opportunity... the Showrunner said, "Yes! I'm offering you one right now! Come to LA and be a Writer's Room PA!" The PA said, "Absolutely!" And by season four of the show, the PA had worked up from intern, to Office PA, moved to LA to work as the Writer's Room PA, then to Script Coordinator, and finally Staff Writer!

The career mover

Not so long ago, there was a banker who was a little older than the recent college graduate. They had already worked ten years in banking but loved film so much. The banker had a client who worked in the film business and who one day offered them a PA job. Excited to try out the new path, the banker turned Office PA proved they were hardworking and had a great attitude when working with other people in the office. Though they struggled to understand office operations and production documents, they didn't give up trying to learn.

As their first Office PA job was ending, the PC asked them if they were still interested in working in film – they were! The PC offered them a Production Secretary job on their next show. The Office PA moved up to Secretary, and over the next three years worked hard to join the Union as an APC. After two seasons, the PC on the show moved up to Production Supervisor and promoted the APC to PC!

UNIONS AND GUILDS

Unions and Guilds exist to protect workers from employers who may otherwise overwork and underpay their employees. A Union contract with an employer can dictate minimum pay rates, including overtime compensation, rest periods, staffing requirements, as well as things like working conditions and conditions when being traveled. When a Production Company signs an agreement with a Union or Guild and becomes a signatory, they are agreeing to employ members of that Union or Guild and abide by the terms of the contract. As a member of a Union or Guild, the employer contributes to the members' health insurance and a retirement plan. As we've reiterated in previous sections of this book, Production Assistants are considered entry-level, and therefore are not represented by a Union or Guild. If you intend to work in the business professionally and long-term, at some point you will likely need or want to join a Union once you find a track that fits you best. Each Union and Guild has joining criteria for new applicants unique to the positions they represent. Speaking to your crew, you can learn how to gain the skills and meet the requirements when you're ready to apply.

For a group to be considered a Union or Guild labor organization, they have to be a collective bargaining unit, meaning they negotiate on behalf of their members to ensure the employer is not taking advantage of them. Film and television related Unions or Guilds negotiate with the Alliance of Motion Picture and Television Producers (**AMPTP**), aka the major Studios, often just referred to as the "Producers." Even though the word "Producer" is in the name, this is somewhat misleading. The Studios hire Producers, as employees, to produce the show, and the Studio is usually serving as the financier, with creative oversight of the project as a whole.

When a Studio or independent Production Company signs an agreement with a Union or Guild, their productions are required to hire their members to perform services that fall under the scope of that Union, and they have agreed to produce the show under the terms of the agreement. The agreements are also very specific about the work that is to be performed by their members and shouldn't be performed by others. You, as a proactive and eager PA, need to be aware that there are times when you could be reprimanded for accidentally doing work that a Union employee is hired to do. That is why it is important you don't touch equipment on set, and you respect every crew member and their job. Just as you are hired to do a very specific job, with very specific assignments, so is everyone else on the crew. Conversely, on a non-Union show, where the Production Company is not employing Union crew members, it is often all-hands-on-deck to complete the work. It's important to recognize the difference between working on a Union vs. non-Union show. On a non-Union production, be ready if your supervisor says, "you're driving the pass van today!"

Although you won't be a member of a Union or Guild at the start, you will definitely be interacting with Union and Guild members regularly on most shows. It is also not uncommon for a Union representative to call the Production Office or visit the Production Office or set. These individuals are considered VIP and will want to speak with your Coordinator, UPM, or Producer.

There are five leading film and television Unions or Guilds in the US: IATSE, DGA, WGA, Teamsters, and SAG-AFTRA. definitions of each are identified here. Noteworthy to mention is the Producers Guild of America (PGA). Though not a labor Union, they are the largest professional trade organization in the film and television industry.

IATSE

The International Alliance of Theatrical Stage Employees, or IATSE, is a labor Union representing technicians, artisans, and crafts persons in the entertainment industry.

Most of the filming crew are members of the IATSE. They are the ones dressing the set, clothing the cast, exploding buildings, lighting the scene, shaping the light, building the sets, recording the sound, and capturing the images. They are often identifiable by the tape rolls at their hips, the makeup kits in hand, pushing a rolling rack of clothing, or carrying a camera.

The IATSE has various local branches, or "locals," that are identified by numbers. Locals can be found in different cities and regions nationwide and represent certain crafts. For example, IATSE Local 52 in New York represents studio electricians, but in Los Angeles, studio electricians are members of Local 728.

DGA

The Directors Guild of America represents the Directors and members of the directorial team.

Directors, Assistant Directors (remember, the *other* Production department), Unit Production Managers, as well as Stage Managers and other stage-based crew are a part of the Directors Guild. In New York and Chicago, this also includes Location Managers. They are typically the ones running various aspects of the set and production.

Teamsters

The International Brotherhood of Teamsters represent below-the-line skilled workers that are not members of IATSE. Crafts covered by the Teamsters can vary from region to region.

Often the term "Teamster" is synonymous with the word "driver" or when referring to the Transportation department. Teamsters are comprised of the crew members driving the trucks, vans, taking care of the trailers and work trucks, and coordinating vehicle movements. In some locales, Casting Directors, Animal Wranglers, and the Locations department staff are also Teamster members; this can vary from state to state.

SAG-AFTRA

SAG-AFTRA combines the Screen Actors Guild and the American Federation of Television and Radio Artists.

This is your cast, stunt performers, background actors, anyone performing in front of the camera or you're hearing their voice on screen. Airplane and helicopter pilots that will be seen on camera are also required to be part of SAG-AFTRA.

PGA

The Producers Guild of America is a nonprofit trade organization that represents members of the producing and production management teams in scripted and unscripted entertainment.

This could include Executive Producers, Line Producers, Associate Producers, Post Production Supervisors, and your boss, the Production Coordinator, who could be a member of the PGA but also an IATSE member.

WGA

The Writers Guild of America represents the writers.

It's not always a requirement for writers to be WGA members, but often they are. The Director or a Producer might be the Writer and could be represented by both the WGA and DGA simultaneously for each of their skills.

In the movie industry, no two experiences will ever be exactly the same. Not every job requires Union membership. It is entirely possible to have a successful career and never need to join a Union. Conversely, you may end up a member of multiple ones depending on your path, and if you do choose to join one, it doesn't mean you can't alter course and join a different one down the line. Consider the work of an Office PA as a whole pie that includes the responsibilities, skills, experiences, and care – for yourself and others – that need to be baked together. Your job is to create a complete pie so your experience can be well-rounded and applied to whatever future goals you may have in the industry.

KEYS TO SECTION 7

- Know the terms of your employment when you begin a job.
- Look out for yourself. Ask the right questions.
- Unemployment is part of being employed.
- Mistakes are human. Learn from them and don't repeat the same mistake twice.
- There are many ways to the top. Take advantage of as many opportunities as you can on the way up.

8 RESPONSIBLE PRODUCTION INITIATIVES

Whether an audience member sits in a movie theater or on their couch to watch a movie, they connect with the story told onscreen. They laugh, cry, get scared, learn, become inspired…immersed in the show. However, what they don't see is how that story came to be on the screen and the craftspeople who brought it to life. The industry has a responsibility not just to tell a good story to the viewers, but to make sure those who create the content behind the screen can go home safely to their families every night, and that they don't feel afraid or belittled in the workplace. The film and television industry also has a responsibility to the world, to make decisions in the production of content that don't cause harm to our planet. The show must go on, but not at the cost of people's lives.

PRODUCTION SAFETY

Moviemaking can be dangerous work. Whether a stunt guy is strategically flipping a car or you are driving while drowsy after a long day, safety should be considered the number one priority of every production. You'll hear it all the time, "safety is everyone's responsibility," and everyone deserves the right to a hazard-free workplace. If the cast and crew perceive themselves to be in unsafe conditions on the job, they may be distracted from doing their best work. Both the employer and employee are responsible for maintaining a safe work environment.

What does it mean to be safe? At the basic level, safety means the protection of people, locations, and equipment. Additionally, safety can be associated with how you feel in the workplace. Are you and your coworkers treated with respect? Is there someone who says or does things that make you feel uncomfortable? Is someone throwing staplers at you? Every Studio, Network, and Production Company issues safety guidelines at the start of each show that you will be required to read and agree to comply with while working for the company. For the Studio, it is a liability concern. They want to take every precaution and don't want to get sued if something goes wrong, but that's just one aspect of why we encourage production safety. If there is a known potential hazard associated with the job, the employer is required to educate you on the ways the risk is being eliminated, mitigated, or controlled, and you are part of reducing that risk.

Per the Occupational Safety and Health Administration (OSHA) General Duty Clause, each employer;

> *shall furnish…a place of employment which [is] free from recognized hazards that are causing or are likely to cause death or serious physical harm to their employees.*

DOI: 10.4324/9781003252825-8

Just like most industries, film and television productions are required to adhere to federal and state OSHA guidelines. Under these guidelines, employers (i.e., the Studio, Network, or Production Company) adopt or develop a production safety plan, also sometimes referred to as an Injury Illness Prevention Program (IIPP) for each of their productions. The production safety plan is created to reduce risk and will outline the way production safety will be handled for the show. It applies to all cast, crew, and third-party vendors employed to work on the production.

The OSHA guidelines are interpreted specifically for the entertainment industry by the Industry-Wide Labor-Management Safety Committee, which is comprised of Guild, Union, and management representatives (i.e. AMPTP and their attorneys). This committee generates "safety bulletins" that have been adopted as standard practice by productions nationwide. These bulletins are designed to be part of a specific safety plan for everything from performing a major stunt to cautioning the crew about indigenous critters that live in the filming location (snakes, bears, and alligators, oh my!). The safety bulletins can be found online via the Contract Services Administrative Training Trust Fund (CSATTF), a California-based administration and training company that recommends production safety practices for the entertainment industry. https://www.csatf.org/production-affairs-safety/safety-bulletins/.

Productions need to plan for everything to go right and have a plan for when things go wrong.

Office ergonomics has become much more prevalent over the last decade or so. While you may already know not to stand on a rolling chair while trying to reach a top shelf, you may not recognize that the extensive hours in front of your computer may cause hand, neck, or eye strain. Consider what ways you can lessen your risk of a workplace injury. One way to reduce potential injuries is through a safety plan. Safety plans can be broad, to cover a wide company policy, or they can be specific and drill down to the details of performing a "movie magic" trick such as a stunt or special effect. Harassment and discrimination policies are also a type of safety plan. As a responsible Office PA, take the time to review the safety plans, help identify potential hazards in your workplace, and make safety a priority of your own.

Types of Safety Plans

Safety plans focus on navigating ways to reduce the risk of potential hazards. Basically, the goal is to prevent an accident or injury! For instance, a plan may address common perceived daily workplace risks, such as the potential for a fire to break out on the soundstage. It will outline methods to reduce the potential for harm, such as requiring that four-foot fire lanes are maintained around the perimeter of the stage and that all fabrics and drapery are to be sprayed with fire retardant. Plans can be designed to address a specific situation, like needing to provide cooling tents when working in high temperatures, or for large-scale events such as a natural disaster or severe weather that would require an Emergency Action Plan (EAP) of how the situation will be handled should an incident occur. There are any number of reasons for safety plans to be created, and they may need to be presented to the Studio and/or insurance company in order to obtain coverage for various scenarios. Here are a few types of plans you may see on a production:

> General Production Safety – These will be the production's general safety guidelines, such as recommending closed-toed shoes, fire safety protocols in the office, or the injury/illness reporting protocols.

Set Construction, Power and Stage Safety – This will provide information about safe practices in the construction shop, working with generators on location, and when working on stage.

Disaster and Emergency Action (EAP) – When filming in locations with the high probability of natural disaster situations, such as hurricanes, tornados, or snowstorms, you will need to have a plan to evacuate and/or shelter cast and crew.

Stunt Safety – Developed by the Stunt Coordinator, this plan dictates what safety measures will be taken to support necessary scripted stunts being filmed.

Special Effects / Pyrotechnics / Firearms – Developed by the Special Effects Coordinator to outline safety measures to support special effects work, such as fire, smoke, or when firearms are being used on set.

Aerial Work – This plan is specific to work with helicopters, planes, drones, etc.

Vehicle Work – This plan will be drafted to outline safe practices for filming with custom vehicles, such as using process trailers, specialized mounts for driving shots, moving cranes, etc.

Marine / Water Work – This is specific to work that involves bodies of water, filming in, on, or near water with boats, when swimming, or when underwater photography and diving is required.

Location and Environmental – Similar to the EAP for severe weather, advance planning is required when working in any type of weather and/or challenging environmental conditions such as extreme heat, high wind or when there may be poisonous plants in the area.

Graphic 8.1 PA safety hazards in cartoon graphic.

Plans will outline safeguards for specific scenarios such as these and other high hazard work conditions. Some may also include working with animals and local wildlife or working with child performers. These plans may require the production to hire experts to supervise the work and the work may require specialized certifications and permits. While you, as an Office PA, are not responsible for knowing all of these intricate plans, you do need to know that they exist and where to find them. When a potentially high-risk activity is scheduled for filming, it is the responsibility of the Production Manager and AD's to help design a safety plan that is approved by the Studio and insurance company. On that day, a safety bulletin identifying the activity and safeguards production has implemented for mitigating risk will be attached to the call sheet for that day's work. If you are copying or distributing the call sheet, it will be part of your responsibility to attach the safety bulletin about that particular activity. The 2nd Assistant Director or Production Coordinator will advise on the proper safety bulletin to attach.

As an Office PA, knowing the safety protocols will help you support the Production Office and the show as a whole by keeping yourself and your coworkers in a safe workspace.

Production Safety and You

So what does production safety mean for you? How do you know if a situation is potentially unsafe and when to speak up? Much of safety is common sense, and over time you will develop an awareness of potential risks and hazards. Practicing production safety will become second nature. "Practice" in this use means how you function while completing your work, day to day. Are you looking out for yourself and the actions you take while completing tasks in the office? Are you remaining aware of your surroundings to maintain a safe work environment for all?

As an Office PA, the majority of your safety purview will apply to your work for the Production Office. Things like fire hazards, slips and trips, workplace cleanliness, and sanitation, as well as long work hours and driving fatigue, are the most common ones you'll encounter. Some examples of your duties include making sure fire exits are clear, not piling the paper boxes too high in the storage room, where they may fall and hurt someone, and avoiding buildup of trash and debris that can attract vermin. You may also be responsible making sure first aid kits are continually stocked and easily accessible in the event someone hurts themselves.

Fire Safety
- Are the fire exits clearly labeled and well lit?
- Are there fire extinguishers located throughout the office?
- Are emergency procedures posted in visible areas? If not, post emergency information around the office. It should include the addresses and phone numbers of the nearest fire department and police station as well as the nearest hospital.
- Are electrical kitchen appliances safe from water exposure?

Office Safety
- Don't keep heavy items on top shelves.
- Store sharp objects such as scissors with points facing down and paper cutters with their arms closed.

- Have extension cords been taped down or covered with a mat to prevent tripping?
- When using a ladder in the office, have another PA as a spotter.
- Is the file cabinet balanced? The bottom drawer should be heavier than the top drawer to prevent tipping.
- Where is the first aid kit located? Is it stocked?
- Keep walkways clear.
- No fooling around: games and horseplay are not appropriate in the workplace.

Driving
- Take proper precautions when driving. Follow the rules of the road.
- Don't drive drowsy.
- Be cautious of obstacles such as bicycles and pedestrians.
- Make sure the vehicle is in good working order.
- In the case of severe inclement weather, determine if the run can wait.
- DON'T TEXT AND DRIVE!

Sanitation
- A clean working environment keeps cast and crew healthy.
- Wipe down commonly used surfaces throughout the day, including door handles and phones.
- Are cleaning supplies properly stored and away from food?
- Placing tissue boxes around the office can help contain germs.

<u>If you need to call 911</u>

In the event there is an emergency and you are asked to call 911, here are a few things to keep in mind:

- Stay calm.
- Make sure you know how to dial out if you are using a landline connected to the office phone system. Many landline phones require dialing "9" to reach an outside line.
- When speaking with 911 dispatch, have the address of the location, major cross streets, and any specific information for how to find you upon arriving on the scene.
- Provide any information about the incident that you can, follow the instructions of the dispatcher, and always let the dispatcher hang up first.

Depending on the location of the emergency, make sure emergency vehicles can access the building. Do you need to notify the Studio lot that an ambulance is on its way? Is there a clear path to the injured person from the entrance?

Make sure your supervisor knows there was an emergency and that a medical response team is on their way. Proper action and communication are key to saving lives.

Employer Responsibilities

In general, the overall responsibility for production safety falls to the Producer, Production Company, and Studio or Network. However, the Producer may delegate the responsibility to an expert. On set, production safety is traditionally designated to the 1st Assistant Director and Key Grip. Off-production worksites fall under the oversight of a **Shop Steward** or a specifically designated department representative.

The Producer is responsible for creating the safety culture of the show. As much as it is the responsibility of the crew to practice working safely, the Production Company, Producers, and Production Manager are all ultimately responsible for overseeing and maintaining a safe work environment. As managers, they should set the precedent from the top. Through their actions and communication, they define the production's commitment to safety, which demonstrates how they intend to provide a safe work place. In addition, they should create a system for ensuring employee compliance with safe work practices, a means for encouraging employees to report unsafe conditions, and support ways for them to work safely. The production budget, managed by the Line Producer/UPM, should include money allocated for labor, supplies, and materials, in order to implement all safety guidelines.

The safety meeting

The 1st AD, in collaboration with department heads, should conduct a risk assessment for each day of work to identify potential safety issues. Is the filming location secure? Does the Special Effects team have the proper permits? Does the stunt team have safety gear for the activity being performed? Are water stations and tents set up nearby to protect crew from hot temperatures?

At the start of every day of filming, the 1st AD will conduct a safety meeting on set for the entire cast and crew. They review any potential hazards that might be encountered throughout the day. This can include the scheduled use of smoke, weapons, special equipment or machinery, stunts, driving shots, special effects, location concerns, and so on. If the company moves to a new location or new set, a second or third safety meeting may need to be held to continue to keep everyone informed of the safety plan.

As an Office PA, ask questions and stay informed. Rather than assuming a safety issue exists, ask about it at an appropriate time.

Studio policies

Most major Studios will have an existing Injury Illness Prevention Program (IIPP). The Production Coordinator will obtain this at the start of the production, and it's the job of the Production Office to disseminate the information. There may be an acknowledgement form requiring the signature of every cast and crew member, indicating they have read the Studio safety policy included in the IIPP manual. Often this form will be included in the start paperwork, along with the Studio/Network's corporate policies and anti-harassment protocols. The Studio safety handbook may be a physical book or completely digital. A complete copy should be kept in the Production Office and with the AD team on set. Take the time to read through the topics in the production safety handbook. It will usually include a list of safety contacts at the Studio or Network and a phone number for anonymously reporting unsafe work conditions. Get to know how your company manages workplace safety and become familiar with how to identify and report a hazardous or unsafe situation.

Most of the major Studios now have their own production safety departments, which will provide support to producers to ensure the guidelines are met. These Studio Safety Managers will make their presence known and should be invited to production meetings and any stunt or special effects meetings Production may hold. Often, they will be present on the filming days where the potentially hazardous activity will be taking place, to ensure all proper safe practices are being followed.

Safety Training

OSHA training is required for a number of Union-covered positions, though not mandatory for those working in the Production Office. Crew that are members of a Union or Guild are required to complete safety training before accepting a job in their specific craft. Online and in-person craft-specific classes are available through CSATTF. This program came about as part of the collective bargaining agreement between the Unions, Guilds, and Studio Producers (AMPTP) to meet the requirement that employers provide safety training. Some vendors also offer training on proper use of their specific equipment. A crew member may need to show proof of having completed their training at the time of employment, the Production Office may be asked to check an online database to confirm their classes are up-to-date.

Unsafe work condition reporting

Just practicing safety in the workplace isn't enough if you don't say something when you see something. It is important to communicate to your supervisor if you notice an unsafe condition in the office. In some instances, the issue may be an easy fix – you can clean up a spill to avoid someone slipping or hang a new sign designating fire exits. Other times the safety hazard may be more serious, such as a water leak near some electrical wires. When you take the time to report an issue, it can be reviewed and handled safely and efficiently before becoming an emergency.

As part of the safety plan found in their production safety handbook, major Studios will have specific documentation required to report and track unsafe work conditions. They will have an anonymous safety hotline, where anyone on the cast and crew can report a hazard if they are not comfortable taking it to their immediate supervisor. This number should be listed on the call sheet and posted in high-traffic areas around the office. You should never feel ashamed or embarrassed to report a safety issue if for some reason your supervisor does not take your concern seriously. Instructions for how to complete and submit these reports are generally found in your production safety manual. Independent, non-Studio productions may not have a formal safety manual or a hotline to call. This doesn't mean safety isn't important. Discuss with your PC how safety issues will be handled on the show. Document 8.2 is a helpful checklist to assess safety in your work area.

PRODUCTION OFFICE
SAFETY AWARENESS GUIDE

☐ Emergency Procedures

In the office, production should have the emergency action plans posted or available and they should be discussed at safety meetings and with the entire office staff. This includes what to do in the event of a fire, earthquake, hurricane, snowstorm, or any other emergency situation. Know the plan for the production office and how to react in an emergency.

☐ Safety Equipment, Materials & Supplies

Every Production Office should be equipped with the appropriate safety materials such as fire extinguishers, first aid kits, signage for fire exits, sanitization supplies, rubber mats to cover extension cords, enough power outlets so as not to overload a single outlet, etc.

☐ Cleaning supplies

Safety guidelines for cleaning products should be followed. Products should be kept away from food, and flammable items should be stored in approved safety cabinets and properly identified and disposed of.

☐ Clothing

Avoid wearing open toed shoes or clothing that can get caught on things or cause tripping.

☐ Office Upkeep

Keep hallways, exits, and doorways free of obstructions and clear of trash, boxes, furniture, and other items that may pose a safety risk.

☐ No Smoking

Smoking is not permitted in the Production Office. Smokers must use designated areas. Make certain the smoking areas are marked and ensure there are butt cans available for proper disposal.

☐ Cables & Power Cords

Cables and power cords should be neatly run, taped down, or covered with a mat to avoid a tripping hazard.

Document 8.2 Production Office safety awareness guide.

- [ ] Lifting and Moving Objects

    Work smarter not harder. Avoid injury by getting help or using dollies or carts when items are too heavy or awkward to move or lift alone.

- [ ] Environmental Concerns

    Bugs, rodents, mold, bacteria, and waste are all types of biological hazards that can pose environmental safety issues in the office if not properly handled.

NOTES & REMINDERS

_____
_____
_____
_____
_____
_____
_____
_____
_____
_____
_____
_____
_____
_____
_____
_____

Document 8.2 *(Continued)*

Pandemic Safety

In March of 2020, the world officially began the battle against the global pandemic COVID-19. Federal and state governments temporarily shut down non-essential domestic businesses, and the international film and television production industry was brought to a halt. In the face of the pandemic, it required Studios and Production Companies to rethink their approach to cast and crew health and safety. At the time of this publication, information about COVID-19 is continuously changing.

The AMPTP/major Studios, Production Companies, and Unions and Guilds have all drafted policies and implemented procedures to keep production going while protecting their cast and crew from this virus. It is unclear at this time how these changes may permanently affect production practices as have been described in this handbook. Some of these changes include considerations regarding how Production Offices are laid out. Many offices now require more space or plastic partitions between crew members so that they can work together and apart safely. Virtual meetings and remote work are being recommended and done whenever possible. This may eliminate many in-person meetings and require more technological support. Less printing and more electronic distribution are encouraged, as well as required use of personal protective equipment (PPE) such as face masks. Repetitive cleaning of high-contact surfaces and shared equipment, such as office machines and phones, may be done to ensure the virus doesn't easily spread. A Health and Safety Manager and support team may become a permanent addition to the Production departments on every show. At this time, it is assumed that the Production Office will have a hand in supporting the work necessary to enact these precautions. Efforts to source and provide safety and cleaning supplies, as well as helping to secure PPE for the cast and crew, may fall to the Office PA. You may also be responsible in assisting with its distribution to departments and ensuring there are cleaning supplies available throughout the office and on set.

HARASSMENT AND DISCRIMINATION

Hazards aren't always a physical risk; some can take a more psychological form, such as the effect individuals can have on one another in the workplace that may cause discomfort or concern for one's safety. A hazardous work environment includes one with offensive or abusive conduct, or where inappropriate comments and hostile actions are made toward you. It is unacceptable and potentially unlawful. Every cast and crew member, from Producer to Office PA, deserves to be treated equally, fairly, and respectfully. Most Studios, Networks, and Production Companies will have a strict code of conduct for cast and crew as well as policies prohibiting all forms of harassment and discrimination.

Harassment is any form of unwelcome conduct, be it sexual, verbal, physical, or discriminatory based on race, gender, religion, sexual orientation, national origin, medical condition, age, or disability.

Harassment

Quid Pro Quo Sexual Harassment, per the Producers Guild of America Anti-Sexual Harassment guidelines, is defined as "when a job, promotion or other professional benefit is conditioned on the recipient's submission to sexual advances or other conduct based on sex, or such benefits are denied to an individual because they refused to participate in a romantic or sexual activity."

Example: Asking or being asked to perform sexual favors for workplace advancement or benefits.

Hostile Work Environment, per the Producers Guild of America Anti-Sexual Harassment guidelines, is defined as "unwelcome verbal, physical or visual conduct that is severe or pervasive and which creates an intimidating, hostile, or offensive work environment or interferes with work performance."

Examples:

- Unwelcome sexual advances, unwelcome flirting, touching, or the use of sexual comments, which can or may cause discomfort, even if said in a joking/teasing manor.
- Verbal abuse, insults, derogatory language, or obscenities, which may demean or shame someone for their race, gender, sexual preference, disability, attire, work performance, medical condition, or age.
- Physical abuse, slapping, punching, kicking, or throwing of items that may cause physical or emotional harm.
- Bullying.

Everyone has a bad day or suffers the occasional bad mood. While this is not an excuse, it happens from time to time. As the Office PA, a fellow crew member may on occasion raise their voice to you. Likely it is due to stress and frustration that has nothing to do with you, and as long as it isn't consistent and isn't a personal or a racial attack, unfortunately it may be a circumstance you face. In those instances, it is best to not take it personally, be polite, and assist if you can. If the situation escalates or makes you uncomfortable, be sure to approach a supervisor for support. There is no end to the horrible things people can do or say to one another. It is not acceptable in daily life, nor is it acceptable in the workplace. You should neither participate in it nor be subject to it in any form.

Reporting

Whether you are the victim of harassment or discrimination directly, or you are witness to it in the Production Office or on set, you should report it to your supervisor. If you are working on a Studio show or for a large Production Company, you or your supervisor may be able to report the incident to Human Resources (HR). In some minor cases your supervisor may be able to mediate the situation and/or bring in the UPM or a Producer to assist. It is generally best to ask for help and report an incident rather than trying to face the offender on your own. Consult your Production Company's anti-harassment guidelines.

Human Resources often works in-house with a Studio or Production Company, though it sometimes can be outsourced to a third-party firm on smaller productions. They are a designated team whose job it is to help build a more efficient and effective workplace by encouraging employee performance and helping to mediate workplace challenges. In the absence of a formal HR department, the responsibility may fall to the Producer. HR will provide guidelines on how to file a complaint or document it when harassment or discrimination is reported. Additionally, they will provide Production with an anonymous hotline for reporting complaints, so you never need to feel exposed or uncomfortable for speaking your truth. HR will investigate all reports completely confidentially and make recommendations for a resolution when possible.

Respect

Everyone you come in contact with deserves your respect, no matter their background, race, gender, or position on the film crew. Harassment and discrimination can no longer be tolerated in the film and television industry. It is your ethical duty to participate in systemic change. That change starts with you in your everyday life and treatment of others. Do not underestimate the influence of being kind. Respect cannot be bought; it must be earned. Disagreements happen in the workplace, but with mutual respect for each individual, you help create a constructive and creative environment rather than a hostile one.

Remember that you are in an industry that has the mentality to "go big" or "go home." Just because you are working on a movie or TV show does not give you the right to be disrespectful to the general public. Maybe you are filming on a public street, or maybe you are sharing an office building with multiple companies. Either way, your attitude should be humble rather than arrogant. Be grateful they are sharing their space with you, not the other way around.

Discrimination

Discrimination goes hand in hand with harassment and is not tolerated in the workplace. No one has the right to discriminate against you, nor you against any other, for reasons of race, religion, ancestry, color, gender identity, age, political opinion, or any other reason. We work in an industry of storytellers and must hold each other accountable for our actions to help create change. The film industry is rapidly developing initiatives from all the major Studios, Networks, Unions, and Guilds to foster more equitable work environments. But every cast and crew member must do their part to change this story and strive for equality and equity in all aspects of the workplace. If you feel you have been discriminated against, witness, or are experiencing an act of discrimination, you should report it to your supervisor or to HR.

GREEN PRODUCTION INITIATIVES

Film and television production is notorious for being wasteful: paper, food, carbon emissions, you name it. Photo 8.3 is an example of the amount of paper a TV show wastes during the course of a season. It is a business about efficiency, convenience, and comfort. Fortunately, there have been many efforts to help productions change these practices and go green. The major Studios now have sustainability departments and "green" policies that govern how their shows need to be produced. Taking care of our planet is important; it's where we live! If each production does their part to help reduce their environmental impact, it is a step in the right direction.

Responsible Production Initiatives 177

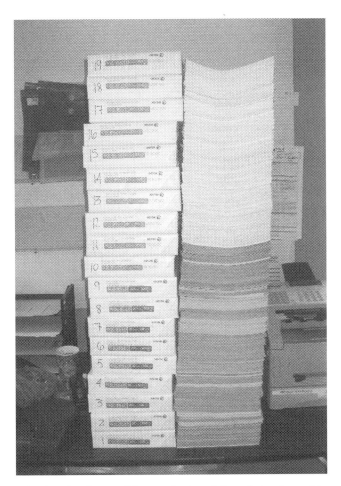

Photo 8.3 Photograph of stacks of paper. Fifteen episodes of discarded script revisions was equal to 19 reams of paper on this show. That's 9,500 sheets of paper!

Check with your Production Coordinator on the green production initiatives your office will adopt. Some shows will designate a "green" department, usually comprised of Set PA's with sustainability training to help arrange for green initiative actions on set. A lot of green practices can and will be managed by the Production Office. Some tasks can be as simple as making sure there are recycling bins in the office. Other initiatives might track a production's carbon footprint, which requires departments like Transportation to document the type and quantity of fuel being used for production vehicles. Digital workflow software can significantly cut down on the need for excessive paper distribution while also supporting production efficiency and eco-friendly goals.

Here is a list of some initiatives you as the Office PA can adopt to help save our planet. Be sure these are also communicated to the cast and crew so they can participate.

- *Set up battery recycling stations.* As they fill up, collect them and figure out where they can be properly disposed of instead of in a trash can.

- *Recycle printer toner cartridges.* Some companies provide mailing labels for you to ship a used cartridge back to the manufacturer for reuse. Large office supply stores also offer recycling.
- *Make double-sided copies.* When approved by the Production Coordinator, copy documents double-sided.
- *Repurpose single-use paper.* Put a box in a central location in the office and on set where cast and crew can drop their no-longer-needed one-sided paper. Collect it once a week and use it as scrap for petty cash receipts or for sides. Some printing companies can make inexpensive notepads out of a stack of single-use paper. (Double check that no papers have staples, confidential information on them, or are torn.)
- *Purchase reusable water bottles.* Many productions are cutting back on single-use plastic bottled water. You may be asked to research where to buy reusable water bottles for the cast and crew as well as find the best deal on water dispensers.
- *Electronic distribution* of production paperwork is an easy way to cut down on paper use. Check with your Coordinator about implementation.
- *Recycle bottles and cans.* Make sure there is glass or plastic bottle and aluminum can recycling in the Production Office kitchen.
- *Consider bulk vs. single-serve craft service.* Buying craft service in bulk and refilling reusable containers can also cut down on single serving waste. However single serving portions are considered more sanitary to reduce the spread of germs. Definitely ask your PC for their preference.
- *Donate office supplies.* At the end of a production, seek out other shows in your area that are starting up or even local schools, as they might be interested in your unused or gently used office supplies. This is an alternative to tossing them into the trash or into storage where they will never be seen again.
- *Purchase reusable kitchen supplies* such as plates, mugs, and flatware for the kitchen that can be washed, rather than disposable paper products. Alternatively, there are eco-friendly compostable paper products on the market that can be considered for both the catering department on set and in the office.
- *Turn off lights and machines.* Make sure lights and office machines are turned off before leaving each night. Encourage "task lighting," if you don't need a light, turn it off. Replace incandescent light bulbs with compact fluorescent ones that use less energy, generate less heat, and last longer. Some offices may also have automatic light switches that turn off if there is inactivity.
- *Make recycling easy.* Ensure every desk has a recycle bin and there is one near the copy machine as well. Check with your PC on how office recycling will be handled.

The Producers Guild of America in collaboration with major Studios and industry organizations has created the Green Production Guide (www.greenproduction-guide.com) as a valuable resource to assist productions in making more ecologically friendly decisions. Learning about green initiatives can add value to your work in the Production Office. If you see an opportunity for green improvement, say something!

KEYS TO SECTION 8

- Practice recognizing unsafe workplace conditions and take responsibility for your safety.
- Much of safety is common sense.
- Workplace discrimination and harassment are considered safety hazards and are unacceptable and unlawful.
- If others' behavior causes you harm, whether mentally or physically, report it and/or remove yourself from the situation.
- Implement the Safety Awareness Guide in your office.
- Eco-friendly initiatives are easier than you think. A few small changes can help save the world.

Bibliography

AMPTP/Industry-Wide Labor-Management Safety Committee General Code of Safe Practices for Production, October 17, 2002, https://www.csatf.org/production-affairs-safety/safety-bulletins/

United States Department of Labor, OSHA Act of 1970, https://www.osha.gov/laws-regs/oshact/section5-duties

Producers Guild of America, IPSI Anti Sexual Harassment Guidelines, https://producersguild.org/ipsi/

9 THE BIG SCREEN VS. THE SMALL SCREEN

And now for something completely different. We've been hammering you with information about being an Office PA but thought it might be helpful to give you a frame of reference for how a show comes together on a larger scope. How do all your hours of hard work translate to the big or small screen? And ultimately, how does this influence your employment on a particular project?

These days, it is common for content to be viewed on a variety of platforms and devices. However, movies shown in a theater are still referred to as being on the "big screen," and content predominantly intended to be viewed on a television is considered to be on the "small screen." While there are more similarities than differences in how content is produced for the big and small screen, one aspect you will want to evaluate when considering your job opportunities is what *type* of show you're applying for. This can help determine the duration for employment on a particular project and how your work will be adapted during the production process. It may also influence how you decide your career path.

By type of show, we're not referring to genre, an action-comedy vs. a family drama, but to the distribution expectation of the project. Is it intended to be released in a theater, on television, or a streaming platform? When you consider the type of show and length of employment it could offer, you will better be able to create a career strategy and manage your work as a freelancer. Traditionally, feature films and television shows operate at a different pace. TV production can be considered more fast-paced due to the repetitive cycle of prepping and filming simultaneously, versus a feature film that preps in a single dedicated time frame and can then focus on principal photography. For this overview, examples of types of shows will include **episodic television series, limited-series television, high-budget feature films,** and **low-budget feature films**. With the digital landscape growing and changing how viewers consume content, the definition of these categories is evolving; here, we will just scratch the surface of how these types affect you.

PRODUCTION PATTERNS AND SCHEDULES

Television has changed dramatically over the past nearly 100 years, and with it the viewing platforms have expanded from Network, Cable, and public broadcast channels to now include social media platform channels and countless streaming services.

Regardless of the distribution platform a show is released on, each type of television show will typically follow a particular production schedule that delivers the show on time for a predetermined air/release date or Network deadline. The production schedule can also be dictated by the **production pattern,** which defines the number of days or weeks needed for each episode to be prepared, filmed, and complete post production. Very often the Studio or Network will have an established formula based on their experience with similar types of shows. The season is budgeted to this pattern.

The correlation between the number of episodes to be filmed, the number of days it takes to film them, and the type of show you are on will give you an idea of how long the principal photography period will be, and may influence your decision to take certain jobs.

On a feature film, there is no uniform production pattern. Some low-budget independent films can film an entire 110-page script in 14 days, whereas a high-budget feature film may complete the same number of pages in over 80 days or more. A low-budget independent feature film will prep and film in a shorter duration than a high-budget Studio film, and the number of days and weeks in the schedule will be dictated by the creative needs of the film and budget. As mentioned in Section 3, feature films will have a designated prep period that for the most part ends when filming begins, unlike in television, which has a cyclical prep, principal photography, and wrap schedule. In both instances, once principal photography begins, it generally continues until all filming is complete. Exceptions to this might be when filming needs to shut down for an actor to physically make a transformation (look up Tom Hanks in *Castaway*) or when a television production schedule builds in two or three **hiatus** breaks during the principal photography period (often to help post production and the Writers not fall behind once filming has started). In addition, if a film has multiple units in various locations, the Producer may choose to prep-film-wrap each unit separately or elect to have multiple production teams working simultaneously. The common denominator in both television and feature films is that they all will have a prep period, a principal photography period, and a wrap/post production period. Refer to Diagram 3.2 regarding the cyclical production process on feature films vs. television.

Each Network and Studio will have their own production pattern for various TV content they produce. Many factors can affect when official prep will start; the budget, complicated set builds, the script, etc. The first season of a show may help determine the production pattern, as it is traditionally the most challenging, and often more prep time is required to get the show up and running than future seasons may take. The crew is getting used to each other, new sets might need to be built, the Production Offices are being set up for the first time, the "movie-making machine" is warming up. The production pattern may also be determined by the time slot the show is assigned by the Network. Television time slots are considered **primetime** or **daytime** depending on the time of day they air and the number of viewers they attract. Shows that air in the evening, when audiences are presumably home from work, are considered primetime and draw considerably more viewership. In light of this, the Network may allocate more funds to produce content of a higher **production value** to fill these slots. This is intended to achieve higher ratings and

182 The Big Screen vs. the Small Screen

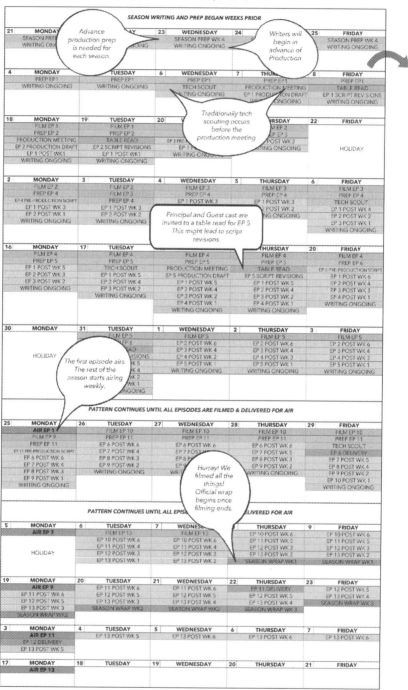

Chart 9.1 Sample production pattern – Primetime drama.

The Big Screen vs. the Small Screen 183

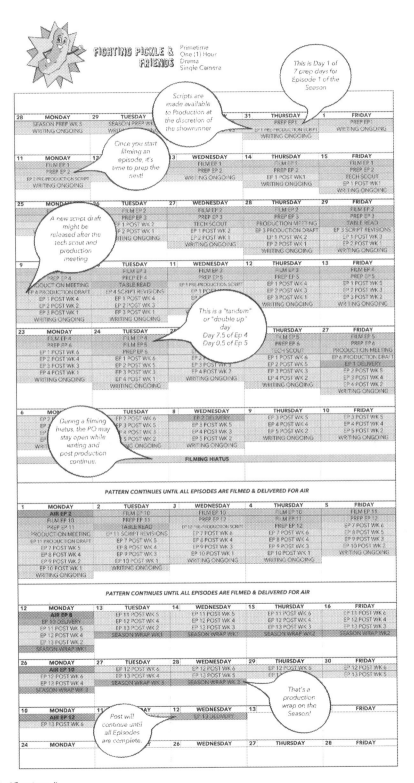

Chart 9.1 (Continued)

draw big advertisers. Conversely, daytime television shows may have less viewership, since audiences are assumed to be at work at this time, and the production value might be reduced to accommodate a smaller budget. Therefore, a one-hour primetime cable television drama that airs at 9 p.m. every Monday may have more days to film an episode than a one-hour daytime network television drama, such as a soap opera, that airs Monday–Friday at 12 p.m., which may film an entire episode in a single day. However, in this age of content streaming, shows may no longer fit a primetime or daytime label, and their production patterns may be dictated by a variety of other factors.

Conventional Studio and Network produced shows may have a production pattern that is more compatible with the style in which the show is intended to be filmed. Shows such as audience **sitcoms** (and daytime dramas) traditionally use up to three or four cameras to film most of the scene in a single take. This style of filming is referred to as "**multi-camera**" and allows for principal photography to be completed faster. A half-hour network television multi-camera audience sitcom that airs once a week may film an episode in one and a half days by using this filming style. The other traditional style of filming is called "**single camera**." Shows that film using this style (as primetime dramas often do) for the most part will only use one or two cameras. Shot structure might be more stylized and therefore needs more time to complete. Using this filming style, a half-hour cable television single-camera comedy that airs at 6 p.m. on Thursdays might film an episode in three to five days, and a primetime one-hour single-camera drama may film an episode in seven to ten days. This may not be discussed in your interview, but it might be good to ask your prospective employer about the structure of their show so you can have a better understanding of their needs and the potential length of your employment.

Charts 9.1, 9.2, and 9.3 are sample production patterns for different types of episodic television shows. This will give you an idea of how the prep, principal photography, and post production processes vary in each type of production schedule from script writing to airing.

Production schedules can also be dictated by the **release** (or distribution) **platform,** which provides the **release date,** the day the content will be available to viewers, as well as the **release schedule,** whether the show airs daily, weekly, or all episodes are available at the same time. A one-hour episodic drama produced for a streaming service where all episodes will drop on a specific date will have a different production schedule than a one-hour episodic drama made for a major broadcast network that airs a new episode weekly. In the latter, principal photography and post production can still be in progress as the show starts to air, whereas when an entire season is "dropped" on a single day, all episodes need to be completed and available for viewing on a single date; thus, the production schedule is more similar to a feature film. A half-hour multi-camera sitcom airing weekly can prep, film, and wrap an entire episode in five days. A soap opera that airs daily will have an even tighter production pattern. Less time for prep, less time to film, less time for post, because the show has to be on the air every single day. Chart 9.4 lays out a sample production schedule.

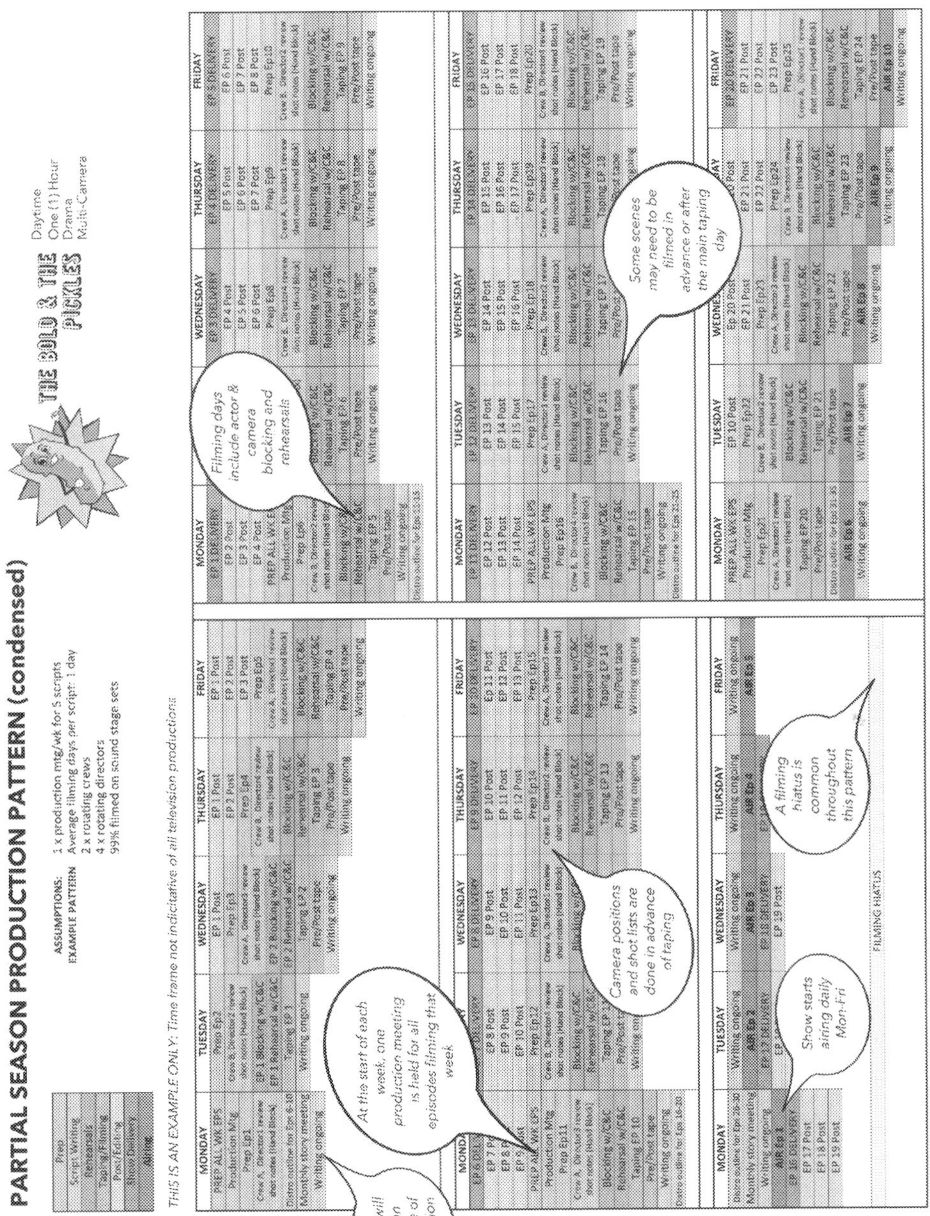

The Big Screen vs. the Small Screen 185

PARTIAL SEASON PRODUCTION PATTERN (condensed)

ASSUMPTIONS:
- 1 x production mtg/wk for 5 scripts
- Average filming days per script: 1 day
- 2 x rotating crews
- 4 x rotating directors
- 99% filmed on sound stage sets

EXAMPLE PATTERN

THE BOLD & THE PICKLES — Daytime, One (1) Hour Drama, Multi-Camera

Legend: Prep | Script Writing | Rehearsals | Taping/Filming | Post Editing | Show Delivery | Airing

THIS IS AN EXAMPLE ONLY. Time frame not indicitative of all television productions.

(Three-week schedule grid showing Monday–Friday production activities across multiple episodes, with annotations:)

- "Writers will begin in advance of production"
- "At the start of each week, one production meeting is held for all episodes filming that week"
- "Filming days include actor & camera blocking and rehearsals"
- "Camera positions and shot lists are done in advance of taping"
- "Some scenes may need to be filmed in advance or after the main taping day"
- "A filming hiatus is common throughout this pattern"
- "Show starts airing daily Mon-Fri"

PATTERN CONTINUES UNTIL ALL EPISODES ARE FILMED AND DELIVERED FOR AIR

Chart 9.2 Sample production pattern – Daytime drama.

186 The Big Screen vs. the Small Screen

ONE WEEK PRODUCTION PATTERN

FIGHTING PICKLE & FRIENDS

Half (1/2) Hour
Sitcom
Multi-Camera

Prep	Rehearsals & Run through
Studio/Network Involvement	Taping/Shooting
Script Writing	

EXAMPLE PATTERN ASSUMPTIONS: Average Prep and Filming days per script: 5 days

THIS IS AN EXAMPLE ONLY: Time frame not indictative of all television productions

	MONDAY	TUESDAY	WEDNESDAY	THURSDAY	FRIDAY
	Production Meeting	Rehearsal blocking w/Director	Rehearsal w/Director	Rehearsal for marks w/Cast & Crew	Camera Blocking refresh
	Table Read	Producer or Studio Run Through	Studio/Network Run Through	Camera Block Pre-Shoot scenes	Dress Rehearsal or Speed Read
	Director/Actor Rehearsal	Producer Notes	S/N Notes	Pre-Shoot playback scenes	TBD addit'l run throughs
	Network Notes	Revised script issued	Shooting script issued	Cut playback scenes for Fri taping	Audience filming day (stage)
	Revised Script Issued	Writers working on next week's script	Set Dressed	Lighting tweaks if needed	Writers working on next week's script
			DP, lighting, grip tweaks	Camera Block Audience scenes	
			Writers working on next week's script	Writers working on next week's script	

Production mtg & table read might be on Day 1 of prep.

Script revisions might be issued daily as the episode is developed with the director and actors.

"Run throughs" put the script on its feet with the actors and director.

Some scenes may need to be filmed in advance of the main taping day.

Audience sitcoms are often filmed on the same basic sets on a sound stage.

Often an entire episode is filmed in a day or a day and a half.

Chart 9.3 Sample production pattern – Half-hour sitcom.

		1 HOUR EPISODIC / SINGLE CAMERA / NETWORK PRIMETIME TELEVISION PRODUCTION SCHEDULE SEASON - BLUE REV - 3/9/XX		PRODUCTION DAYS OFF Good Friday 4/22 Memorial Day 5/30 Independence Day 7/4 Labor Day 9/5		

EPISODE#	PRODUCTION TITLE	WRITER(S)	DIRECTOR	PREP DATES	SHOOT DATES	AIR DATE
201	MEET TOMATOSAN	KIM SHOWRUNNER	W. MAXWELL	3/31 – 4/8	4/11 – 4/20	7/25
202	NO ROOM FOR MUSHROOM	BEN SCRIBE	S. LOBEL	4/11 – 4/19	4/21 – 5/3	8/1
203	MEET THE BEAN TEAM	SHELIA COMPOSE	G. HAIRE	4/20 – 4/29	5/3 – 5/12	8/8
204	LETTUCE REVENGE	ARCHIE WRITER	S. CRANDALL	5/2 – 5/10	5/13 – 5/24	8/15
205	MEET THE YAM CLAN	TATIANA LETTER	D. DECERBO	5/11 – 5/19	5/24 – 6/3	8/22
206	CRYIN' ONION	BEN SCRIBE + KIM SHOWRUNNER	A. JOHNSTON	5/20 – 5/31		
HIATUS				6/6 — 6/10		
206	CRYIN' ONION	BEN SCRIBE + KIM SHOWRUNNER	A. JOHNSTON		6/13 – 6/22	8/29
207	MEET AND POTATOES	JAVIER NOTE	H. JAXTON	6/13 – 6/21	6/22 – 7/1	9/5
208	EGGPLANT FACE OFF	KIM SHOWRUNNER	G. HAIRE	6/22 – 6/30	7/5 – 7/14	9/12
209	MEET THE CABBAGES	ARCHIE WRITER	S. LOBEL	7/5-7/13	7/14-7/25	9/19
210	SQUASHED	TATIANA LETTER	L. HAYDEN	7/14-7/22	7/26-8/4	9/26
211	ASPARAGUS DREAMS	SHELIA COMPOSE	J. CONNELLY	7/25-8/2	8/4-8/15	10/3
212	BROCCOLI TO MEET YOU	JAVIER NOTE + ARCHIE WRITER	W. MAXWELL	8/3-8/11	8/16-8/25	10/10
213	BEET DOWN BRIGADE	KIM SHOWRUNNER	K. SHOWRUNNER	8/12-8/22	8/26-9/7	10/17

Chart 9.4 Sample production schedule.

RELEASE PLATFORMS AND SCHEDULES

Release platforms

Some feature films and television shows will already have a designated release platform when they start production. The release platform is where the project can be seen and is what will determine the number of episodes being purchased for production, in other words, how many episodes they want to order per season. A season is considered the number of episodes of a television show a Network agrees to produce and air, usually within the span of a year.

For a Network television primetime show that airs once a week, such as the *Grey's Anatomy* series, an order can be for up to 22–24 episodes in a season. A Network television daytime drama airing daily, such as a soap opera, may have as many as 124 episodes, cable television may average 13–15 episodes of a show, and an over the top (**OTT**) or streaming platform may only commit to 6–10 episodes in a season. However, while these orders are the current Hollywood industry standard, as demand for content increases, technology advances, and viewing habits change, so may episode orders in a season and production schedules. Many Studio and television Networks have launched streaming services in order to make their content available in the digital space. This may also impact the pattern by which the content is produced.

Table 9.5 offers some examples of release platforms that are producing original content; this list is not exhaustive.

TABLE 9.5 Examples of Release Platforms

Platform Type	Examples
(Disclaimer: These platforms are examples available as of the date of this publication. As the landscape continues to evolve so may the ones listed here.)	
TELEVISION	1. Network/broadcast (ABC, CBS, NBC, Fox, The CW) 2. Cable television channels (AMC, FX, USA, TNT) 3. Premium Cable television channels (Epix, Starz, Showtime) 4. Public Broadcasting Service (PBS)
OTT AND STREAMING	Netflix, Amazon, AppleTV+, Disney+, Paramount+, Peacock, Hulu There are also content-sharing sites such as, YouTube, Facebook Watch, and Snapchat.
THEATRICAL	Feature films are often produced for an intended theatrical release in movie theaters; however, the industry is moving further in the direction of OTT platforms and is producing content for both the digital space and theatrical. (For example, Disney has done simultaneous day and date multiplatform releases both theatrically and on their streaming service, Disney+).

An independently (non-Studio/non-Network) produced film or TV show may not have a distribution deal for release when they begin production, but their ultimate goal will be to sell to a TV network, streaming platform, or a theater chain.

Doing a little homework about where the show you are working on will be released can inform how you approach your work, both as an Office PA and as you grow your career. Some employers may prioritize hiring someone who has worked in their system in the past, advertising "Feature experience a plus" or "Familiar with [major TV Studio] preferred." (Plus, you need to know where and when to tell mom to watch your show!)

Release schedules

How often and when a show is available for viewing is considered its release schedule. There are five main types listed here and as shown in Graphic 9.6:

Weekly: A show that airs one time a week, on the same day and at the same time each week. Common to primetime dramas and sitcoms.

Daily: A show that airs daily, often Monday–Friday, at the same time each day. Common to daytime talk shows and soap operas.

Parts: A show that airs as parts of a whole. Common to limited series television.

Drop Release: Used on some streaming/digital platforms where an entire season is released on a single date.

Day/Date: Theatrical feature films and some streaming platforms will open a movie or drop an episode of a TV show, or the entire season, on a specific day and date.

The Big Screen vs. the Small Screen   189

Graphic 9.6 is a calendar of how different types of shows are released.

PA WORK LIFESPAN ON A SHOW

Now that you are familiar with the broader scope of how a show's production schedule is determined, let's take a look at how the timeline plays out through your potential employment lifespan on a television show. Refer to Charts 9.7 and 9.1 as reference. Chart 9.7 shows a calendar of the possible duration of your employment, and Chart 9.1 offers a more detailed look of the production cycle during your employment period.

SCENARIO:
  Type of show: one-hour primetime cable television.
  The Network ordered 13 episodes of "Fighting Pickle and Friends."
  The season was budgeted for six weeks of prep.
  The season was budgeted for three weeks of wrap.

Production pattern assumptions:
  Each episode gets seven days of prep.
  Each episode films in seven and a half to eight days (Episodes 1, 12, 13 are eight days.)
  Post Production takes approximately six weeks per episode. (This does not affect you.)

190 The Big Screen vs. the Small Screen

There is one principal photography "hiatus" (non-filming) week.
You are the first PA hired on and last to be wrapped.

Here's how to calculate your maximum expected work timeline:

+ 6 weeks = number of season prep weeks
+ 20.6 weeks = number of filming weeks (3 x 8 day episodes, 10 x 7.5 day episodes = 99 filming days + 4 holidays = 103 days ÷ 5 days per week = 20.6 weeks)
+ 1 filming hiatus week (Production Office stays open)
+ 3 weeks of wrap

Total weeks: 6 + 20.6 + 1 + 3 = Over 30 weeks of work out of a 52-week year! That's seven months of work on one show!

(A note of clarification: in this example, the number of days in a five-day week are indicated by a fraction of ten. 0.2 weeks is equal to one day, 0.4 weeks is equal to two days, and so on).

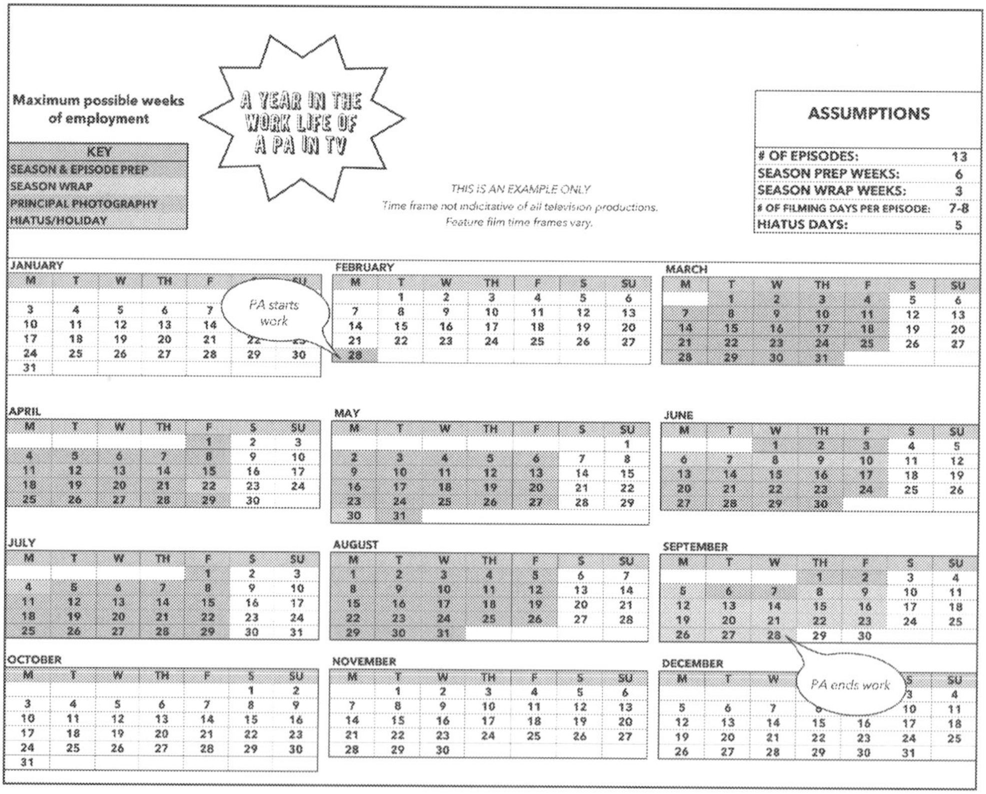

Chart 9.7 A year in the work life of a PA in TV.

Holiday scheduling

In general, most Studios recognize all the big holidays (think Christmas, New Year's, Memorial Day, National Pickle Day [just kidding, it's too close to Thanksgiving], etc. ...). There are often a couple of weeks of hiatus (unpaid vacation) in December. The production schedule of a film or television show will adjust to accommodate the holidays and maintain the number of expected filming days needed for each episode.

There is no single strategy for all the various production schedules or patterns. However, it's good to have this basic knowledge to help you navigate the kinds of shows where you may ultimately get work. You may find you're more suited for short-term work on feature films with a three- to four-month filming schedule, or perhaps you prefer the stability of a long-running ten-month TV show. All of this information is to give you insight into what it takes to produce your favorite shows, whether enjoyed in the movie theater or from the comfort of your couch.

KEYS TO SECTION 9

- A television show will have a production pattern that dictates the number of days to complete an episode, which builds the production schedule.
- The release schedule, determined by the distribution platform and type of show, contributes to the production pattern.
- Your length of employment on a show can, in part, be determined by the type of show and the number of episodes.
- You may decide to take certain jobs based on a certain type of show and its production schedule.

10 WHERE YOUR STORY BEGINS

Look how far you've come! You've shown your commitment to working as an Office PA through your dedication to this book and learning the tools of the trade. This initiative indicates you may be ready for the workplace! All you need now is the job.

Breaking into the entertainment industry is just that: you will likely need to pick-ax, climb, and backflip your way in by every means at your disposal. Other than the rare circumstances where you are a relative of someone already in the industry who can offer you a way in, no one is going to just hand over a job to you. You need to set yourself apart.

What is your story? Did you just graduate from college? Or from a film school or training program? Are you looking for a career change and want to give film and television a try? Did you skip university and go straight into the workforce? No matter what life avenue you are coming from, it is possible to find a way into the industry. As with getting any new job, a few basics will apply. You'll need to know where to look for jobs, who can help connect you to jobs, have a resume applicable to the work, and be able to demonstrate to others why you are the right person for the job. In addition, taking advantage of opportunities to learn and advance your skills will make you a more sought-after candidate. A job might come through a referral of someone you know, or by becoming active and networking in your local filmmaking community. Attending industry events, exploring connections through your college classmates, using online resources, taking an internship, or getting a gig with an industry support vendor are also side doors into the business. Determining the right job opportunity in a sea of options might just be the hardest part.

NETWORKING

Networking is work and is a door to job opportunities no matter the field. It is a vital part of building a film industry career, but it's not easy for everyone. There are extensive articles, videos, and books devoted just to the art of networking, so we won't reiterate everything here, but we will highlight some avenues and tips most applicable to this industry.

1. *Using your alumni community.*
    If you just graduated from a college program, perhaps your university has an alumni group you can reach out to and connect with others working in film and television. In addition, your classmates and sometimes professors while you're in college can be excellent resources for job opportunities. Make sure you make and maintain relationships with those you've worked with in school. That

connection could be the "in" you need when trying to land your first job. Stay in touch with them, let them know what you are up to, and find out where their path is leading them.

2. *Connecting with your coworkers.*
From the first day on your first job, you'll be building professional relationships with your coworkers. By working hard and having a good attitude, you will prove yourself as a valuable asset to the team, and one they will want to work with again.

Once you've done a job or two, don't forget to start the cycle of following up with your previous employers and fellow office staff. Drop them an email or text saying hello and say that you are checking in. Casually let them know you are available for work and just had such and such experience. If you ended the show as friends, this should be a relatively easy exchange. Stay in touch with your Production Coordinator and Assistant Production Coordinator from each job. A short and sweet message that essentially says "Hi! Remember me from that show we did?" can be a great reminder for them to give you a call about their next show.

3. *Attending or volunteering at industry events.*
Seek out industry events in your local film community, be it through your local film office, film forums, alumni program, or filmmaker groups. Try to meet at least five new people at each event. If you live in a production hub like Los Angeles or New York, all year long there are **screenings**, panels, workshops, and more for members of professional industry organizations (Unions, Guilds, Alliances, film groups, etc.). Chances are you know someone who is a member of one of these. If you've established a rapport with them, maybe you can ask if you can join them at a screening or panel where guests are allowed. In some instances, you can join these groups yourself and begin to meet people.

Look for events being sponsored by industry vendors. Sometimes a new business might offer an open house for new clients. Maybe a lighting company or **camera house** just opened up in your area and is offering a tour or workshop, or the film commission is putting on a speaker panel. Once you start digging, the opportunities to meet people could be more numerous than you think.

Many cities host **film festivals**. These are another great way to meet both established and up-and-coming filmmakers. Seek out one or two festivals closest to you and check them out. They often have workshops and panels in addition to the film screenings. Attend some of the parties and start introducing yourself!

If you are not in a major production hub, research local film groups via social media, and reach out to them about opportunities. Some cities also have local communities of arts-based clubs. Join them, make friends. You may even want to consider getting involved in local theater groups. Performers and artists will always find outlets for their work. The more people you know, the more likely you'll get a call when a project is greenlit.

Introduce yourself to the event organizers. Volunteering at events is also a great way to meet people connected to the industry. And it is a way to demonstrate your skill set. If you help to organize an event, you may get to show off your excellent spreadsheet-making or public relations skills. If you volunteer in person for an event, you may get to interact with the attendees directly. Don't underestimate the value of putting in some "free" time for an industry you are passionate about. You never know who you may meet.

4. *Know your pitch.*
   When you are meeting new people, you'll want to be able to give them a ten-second pitch about yourself as a way of introduction. Make sure to clearly pronounce your name when introducing yourself, and don't be afraid to tell someone you are just getting started and are looking for your first in. If you have some experience, i.e., you just finished a short film, are fresh out of film school, or even just moved to town, mention it. But let the person you are speaking with ask for details before you launch into a monologue. Keep it short. Talking yourself up can be intimidating, and you want to be careful not to come across as desperate or begging. Present yourself as already having a plan. You're "trying to meet people in the industry," or trying to learn more about an area of the industry that interests you, and this is how. This will reveal your determination and desire to break in and your confidence in doing so.
5. *Contact information.*
   If you are connecting with someone and the situation seems right, ask them if you can follow up with them, or if they have a business card. In this instance, if you can get their contact info, then the responsibility is on you to reach out. Unless they specifically ask you for your information, it is unlikely that offering your business card or giving them your email address will do anything more than get lost and you, forgotten. Give yourself the advantage of being able to follow up with them.
6. *Following up.*
   When you've successfully met a new industry contact always be sure to follow up. Email is the least invasive method, and again, you'll want to keep it short. Remind them where you met, what your plan is, and perhaps they can keep you in mind if they hear of any opportunities. Attaching a resume also doesn't hurt so that they have it handy. You may or may not get a response. Don't fret. People are busy, emails are constant. But sending a friendly, short note to "check in" and let them know what you are up to a few times a year can keep you fresh on their mind without being invasive.

Again, there are many other resources available that offer more in-depth details on this topic. Do your homework on how to master the art of networking.

OTHER JOB SEARCH TIPS

In addition to networking, you'll need to devote some time to other methods of searching for work. This includes using online databases, production listings, and seeking out related work.

Local resources

Is there a film or television show filming in your community? Do you know someone who might know someone working on it? Can you get them your resume? Many cities and states with a production community will have an online database of ways their state can provide support to incoming shows. They may have a photo gallery of potential filming locations, a listing of local equipment and supply vendors, as well as a catalogue of local crew by job. Often, they also have a list of job openings. Many times, this can be found through the film commission website or on their social media page. Check it out, get listed! When just starting out, listing yourself as a Producer, Director, or any key department head for that matter, without the experience to back it up, will not be beneficial to you or someone looking to hire for that position. Be honest, you are looking for PA work. You are more likely to get a call for a job using that listing than putting your name under every department and expecting to "get lucky." Someone associated with too many jobs is often a deterrent to employers. They may think either you do too many things and none of them well, or you don't know what you want or can't decide. It's okay to have some varying experience, it shows you are trying jobs out to find your place, but your resume should be focused. As you gain experience and find your path in the industry, you'll be able to add more credits and job titles.

Online resources

There are various online resources that can be used to search for jobs. *Keys to the Production Office* does not endorse or promote any of the services included here; however, as an example of some options available, we will list a few. Some require a fee; some allow free listings. Production Weekly is one of the largest industry resources and is a list of productions in development, prep, or in principal photography around the globe, and for a monthly fee you can subscribe to it. Often, it lists key persons, such as the Producers, Director, and lead cast. At times it may list the Production Coordinator and a contact email or phone number. The contact info may be for the Studio entity, or, if you're lucky, the Production Office itself. If an email address is listed, the show is expecting that resumes will find their way to it. It can't hurt to send one in.

These are online job search websites specific for the entertainment industry:

- ArrayCrew.com is an industry database for crew members of diverse backgrounds.
- Crewmeup is an app for finding and booking work based on your posted availability and job type.
- Crewvie.com is an international crew list serve database for entertainment and technology industry members.
- Entertainmentcareers.net offers assistance with resume-building, a weekly newsletter, and job listings.
- Hollylist.com is a subscription-based list of jobs and internships.
- LinkedIn.com is a professional networking site, not specifically geared toward the entertainment industry.
- Mandy.com offers an online community, a place to create a profile, as well as job listings.
- Productionhub.com offers a variety of paid profile options, including one for "newbies" just starting out.
- Staffmeup.com is a job listing and networking site for a variety of production jobs across various entertainment platforms.
- Showbizjobs.com is geared a little more to staff or in-house Studio, Network, and Production Company jobs, often on a corporate level.

Give yourself as many options as you can to get your name out there into the production community. But also have a strategy and be specific as to the type of entry-level job you are looking for. The listings could vary from a non-paid student film to a recognizable Production Company. Some may be more legitimate than others, so get details before committing to a job.

Industry-related work

Another direction you can take is to find a flexible gig for an industry-related vendor. Perhaps a local equipment rental house or soundstage could use part-time staff. Taking an opportunity to learn from an industry-support vendor not only educates you on how other aspects of the industry work, but you'll be around industry professionals and crew members working on the shows you want to be on. However, it is important to be upfront with the employer. Find a nice way to make sure they know you are ultimately looking for production work but would appreciate the opportunity to learn from them. You don't want to burn bridges with a vendor you'll need to have a relationship with once you are on a show.

Resourcefulness is how you will get your foot in the door, and even if the first door doesn't open, keep looking for places to knock.

Availability

One of the hardest aspects to balance when looking for freelance work is figuring out your availability and how to take the right job vs. taking the job right now. Gig employment is tricky, and if you don't have enough money saved to get you from one job to the next, you may find yourself in need of taking any job that keeps the roof over your head. This means, however, that when you do get the call from the next show, you will need to be able to make yourself available (sometimes within 24 hours or less) for an interview or even to start the job. If you are already in a part-time "pays the bills" type job, this may be harder than you think to get out of. There is no magic "in between" job that can be recommended, and every employer will vary. Some may allow the flexibility for you to leave for an interview or come work for them on your downtime between shows. Others will not be as accommodating. But in the 24 hours it may take you to get approval to have a couple of hours off to interview for a show, that job might be gone. They simply come and go that fast. When the Coordinator is looking to bring someone on, they usually needed someone yesterday.

This applies to time off as well. In our industry, the universe is notorious for the phone to start ringing off the hook with job offers after months of not a single nibble. Usually it happens right when you decided to join your parents for that two-week, non-refundable vacation cruise. A missed call or an unreturned message will be interpreted to mean you aren't available, and the PC will likely move on to the next candidate in line for the job. Consider your priorities, be available to take the job when it comes, or make the decision to wait for the next one (there will always be a next one!).

YOU DON'T KNOW WHAT YOU DON'T KNOW

Getting a job is often the old Catch-22. You need experience to get the job, but you need a job to get experience. There will always be ways to learn and always someone willing to give you a chance. Perhaps, while attending a panel at your local film festival, you meet a cool up-and-coming Producer in the audience who's looking for an intern. Maybe you can attend a training workshop for PAs through a local education program in your community. Or, perhaps you are reading a handbook to learn the tools of the trade on getting started in the industry? Your experience is unique, and how you gain that experience is different for everybody. Open every door to learning and look for different ways to gain the education and experience you may need.

Internships

It is a privilege to work in a field you love. However, that privilege isn't always easy to come by and must be earned. Sometimes that means taking an internship for little or no pay to gain experience and to prove yourself in order to get your foot in the door. When you are first starting out, almost any opportunity can be a good opportunity. One of the best ways to learn about the business is to do it! Interning will give you first-hand experience of the job and at the same time you'll be meeting people who are working in the industry. Consider an internship as on-the-job training so you can better perform in the workplace. In some internships, you may even be paid to learn!

Wearing the "intern" hat automatically tells people you are still learning. This is your time to ask questions and make a few mistakes. You'll be able to connect with different departments and watch as crew complete tasks you may one day be responsible for. Demonstrate your enthusiasm for the work by helping out everywhere you can. Internships really are a phenomenal way to start your career.

There are a couple of traditional internship types. One is the "learning by doing" method where you may be working alongside members of the office staff, having direct involvement in the work being done such as answering phones, making copies, setting up meetings, etc. Other internships allow more of a "shadow" experience where you observe specific members of the key production team as they conduct their work. You may end up attending meetings and scouts, listening in on phone calls, and essentially taking part in their day-to-day, but it is unlikely you will be doing much more than watching and listening.

In recent years, there have been some strict regulations established for interns to ensure their experience is educational and not used as free labor or to replace a paid position. Many Studios no longer allow unpaid internships, and interns will be paid a minimum wage. Most require you to be receiving college credit, and there are usually specific requirements governing what learning opportunities will be available to you while at the company. Be sure you understand what is expected of you by the company and what you expect to get out of it. You can find these internships directly through the Studios and some of the job search websites we previously listed, as well as from career counselors at your university.

Here are some important questions to consider when applying:

- Do you need to be in college and receiving credit to be considered for the internship? Will you receive college credit for this internship?
- How will that credit be managed and calculated?
- Is the internship paid? What are the terms? How will that payment be handled?
- What are the expected daily or weekly hours of the internship? What is the time frame? Will you need to commit for a few weeks? Months? Longer?
- What are the goals set for the internship? What will you be learning, and how will you learn them in the workplace? Are you shadowing a specific person or working across multiple departments?
- How will you then be able to apply these learned skills to your future work? Is there the possibility the internship can lead to a job?

Not all internships are advertised. If you see an opportunity to learn, consider asking if you can work for the company for a week to show what you are capable of. No strings attached. You get on-the-job experience and some new contacts; they get an extra pair of hands.

Unpaid internships

Generally, you'll see opportunities for unpaid internships on low-budget or student films; these are still great places to learn. Often the project will offer screen credit, a meal, and possibly gas reimbursement if you are asked to do runs. Make sure you are clear on the terms and get it in writing before starting. Ask the same questions previously mentioned. Technically, you should not be asked to do work that would otherwise be done by a paid employee. Set boundaries for your work hours, and if an assignment seems a little out of the ordinary, ask about it. Internships should never cost you money. You'll also want to find out if the company has workers' compensation insurance for interns. If you get hurt on the job, the costs might come out of your pocket. It's important, even in an internship, to make sure you are protected.

With any internship, remember that you are there to learn, so ask questions! This is a great place to start building your career and no one is above gaining valuable experience to better excel in the workplace – that includes you. Be willing to dedicate yourself for the career you want, and you'll earn your place.

Educational Programs

College/university programs

While it is not required, some individuals choose to get an education in filmmaking through a college or university. Many of these individuals are aspiring Directors, Producers, Editors, Screenwriters, and Cinematographers. An education focused on these creative crafts can be very beneficial, but they are not the only path forward. There are some great colleges and universities across the nation that offer remarkable programs for both undergraduate and graduate students (each year, *The Hollywood Reporter* and other industry publications rank top film school programs). If this is a path for you, explore the schools that offer a focus in the areas of film that interest you most and will help give you a well-rounded filmmaking experience.

Training programs

Perhaps committing to film school isn't for you. Many cities and states support programs that offer crew training, such as in New York, California, New Mexico, and Georgia. These programs vary in structure and content and may offer basic skills training for working on-set or in specific departments. You can usually apply through the states' film office website. Your city, community, or local arts center may even offer educational opportunities on industry basics. Film festivals tend to offer panels and workshops. There are also numerous organizations that offer film classes and training in order to make film education more accessible. Explore industry vendors who host training classes on the use of their equipment and other technical skills, such as in camera and sound. There are countless online resources, such as articles, videos, and virtual classes available regarding any aspect of the industry you want to know about. Take the time to stay educated.

When considering training programs, review what the course offers. Is it working hands-on with equipment? Is it a virtual production workshop or focused on-set? A good training program will offer you tangible skills that you can carry with you from job to job. It's also a great way to network with other passionate filmmakers in your community.

Mentors

Finding a mentor is another way to learn and explore ways to advance your career. Mentorships can look different to many people. Sometimes it's having a skilled professional provide you career advice. Other times it's an opportunity to shadow that person in their own workplace and learn from watching them work. If you think you've identified your job aspirations or focus, find someone working in that job whose career and achievements you admire. Be realistic and resourceful. It's unlikely that J.J. Abrams will be your mentor because you sent a nice email to his assistant; however, maybe the Producer, Director, or Cinematographer you met at your local film festival is interested. Do your homework about the work they have done so that when you start a rapport with them, you can comment on it and let them know you are interested in a similar path. Find out if they would be open to chatting with you about what their job entails. And would they offer advice on what they feel it takes to get there?

Mentorships are not internships, though an internship with the right person could lead to a mentor. Nor are they job-hunting opportunities. You are not approaching a potential mentor for a job, but rather for guidance and a sharing of experience so you can be better-educated on your own career path. However, it won't hurt to communicate with your mentor about the job opportunities you're seeking. As you build trust, they may recommend you should an opportunity arise. As long as you are always approaching your mentor-mentee relationship from a learning perspective, a potential mentor will be less likely to shy away.

LANDING THE JOB

There are countless resources available on resume-building and job-interviewing. Rather than reiterate the exhaustive work of others, here are a few select tips that most aptly apply to the film and television industry.

The Resume

There isn't an industry standard for the perfect resume. However, when you are just starting out, no one is expecting an extensive work history. If you have never worked as an Office PA but have experience in another type of office, list that. Include what your responsibilities were in that office. Be clear and concise. If you are fresh out of film school and have directed or produced short films, it's okay to list them and any accolades received, but preface the resume with your goal being to work in a Production Office rather than to immediately take on a Director role. Almost any job skill you have used in the past, whether paid, volunteer, or after-school extracurriculars, can translate to your work as an Office PA. Think through the type of tasks you were assigned, or a supervisor role you played. Align your experience and tangible skills with the work this book has outlined. See where there is overlap in your experience and list it.

Your work experiences may vary as a freelancer; this will affect how you organize your resume. A resume should express that you want the job and that your experience correlates to the job.

- It should go without saying, but make sure your name and contact information are clearly visible on the top of your resume.
- Cater your resume to the job to which you are applying.
  Have alternate versions of your resume, or edit it as needed for each application. If you are applying for a job in the Production Office, list relevant experience first, then any other production experience second. Focus the resume to the job.
- Give yourself a job title.
  When you are applying for an Office PA job, you'll want to identify yourself as such. "Dede Rocks, Office PA" vs. "Dede Rocks, Director" can indicate you are not serious about the job you are applying for. If your work history is in a variety of jobs, this can confuse an employer as to what kind of work you are looking for if you don't have a job title listed.
- List the most relevant and current experience first, then backtrack through other work experiences.
  Direct production experience should be listed before any other work history if you have some. Include the dates you were employed at the job. Employers will want to know what your last show was and when. Have you just come off of back-to-back seasons? What experience is the most recent?
- If listing a production job, include the name of your immediate supervisor and their role.
  This is a business about who you know and who knows you. Perhaps the person you are interviewing with knows your old boss.
- In general, keep your resume to one page. Most will get no more than a quick glance, so make sure the important information is listed first.
- What are your areas of expertise? Do you have any special skills? Are you a PowerPoint genius? Can you speak another language fluently? List something that sets you apart.
- It isn't always necessary to list references, but you should have a list on standby of people who can vouch for your hard work and passion.
- Always send your resume as a PDF document when emailing.
- Resumes should be sent to the attention of the Production Coordinator or Assistant Production Coordinator.

Cover letters

A note about cover letters. The reality is no one has time to read a cover letter, and this is even more true for an Office PA position. Can you do the job? Can you start tomorrow? This is all most employers are trying to answer. However, if a cover letter is requested in the job posting or you have been recommended for the job by a mutual friend, a cover letter may help. It can be in the body of your email as a note of introduction when sending a resume for a job, in order to give it a personal touch. Keep a cover letter short, no more than two or three brief paragraphs: an introduction, your skills summary, and of course, mention the person who recommended you. You are not reiterating your resume, but rather highlighting what isn't on the resume and giving a sense of your personality at the same time. Personalize it to the person doing the hiring and consider that they may not be the first person to receive your resume. Never send a resume email without a subject line and a note about the job for which you're applying, and make certain to include your contact info in the closing of the email.

Once you've sent your resume, follow up within a day or two to make sure it was received. You may or may not get a response, but a little tenacity shows your desire for the job. Hopefully you'll get a confirmation, and then it's a waiting game to see if you'll get the interview. After a few tries, if you don't hear back, let it go. Becoming a nuisance will not work in your favor; there will be another opportunity for a job elsewhere if this one doesn't work out. Don't stop applying.

Your Online Presence

IMDb

One of the most common resources an employer uses when hiring is the Internet Movie Database, IMDb.com. This is a quick and easy work-history reference available for free online. If you've been employed on a television show or feature film, there is a chance you already exist on this site. Some productions will input their cast and crew at the end of the show, and for some projects you'll need to go in and list yourself. The information is internally cross-referenced for accuracy, and all submissions are approved or declined. As you gain experience, this is an invaluable resource to keep up-to-date. Employers can use this to see what types of jobs you've held, on what types of projects, and can find out whom you've worked for.

Social media

It's likely you already have an established social media presence. Maybe you use it to promote your short films, fight for social justice, or just for fun with your friends. It would not be considered uncommon for a potential employer to reference a social media platform in order to get a sense of who you are as a person. In light of this, it is necessary to consider how you present yourself in the digital space. Remember, once you are employed on a show, you will be expected to represent that show in a professional manner. This may include the way you choose to present yourself to the world.

The Interview

Being a good interviewee is a skill that takes practice. Not everyone is comfortable being interviewed. You are being put on the spot and trying to convince a stranger you are the right person for the job. And it's not just about qualifications. Who you are as a person, your work ethic, attitude, and how you fit into the office dynamic are also part of the equation.

Do as much research about the job as you can before the interview. What type of project is it? Is it season three of a television show? An independent feature film? Are they looking for someone for the run of the show or a short-term Office PA? Whom are you interviewing with? Can you find out their past work history?

When interviewing for an Office PA position, present yourself for the job to which you are applying. Maybe you direct short films in your spare time, but remember you are not applying to be the Director for their next project. Unless asked, it is not appropriate to bring it up. Focus on getting hired for the Office PA job.

As part of your interview prep, consider the following:

- What are the strengths and weaknesses you have that are relevant to the specific job position? Did you used to work in retail? Much of working in the Production Office is customer service, personality, and presentation. Talk about how your skills will translate.
- How will your presence help the Production Office team be strong and efficient? Convince them why you are the best candidate for the job. Mention things that can't be found on your resume.
- Avoid exaggerating. Be honest about your previous work experience.
- Never lie.

Here are some things a Coordinator or your interviewer might want to hear:

- You are a local expert; you know where to buy the best bagels!
- You are resourceful; you talked a stranger into letting you borrow their vintage car for your friend's short film.
- You have a valid driver's license.
- You have experience answering phones; you worked for your mother's business as a receptionist while in college.
- You make amazing spreadsheets!
- You're passionate about learning how the Production Office operates because you want a long-running career in the film business.
- Convey that you know what will be expected of you, and what you don't know, you'll learn.
- Share some related accomplishments you are proud of.

Things your interviewer does not need to hear:

- You already directed five short films and a web series and just want this job so you can share your films with the Director. You saw his last film and think you two would make a good team.
- You know how to hotwire a car.
- You applied for a job at a talent agency, but are waiting to hear back, and you figured you'd do this in the meantime, but might need to leave if you get that other job.
- Your dog has the stomach flu and it's gross.
- A bad attitude.

The interview is not social hour. Be careful not to come across as too familiar or casual. This is still a professional interview. Let the person doing the interview lead the conversation and set the tone. They may have many interviews to get through and only a few minutes per person.

Sometimes it is what doesn't get said that can indicate you are the right hire:

- Arrive early for the interview.
  This is a good indication of how you will perform on the job.
- Have a copy of your resume on hand in case the interviewer needs it.
  Show you know how to be prepared.
- Dress appropriately for the interview. Your appearance indicates your attitude toward the job. This is not a suit-and-tie or fancy-dress-type job, but dress as you would on the job. Be clean and presentable.
- Let your ambition and excitement to get started in the industry come through in how you portray yourself.
- Be mindful how your attitude toward the job comes across in conversation. Try to present information from a positive perspective rather than negative.

Be able to commit to the entire project if it is offered to you. If you know you'll be out of town or have a conflict with some of the dates of employment, mention it in the interview. It doesn't mean you won't get the job, and it is better to be upfront than have it be a surprise later.

Don't forget to ask about the details of the job as well. Make sure you know the rate they are offering, when it starts, and if they know the end date. How big an office staff will there be? Will they be filming on a soundstage or mostly practical locations? Asking these questions will reiterate your interest and knowledge of the job.

Most importantly when interviewing, *be yourself*, not who you think you should be. Working production is a lot of long hours. You may spend more time with your crew than your own family. It is essential that everyone working in the office gets along and your personalities click. A good interview is one that doesn't feel like an interview, where you are able to have a conversation rather than a Q&A. Express your motivation for why you applied to the job, and your commitment to doing your best work to support the team and the show.

After an interview, it's a nice touch to send a quick thank-you note for taking the time to meet with you. This could be via email or even regular US mail. This classy touch says you appreciated the time they took to meet with you. It can make a difference.

COMPETITION

You are not the only person who wants to work in the film business or in the Production Office. There are many opportunities, so try not to let a competitive nature overshadow a great interview. You're not going to get every job you apply for; Coordinators are looking for an Office PA who is the best fit for their team. Express how you strive for excellence and that you will bring your dedication to the workplace. It may not work out, but don't give up!

Political hires

On some occasions you may face what are often called political hires or "must hires," where a staff member is hired due to a relationship with someone at the Studio or Producer level. You may be just the right person for the job, but there are only so many spots available, and a "must hire" was just thrown into the mix. It is expected that this person will work hard and perform the job, even if they have little experience, just as would be expected of you. All you can do is give your best interview and an occasional follow-up with the Coordinator so that hopefully you can land the next opportunity. In the event you are hired with a "must hire" they will become your teammate, and the best way to handle this kind of competition is to work together so everyone looks good and the job is done well.

Even when you get the job, sometimes a sense of competition or seniority comes into play within the office between you and the other Office PA(s) or other staff members. This is relatively common but not constructive to the work environment or the team dynamics. Everyone is trying to do their best to achieve what is necessary for the show.

REFERRALS AND RECOMMENDATIONS

The best way to land a job is through a referral or recommendation. This can come from a faculty member at your university or training program, someone you've worked with on a show in the past, or from someone who knows you and your work ethic. It is less common but not impossible to be hired without a recommendation. We work long hours and in a demanding environment. Having that extra vote from a respected colleague of your potential boss could land you the job. We all want to work with people we know are skilled, talented, and make the job more enjoyable. Cultivate relationships with members of the crew that you are comfortable with. Ask them to pass your name on to the Production Coordinator on their next job and if they would give you a glowing recommendation. And of course, make sure your Production Coordinator and Assistant Production Coordinator know that you'd love to work with them again!

If you're just starting out and don't have a direct connection to someone in the industry to help recommend you, ask your community. Let people in your circle know you are looking for opportunities. Perhaps there is a distant family member or a neighbor who knows someone who might be able to help or offer advice. If you put it out into the universe, there is someone out there looking for you, too.

Recommending others

Sometimes on a job you may be asked if you can recommend someone awesome like yourself who is looking for work. When you are offering a recommendation, make sure it is for someone you personally would vouch for and feel has the right attitude and work ethic. If your friend isn't qualified or motivated to do the job, do not recommend them, no matter how fun they might make the office. Whether they perform well or poorly, recommendations can come back to you.

Getting a job is never easy. It takes perseverance, dedication, some salesmanship, and unrelenting passion, but if you want it, it will happen. A Coordinator will see your spark, the Producer will recognize your diligence, a recommendation will get you in the door, or you are simply in the right place at the right time (with the right book!)

No matter how you land that first job, it's through your work that you will prove yourself as a valuable asset. When you treat every job as a learning opportunity and every learning opportunity as part of the job, you can become the most in-demand Office PA that ever existed!

KEYS TO SECTION 10

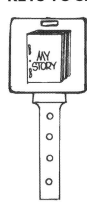

- Network, Network, Network.
- A resume is only half the battle. Presentation is paramount.
- Meet people, learn, put yourself out there for every opportunity.
- Who you know is just as important as who knows you.
- It's called "job search," not "job found." Be patient and consistent. Use all the resources available to you.
- Match your skills with the job requirements. It's okay to be creative when connecting the skills.
- If you truly want to work in this industry, NEVER. STOP. TRYING.

"You never fail until you stop trying." – Albert Einstein

This isn't the end, it's where *your* story begins.

Conclusion

You are amazing. You made it through the book, and by following it, we believe you're going to be a rock star Office PA!

We began this book by explaining that there is no one pathway to ultimate success, and at the risk of sounding like a motivational poster in your high school guidance counselor's office, success is how you choose to measure it. Whether you continue climbing the film industry pyramid or decide on another career, consider this book necessary in building your foundation. Starting in the Production Office allows you to practice and hone skills that apply not just at work, but in life. Determining where to live, what you want the balance between career and home life to be, ways to be of assistance to others, handling of basic finances, navigating different jobs, keeping yourself and others safe, and simply being a professional human in this world can be considered success. The Production Office is one possible path through life. No matter what career route you take in the film industry, you now have a way through the Production Office.

By applying your new knowledge of how the film industry operates, and the increase of content being created, you can decide where to position yourself at the start. You now know the basic job roles of those working both "on" set, "off" set, and in the Production Office, and how important every member of the production crew is to making a film or television show. When you meet an industry member at an event, you can ask them how to connect you with their Production Office team to see if they need to hire someone like you! The workload and dedication required of an Office PA is demanding, but no more demanding than the commitment you would make to any career you are passionate about. If this is an industry you love, it is no longer work, it's your life. It's the satisfaction you get when you see a cast member using a collated script you made, when Accounting thanks you for the morning paperwork distro, or when the catered lunch you ordered for the office is a hit. Whether you've had other jobs in the past or this is your very first, we've given you job basics that always apply. Remember the learning never stops when it's about something that motivates you.

It's no question that being an Office PA can be daunting, but you can use this book as the ultimate resource. No one expects you to know everything on day one; that's why we've outlined so much of the minutiae here for you. Failing will be harder than succeeding! For a century, the Production Office has been kept a secret, tucked away behind the scenes, but no more! When you're on your first job and you walk into that office the first day, you're going to instinctually look around for the signage and make a mental note that the copier needs an instructional "How-To" sign. And if the PC asks if you know what sides are, you can answer with confidence and say, "Yes! Do you and the AD's prefer the sides chronologically or in call sheet order?"

When a shipper drops off a stack of boxes, you'll be ready to sign them in on the shipping log spreadsheet you created from Section 4. This book is intended to be an everyday reference. It's not cheating; it's working smarter by doing your research and being prepared to tackle any challenge that comes your way.

The industry continues to grow and is rapidly evolving, and while it may have seemed out of reach before, we hope this book has now made it more accessible if perhaps you didn't know where to start. It will guide you and inspire you to work harder, strive to be better, and see the next step in your career. That path starts now, just behind that door over there…turn right… No, your other right…someone please put up a sign!

Working on a film or television show can be truly rewarding, and we wouldn't have written an entire book about getting started in it if we didn't think it was so awesome. There's no better feeling than being a part of the team responsible for the creation of a show in an industry where both the work and the product can bring people together, regardless of their background or experience. We're excited to have you in it.

You now have the keys, it's time to open some doors, and up to you to take the first step in.

Sincerely,

Gilana & Jen
P.S. We love you. Don't F$%* it up.

Coordinator Corner

These are tips directly from working Coordinators and office staffers to help you succeed.

It's easy to get frustrated if there aren't clear expectations for the job but use common sense and pick things up along the way.

   Ebony Cawthorne, Former Office PA

I want someone who is a go-getter. Be someone who isn't afraid of the task and is willing to come up with a solution when faced with a problem. We are in the business of not only filling the cup but making it overflow. Don't be the PA who does the job halfway. Learn by listening. Don't assume you have all the answers. Just because you may know the answer, doesn't mean it's right.

   Tanesha Hartsfield, PC

Have a positive attitude and excitement about the job! I'm always looking to hire someone who is ready to learn. Don't be an Office PA who just settles into doing one or two tasks all the time. It's important to be adaptable and willing to try something new. I like to keep the work between PAs balanced, which means everyone gets a chance to learn something. Also, active listening skills are KEY. The best way to stand out as an Office PA is to always pay attention to your surroundings, take note of what's going on, and apply that knowledge to your tasks. This also helps anticipate issues before they happen!

   Mary Hodge, PC

The key trait I look for when hiring an Office PA is positivity. When I'm hiring someone for a job that could potentially go on for 6 months to a year, I don't want to spend 12 hours a day with someone who reads negative. A positive outlook and disposition are essential. Each hire is a puzzle piece. You're trying to create an office space made up of people who complement each other and who are hopefully going to work well together. Positivity and a great attitude are an essential part of creating that. Always be prepared. All the tools are laid out for you. The prep schedule. The call sheet. The crew list. Know what meetings are happening the next day. What time the scouts are leaving. Who the people are that are attending. Getting ahead of things without being asked is always noticed. Those are the PAs that will move up quickly.

   Josh Nadelman, PC

- Don't sweat the small stuff, we're not performing brain surgery.
- Don't ever say "I don't know." Say "I'll check into that and get back to you," and find out.
- Try to have foresight and think outside the box.
- Volunteer to do a project instead of being asked. It shows eagerness.

- Have a good attitude and common sense; it will get you further than being book smart.
- The Production Office is a "team." What happens in the Production Office stays there.
- Always admit if you made a mistake, and we'll fix it. Don't lie or try to cover it.
- Network, network, network.

Joanne Oboyski, PC

Don't be afraid to ask questions or offer suggestions! The PC or APC should be willing to collaborate with their staff to accomplish all tasks & goals. This means that every member of the team should be able to have a voice and be a part of the discussion. Trust in yourself that you are an important part of the Production Office.

Holly Pilch, PC

"Professional Eavesdropping" – I always tell PAs to be alert and listen to everything around them. It helps them to anticipate what could be coming down the pike and prepare accordingly. Plus embracing the awareness factor will help them through not only production, but life.

James Wallace, PC

Always find something to do! There should never be down time. Whether it's cleaning the kitchen, filing documents, answering the phone, keep busy!

Canella Williams-Larrabee, UPM

Acknowledgments

Our journey on this book together started in the fall of 2018 in a New York City hotel lobby. But it wasn't until a global pandemic brought the film and television industry to a screeching halt for half of 2020 that we suddenly found ourselves with an abundance of time. Unsure if there would be a career to go back to, but optimistic that if there was, we wanted to contribute to its future, we started writing. This book allowed us a daily distraction from the unrelenting turmoil happening in the world, and without it we may have struggled to come out on the other side. We shared so many laughs, frustrations, and even a few tears, but with every sentence we wrote, our passion for the industry was reignited. As film and television bounced back and we returned to work, we knew we had to complete the book. It has been a production in and of itself. It took two years, from outlining the story we wanted to tell, to the countless weekly video chats, phone calls, thousands of emails, and hours writing in front of the computer, to its final publication and placement in your hands. In many ways this book began decades ago during our time as Office PAs. As we followed our path and climbed the pyramid, we tucked away each experience, saving it for this, saving it for you. Thank you for being our inspiration.

Thank you to our many past Office Production Assistants. It is because of what we learned from you that we were encouraged and inspired to share this knowledge with others. And of course to all of the Production Coordinators out there who we hope will use this book to train the next generations.

Thank you to our early draft readers whose feedback helped us see what we couldn't. We wrote a better book because of you: Mary Lou Belli, Ebony Cawthorne, Gary Haire, Evie Hornak, Megan Jordan, Cleve Landsberg, Patricia Lobel, April Smith, and Denver Wahwassuck.

Thank you to our artistic contributors who brought our visual concepts to life. To Samantha Osborne Designs and Grace O'Brien for your incredible graphics and illustrations. To Gary Haire for your keys and cartoons. To Rich Clark for your brilliant maps, Mary Colston for your banker's box, and to Ian Hannin for your concept artwork in the very beginning.

Thank you to our academic reviewers who helped convince the publisher our book needed to be in the world.

Thank you to our team at Routledge/Focal Press including, Claire Margerison and Sarah Pickles and to our editors at KnowledgeWorks Global, Suzanne Pfister and Laura Lowder.

And, thank you to the University of North Carolina School of the Arts, School of Filmmaking for a rewarding film education experience and to all the amazingly talented Fighting Pickles who, through their ongoing success, keep our passion for the industry alive. A special thank you to the faculty and staff who have continued to support us beyond our time at school, including but not limited to: David Elkins,

Nicole LaLoggia, Kate Miller, Dale Pollock, and Betsy Pollock. An additional thank you to the school for supporting our use of the Fighting Pickle mascot as a character throughout this book.

A special thanks from Gilana:

First, thank you to my parents Patricia and Steven Lobel, my sister and her family Liora, Jordan, and Romi Rait, and my brother Nate. Their endless encouragement has kept me going even when I was unsure, exhausted, and overwhelmed. Though they may not understand all the layers of my film career onion, they know it's too important to me to give it up.

Thank you to my dear friend and business partner Oliver Brooks, his wife Sarah, and their daughter Ruby whose walks and talks and pizza nights got me through the pandemic. To my friend Heather Levenstone who took my phone calls three times a day.

Thank you to the professional peers, mentors, mentees, Producers, Coordinators, and Office PAs I've worked with over the years who have helped me become a better person and manager: Jared Goldman, Tanesha Hartsfield, Takina Holloman, Ron Lynch, Josh Nadelman, Holly Pilch, Sarah Walker, Canella Williams-Larrabee, and so many others.

Thank you to the PAs who inspired and encouraged me to self-publish the first iteration of this book; *Be On Top Of It*, and who urged me to find a way to write this new one.

Also there is no way this version would exist without the incredible Jen Haire, my Co-Author, who believed there was so much more story to tell about the role of the Office PA. Her patience, diligence, and incomparable attention to detail helped make this book better than I could have imagined alone (also with a lot less typos). Thanks, Jen!

A special thanks from Jen:

Thank you to my parents Gary and Debbie Haire who always supported my passion and encouraged me to follow their example of making things better than I found them. To my brother Matthew, his wife Jamie and my hilarious nephews Jaxton, Maxwell and Rylan who give me an escape from real life and let me play in the moment.

Thank you to my professional peers who provided opportunities along my journey that shaped my career: Yoram Barzilai, Ronnie Chong, Giampaolo Debole, Scott Elias, Rebecca Green, Jason Hariton, Kent Jorgensen, Bernie Killian, Stephen Marinaccio, Michael Miller, Rick Nelson, Roger Nygard, Leigh Paonessa, Andy Sacks, Darius Shahmir, Michael Sledd, Dana Sullivan, Susan Sprung, Vance Van Petten, Matt Zboyovski, and so many more. I am grateful for what I learned from you.

Thank you to my Co-Author Gilana Lobel. One of the most remarkable, generous, and patient people I know. It's been an honor to collaborate with you.

And from us both, thanks to Sue Ellen Crandell because…she's right on top of it, Rose.

Appendix

Appendix 213

A.1 – Crew List

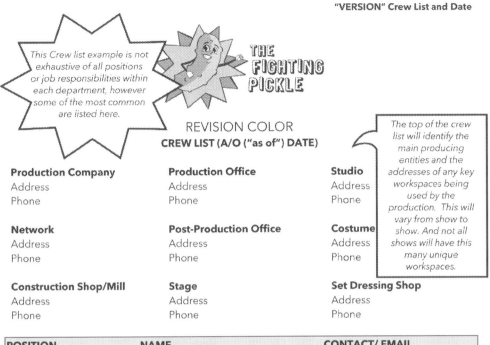

"VERSION" Crew List and Date

This Crew list example is not exhaustive of all positions or job responsibilities within each department, however some of the most common are listed here.

REVISION COLOR
CREW LIST (A/O ("as of") DATE)

The top of the crew list will identify the main producing entities and the addresses of any key workspaces being used by the production. This will vary from show to show. And not all shows will have this many unique workspaces.

Production Company
Address
Phone

Production Office
Address
Phone

Studio
Address
Phone

Network
Address
Phone

Post-Production Office
Address
Phone

Costume
Address
Phone

Construction Shop/Mill
Address
Phone

Stage
Address
Phone

Set Dressing Shop
Address
Phone

POSITION	NAME	CONTACT/ EMAIL
	PRODUCERS/ WRITER(S)/ DIRECTOR	
NAME	PHONE / EMAIL	(C)= cell / (O)= office

EXECUTIVE PRODUCER
Often a Studio, Network or Production Company representative, associated with the entity responsible for financing the show. Oversees the project from creative development through distribution. In television, this may be an additional title given to a key creative role such as the Showrunner, Writer, Director, or a lead cast member.

SHOWRUNNER
Showrunner, often the show creator, is the term for the lead Executive Producer of a Hollywood television series. They typically have creative control of a TV series, combining the responsibilities of the Head Writer, Executive Producer, and Script Editor. In films, Directors typically have creative control of a production, but in television, the Showrunner outranks the Director.

PRODUCER
Oversees all phases of production, from development through delivery and contributes to the integrity of the creative vision of the project. The Producer sources the material, develops the script, secures financing, assembles the Director, cast and other key creatives for the project. Receives the "Produced by" credit.

"VERSION" Crew List and Date

PRODUCERS/ WRITER(S)/ DIRECTOR (continued)

DIRECTOR
Responsible for interpreting the script and creating the overall creative vision of the project such as developing the visual style, selecting the shots, and directing on camera performances.

WRITER (AKA SCREENWRITER)
Responsible for creating the content on the page, writing the screenplay. They collaborate with the Director and/or Producers to develop the story for the visual medium.

CO-PRODUCER
An individual on a production who performs producer functions as delegated by the Producer. Title may be awarded to an individual performing another role on the production such as the Line Producer, UPM, a Financer, Writer, or star.

LINE PRODUCER
Oversees overall day to day production operations from prep through post production. They ensure that all departments are working efficiently, are equipped to do their job, and operating within budget. Often responsible for managing contractual cast needs as well.

PRODUCTION
Refer to Section 2 for more detailed descriptions on these Production roles.

UNIT PRODUCTION MANAGER (UPM)
The manager of the physical production from pre-production through wrap. They are in charge of all organizational, administrative, financial and logistical aspects and must collaborate accordingly with the Executive Producer, Producer, Line Producer, Director and Studio.

PRODUCTION SUPERVISOR
Assists UPM in managing production needs during filming. Often the on-set representation for the production manager when they are needed in the office. The assignments can be similar to the responsibilities of the UPM or more in line with tasks assigned to the Production Coordinator.

PRODUCTION COORDINATOR (PC)
Department head overseeing the Production Office. Facilitates production logistics from pre-production through wrap.

ASSISTANT PRODUCTION COORDINATOR (APC)
Direct support for the PC, manages the day-to-day office needs.

PRODUCTION SECRETARY
Manages paperwork distribution, document filing and assists in overall Production Office support.

Appendix 215

"VERSION" Crew List and Date

PRODUCTION (continued)

OFFICE PRODUCTION ASSISTANT (YOU!)
Assists all aspects of the production from pre-production through wrap. Supports all production office function. Helps everything get done that needs to get done in the office!

TRAVEL COORDINATOR
Works closely with a travel agency or the studio travel department to ensure the necessary employees are traveled and housed for the show.

SCRIPT COORDINATOR
A member of the writing staff, the Script Coordinator is responsible for collaborating with the Showrunner and Writers to incorporate written changes to the script. They ensure formatting, revision color order, and consistency with writing style is maintained. May also be tasked with script distribution. Manages WGA obligations for the show Writers.

WRITERS' ROOM ASSISTANT
An assistant designated to the writer's room and works to support the needs of all staff Writers. Takes notes on story ideas, script revisions, helps Writers track drafts and scripted elements.

SHOWRUNNER/ WRITERS' PRODUCTION ASSISTANT
A Production Assistant designated to the Showrunner and/or Writers who assists with daily office tasks such as managing their schedule, running copies, phone calls, errands, and meals.

ASSISTANT DIRECTORS

The support team for the Director and DP to directly assist in enabling the creative vision during filming. In pre-production, responsible for generating schedules, supervising pre-production meetings and scouts.

1ST ASSISTANT DIRECTOR
Head of the AD Department. Creates and maintains the filming schedule, runs the set for the Director, supports delivery of the Director's creative vision. Prepares the production filming plan and creates shot lists with the DP and Director. Responsible for completion of each filming day, running the production meetings and oversight of on set safety.

2nd ASSISTANT DIRECTOR
Responsible for advance preparation of filming each day and creation of the daily call sheet. Facilitates on set communication between departments, manages cast schedules and readying talent for camera.

2nd 2nd ASSISTANT DIRECTOR
Helps run the set with the 1st AD, assists in placing background and managing set PAs.

ASSISTANT DIRECTORS (continued)

KEY SET PRODUCTION ASSISTANT
A staff Set PA. Head set production assistant, under the direction of the 1st AD and 2nd 2nd AD, assigns the set PAs responsibilities. (Refer to Section 2.)

FIRST TEAM PA
A staff Set PA. The Set PA assigned to work directly with the cast and coordinate production-related needs on set and in basecamp. Assists with cast "wrangling" such as when they are called to/from the set, hair and makeup and wardrobe.

PAPERWORK PA (common to NY)
Works with the 2nd AD to help generate the Call Sheet & Production Report. Also, a staff PA.

BACKGROUND PA
A staff Set PA designated to helping the 2nd 2nd AD wrangle background performers (extras) to get them through hair, makeup, and wardrobe. They may also assist with background voucher (payroll) paperwork and check-in.

WALKIE PA
A staff Set PA. The Set PA responsible for walkie talkie management on set.

ADDITIONAL SET PA / DAY PLAYER
A set PA who has been employed on a short-term basis to assist the production on larger days. Often assigned to "lock up's" and echoing "rolling" and "cut."

ACCOUNTING

The team responsible for managing, budgeting, and recording of production expenditures and financial transactions needed to create a show. The liaison between the financing entity and the production.

PRODUCTION ACCOUNTANT
Accounting department head. Oversees all production expenses, including tracking and reporting. Collaborates with the UPM to manage the budget. Liaises with studio head or finance executive.

1st ASSISTANT ACCOUNTANT
Responsible for set up and management of the accounting office. Manages accounts payable and accounts receivable, petty cash and cash per diem distribution, vendor account set up, accounting forms and PO issuing.

PAYROLL ACCOUNTANT
Handles the processing of cast and crew payroll, including start paperwork.

"VERSION" Crew List and Date

ACCOUNTING (continued)

2nd ASSISTANT ACCOUNTANT
Manages day to day accounting operations, including managing PO's and invoices, tracks petty cash expenses, works with 1st Assistant regarding accounts payable and accounts receivable.

ACCOUNTING CLERK
Entry level accounting department position. Assists all aspects of accounting needs. Majority of the work can consist of managing paperwork, sorting, and distributing mail, and filing of accounting and/or payroll documents.

ANIMALS

Hired as needed per the demands of the script. Responsible for acquiring, training, and supervising the well-being of any animal performers required on a production.

ART

The visual design team. Works with the Director and DP to create the overall look for the sets and locations. Determines what sets need to be built or filmed on a practical location.

PRODUCTION DESIGNER
The creative head of the Art Department. Collaborates with the Director and DP to create the visual look and style of the film. Works with the Producers to determine the budget needed to fit the creative scope.

ART DIRECTOR
Responsible for the organizational and administrative aspects of bringing all artistic elements together on camera. Manages the budget and coordinates with set decoration and construction. Supervises set build plans and Art department needs on location.

SET DESIGNER
Translates concept drawings into practical set blueprints intended to be built by the construction department.

ART DEPARTMENT COORDINATOR
In collaboration with the Art Director, coordinates the administrative and organizational needs of the Art department. This includes tracking materials, purchases, and rentals as well as office set up and strike.

ART DEPARTMENT PRODUCTION ASSISTANT
Supports the Art department in similar ways that the Office Production Assistant supports the Production Office.

"VERSION" Crew List and Date

CAMERA

Responsible for capturing the performances and story through a visual look created by the lighting, framing, camera movement and image focus.

DIRECTOR OF PHOTOGRAPHY
The creative head of the camera, lighting, and grip department. Works with Director and Production Designer to create the photographic visual style and mood for the show. They develop shots lists and design lighting plans for each set.

CAMERA OPERATOR
Operates the camera and framing of the images to capture performances in accordance with the Director and DP's vision.

1ST ASSISTANT CAMERA
Responsible for managing the crew, equipment ordering and the needs of the camera department. On set, handles camera lens changes and keeps the image in focus during filming.

2ND ASSISTANT CAMERA
Assists with wrangling camera equipment, lenses, documenting details from each film take onto camera reports and "slating" takes. They are responsible for ordering expendables.

DIGITAL IMAGING TECHNICIAN
Responsible for on set "live" color correction of images as they are filmed. Collaborates with the DP to set "looks." Ensures media is backed up and delivered to editorial.

CAMERA LOADER/ DATA WRANGLER
Manages the media or film that is capturing the images. Records the amount of footage or data filmed per reel or digital camera card and may be responsible for downloading the media.

STILL PHOTOGRAPHER
Responsible for capturing still images of both on-screen action and behind-the-scenes for studio use and publicity purposes.

CAMERA PRODUCTION ASSISTANT
A non-union entry level position in the camera department. They will learn and train under the direction of the camera team and are often responsible for things like charging batteries, cleaning the truck, and getting food orders.

CASTING

Responsible for sourcing and negotiating the hiring of all on screen performers.

CASTING DIRECTOR
Works with the Director to provide a selection of performer options for consideration for the speaking roles needed in the script. Works with the Producers to negotiate the hiring terms.

"VERSION" Crew List and Date

CASTING (continued)

EXTRAS CASTING
The team responsible for sourcing and casting background actors (non-speaking roles) per the needs of the script and the Directors' vision for ethnicity, gender and general look required.

CATERING
The department responsible for preparing and providing meals to the cast and crew each day.

CATERER
The individual or company hired to manage a staff that purchases, prepares, and serves meals on set during principal photography days.

CONSTRUCTION
Responsible for building, installing, and striking of non-permanent sets that will be filmed.

CONSTRUCTION COORDINATOR
Construction department head. Oversees the budgeting, ordering of materials and the scheduling of workers for the construction of sets. Supervises the building of the sets.

HEAD (KEY) CARPENTER
Determines the most efficient order in which to build the set pieces, supervises the Carpenters and Laborers.

CONSTRUCTION FOREMAN/ CONSTRUCTION GANGBOSS
Essentially a construction "team leader" assigned to oversee the build of a specific set with a team of "propmakers." The term "gang boss" can be applied to a team leader of multiple construction-oriented departments such as paint and plaster.

PROPMAKER (aka CARPENTER)
Construction crew build team member responsible for the actual construction of the set pieces and any wooden props or furniture.

CONSTRUCTION BUYER
Found on larger productions, responsible for tracking purchases and placing material and supply orders to ensure the department has what they need to maintain the build schedule.

PLASTER FOREMAN
In charge of the plaster department, knowledgeable in all phases of plaster application, collaborates with Production Designer, Art Director and Construction Coordinator. Delegates assignments to Plaster Gangboss.

CONSTRUCTION (continued)

PLASTERERS
Members of the construction plaster crew. Responsible for applying plaster to surfaces, creating molds and faux finishes such as brick and cinder block patterns.

GREENSPERSON
Responsible for all landscape, plants, and vegetation on the set including grass or dirt placement.

COSTUMES & WARDROBE

Costumes is responsible for the style and design choices, sourcing and acquiring, fit and alterations of items worn by the cast. Wardrobe is responsible for the organization and continuity of costumes as well as dressing and maintaining the looks of cast members on set.

COSTUME DESIGNER
The creative head of the costume department. Designs all clothing and costume looks worn by the cast per the script and Director's vision. They work with Producers to determine the budget needed to fit the creative scope.

ASSISTANT COSTUME DESIGNER
Second to the Costume Designer, assists with and oversees purchasing and/or manufacturing of costumes per the Costume Designer's vision.

WARDROBE SUPERVISOR
Head of the wardrobe department. Oversees costume preparation and organization of all wardrobe per character per scene as designated by the Costume Designer and ensures their delivery to/from set each day. In the absence of a Costume Coordinator, manages the department budget, logistics and paperwork and oversees department staffing.

COSTUME COORDINATOR (common to NY)
Manages the department logistics including accounting matters such as PO's and budget tracking, as well as expendable and supply ordering, coordination of dept. staffing and runs.

KEY COSTUMER
The head of the on-set costumers who coordinates with the Costume Designer and Wardrobe Supervisor regarding the needs on set to ensure costumes are ready for cast each day.

SET COSTUMER
Provides the assigned wardrobe and assists in dressing cast members for their roles. They work on set to ensure continuity and make costume adjustments for on-camera if necessary.

COSTUMES PA
Supports the Costumes department in similar ways that the Office Production Assistant supports the production office.

"VERSION" Crew List and Date

CRAFT SERVICE

Responsible for assisting various crafts on set, traditionally they provide on set snacks, beverages, and general set cleanliness during filming each day.

CRAFT SERVICE HEAD (KEY)
An individual or company hired to purchase, prepare, and serve snacks for crew during filming.

ELECTRIC/ SET LIGHTING

Responsible for everything power and electrical, including equipment. They provide the light on the set.

GAFFER/ CHIEF LIGHTING TECHNICIAN (CLT)
Head Electrician. Responsible for all things power and lighting including the lighting design and plan needed to support the visual style for the production under the direction of the DP.

ASSISTANT CHIEF LIGHTING TECH (ALCT) / BEST BOY ELECTRIC
Lighting department 2nd in command. Responsible for equipment ordering and tracking, expendable ordering, department labor hiring, scheduling, and submitting work hours.

LIGHTING PROGRAMMER/ DIMMER BOARD OPERATOR
A specialized position in the lighting department responsible for the digital lighting plan in order to control preset lighting looks, most often employed when working on a sound stage.

ELECTRICIAN/ SET LIGHTING TECHNICIAN / LAMP OPERATOR
Sometimes considered the entry level position in the lighting department, though some experience is required. Responsible for executing the lighting plan under the direction of the Gaffer/CLT by setting lights and running cable.

GRIP

Responsible for shaping the light on set and all camera support needs as well as any specialized rigging and set wall movement as needed for filming and lighting.

KEY GRIP
Head of Grip department; collaborates with the Gaffer and DP to supply the tools that help control and guide the light. They work with the camera department to determine the equipment needed to support camera movement and may also oversee car rigs, cranes and assist with on-set safety.

BEST BOY GRIP
Grip department 2nd in command. Responsible for equipment ordering and tracking, expendable ordering, department labor hiring, scheduling, and submitting work hours.

DOLLY GRIP
Specialized technician responsible for supporting camera movement often through the operation of a "dolly", they provide safety assistance anytime the camera is in motion.

"VERSION" Crew List and Date

GRIP (continued)

COMPANY GRIP
Sometimes considered the entry level position in the grip department, though some experience is required. Responsible for supporting the lighting plan and the camera department under the direction of the Key Grip for any non-electrical related needs.

HAIR

Responsible for all hair needs for the production as it relates to performer appearance, hair continuity and touch ups on set as needed.

HAIR DEPARTMENT HEAD
Designs and creates the hair styles, wigs, colors, and facial hair looks for each cast member.

KEY HAIR STYLIST
Hair department 2nd in command, they assist in preparing the hair on cast members for filming per the Department Heads' design as well as Hair Stylist staffing, and ordering hair supplies as needed.

HEALTH & SAFETY

Responsible for planning, implementation and enforcement of health and safety obligations in accordance with the Production Company, Studio or Network production safety plan.

LEGAL

PRODUCTION COUNSEL
The Studio or Production Company business affairs or legal representation responsible for handling all contractual matters, including cast contracts, releases, and vendor rental agreements.

LOCATIONS

Seeks out practical locations that fit in the vision of the Director and Production Designer based on the needs of the script. Responsible for taking the Director and creative team out on scouts to assess the practicality and viability of filming locations. Responsible for the day-to-day management of the location property during filming.

LOCATION MANAGER
Head of the Locations department, they present options for practical film set locations based on what has been scouted to fit the story. Supervises the locations department staff, works with Producers to determine locations budget, negotiates, and manages location rental and logistical needs for filming.

KEY ASSISTANT LOCATION MANAGER
Locations department 2nd in command. Assists with securing location agreements, rental payments, permits and other rental equipment needed to support filming logistics on location.

"VERSION" Crew List and Date

LOCATIONS (continued)

ASSISTANT LOCATION MANAGER
Assists the Location Manager with scouting and managing the location during prep, filming, and strike.

LOCATION SCOUT
Seeks out location considerations under the guidance of the Location Manager and in accordance with the script. Photographs locations and makes contact with owners/representatives in order to follow up if selected by the Director and creative team.

LOCATION COORDINATOR
Manages the locations department office, they facilitate location agreements, help file permits, place equipment and supply orders, help track department spending and sometimes complete location maps.

LOCATION ASSISTANT / UNIT PA (common in NY)
Assists the locations department with on set operations such as trash pick-up, set up and strike of tents, fans, heaters, tables, and chairs, etc.

MAKEUP

Responsible for all makeup needs for the production as it relates to performer appearance, makeup continuity and touch ups on set as needed.

MAKEUP DEPARTMENT HEAD
Plans and designs the makeup looks for each cast member.

KEY MAKEUP ARTIST
Makeup department 2nd in command, assists in applying the makeup on cast members for filming per the direction of the Department Head's design as well as Makeup department staffing, and ordering supplies as needed.

MEDIC

Responsible for basic first aid on the set.

SET MEDIC
Trained in basic life support, treats minor cast and crew injuries that may occur during filming and maintains a well-supplied first aid kit. Assesses medical emergencies as necessary.

"VERSION" Crew List and Date

PARKING

This department is primarily found on productions filming in Northeastern cities such as New York and Boston where additional on-location parking support is necessary.

PARKING COORDINATOR
Responsible for coordinating the parking staff to hold street parking and direct the parking of crew, trucks, and equipment vehicles on location.

PARKING ASSISTANT
Physically holds parking spaces on the street using cones and signage, helps direct trucks to designated parking areas.

POST PRODUCTION

Sometimes broken into two categories "Editorial" and "Post Production".
Responsible for assembling the final product. Cuts together the visual and sound elements to create the final cohesive story.

EDITOR
The creative head of the editorial department. Collaborates with the Director and Producers, cuts the film together from all the footage, oversees the creative vision is maintained through the editorial process.

ASSISTANT EDITOR
Supports the Editor. Works with Post Supervisor to ensure the editing facility and equipment are secured and set up. AE's may be responsible for syncing dailies and organizing clip files.

POST PRODUCTION SUPERVISOR
Oversees the Post Production schedule and budget, logistical set up for the editorial workspace, negotiates deals with Post Production vendors, tracks the entire post production process to delivery.

POST PRODUCTION COORDINATOR
Manages Post Production office function including expense reports, travel coordination and general post production office management.

POST PRODUCTION ASSISTANT
General Post Production office assistance. Similar tasks as that of the Office Production Assistant but dedicated to Post Production and/or Editorial.

"VERSION" Crew List and Date

PROPERTY
Responsible for all the practical handheld items used by a performer in a scene.

PROPERTY MASTER
The head of the Property department. Collaborates with the Production Designer and Set Decorator, responsible for designing and sourcing the physical props including ensuring historical accuracy when applicable. They manage the department budget, prop continuity, and may handle food and weapons as well as picture cars in the absence of a Picture Car Coordinator.

ASSISTANT PROP MASTER
AKA On Set Props. Prop department 2nd in command. Often responsible for prop management on set during filming including prop continuity, pickups and returns.

SCENIC
Under the supervision of the Art and Construction departments, and in collaboration with the plaster department, the scenic/paint department are the visual artisans. Skilled with paint color and brushes, they add realism and the final touches needed to bring sets to life.

CHARGE SCENIC/ PAINT FOREMAN
In charge of the paint department, knowledgeable of all phases of paint application, collaborates with Production Designer, Art Director and Construction Coordinator. Delegates assignments to Paint Gangboss and Scenic Artists/Painters.

SCENIC ARTISTS / PAINTERS
Members of the construction paint crew. Responsible for surface priming, painting, and finishing.

SCRIPT SUPERVISOR
Maintains detailed notes of what and how the script was captured on camera. Ensures that the continuity of the film is coherent. Is the official "timekeeper" during principal photography.

SCRIPT SUPERVISOR
The most detail-oriented eye on the frame, works closely with the Director to ensure the entire script is filmed. Watches for script and screen continuity during filming, records detailed notes of each take filmed, and provides reports to assist the editorial process.

SET DECORATION
Responsible for dressing all sets with furniture and other décor to support the creative aesthetic for the show.

SET DECORATOR
The Set Decorating department head. Reports to the Production Designer. Responsible for decorating the film set. This includes everything from drapery to furniture and wall decor. Manages the department budget, tracks inventory and assets, and coordinates department crew to ensure sets are camera ready.

SET DECORATION (continued)

LEADMAN
Second in the set decorating department. Responsible for dressing and wrapping sets, including coordinating the pickup and return of pieces selected by the Set Decorator for use in the film, and making sure they arrive on the appropriate set. They supervise a team of set dressers to ensure the work is completed.

ON SET DRESSER
Works with the "on" production crew to assist with any set dressing needs to accommodate lighting or facilitate blocking and camera movement on the day. Responsible for placement and replacement of set dressing during filming. Often this means moving furniture.

SET DRESSERS/ SWING GANG
Multiple Set Dressers are employed to prep and strike sets before and after filming. They are responsible for pick up, return and "dressing" of the set to ready it for filming.

SOUND

Responsible for capturing the dialogue and audible ambiance of every scene filmed.

SOUND MIXER
Head of the sound department, records the production sound during filming. Monitors that speaking levels are appropriate and unobstructed by other noises. Creates detailed sound reports to assist editorial.

BOOM OPERATOR
Skillfully operates the boom microphone pole placement to best capture dialogue during a scene. Assists with mic-ing actors.

SOUND UTILITY
Assists with mic-ing actors, cable wrangling and general department assistance, sometimes also serves as a 2nd Boom Operator.

SPECIAL EFFECTS

Hired as needed per the demands of the script. Responsible for all practical effects needed for filming such as running water, smoke, pyrotechnics and other high risk scripted activities.

STAND IN'S

(Inclusion on crew list at the discretion of the PC) Individuals of the same height, skin tone, and hair color, that take the place of principal cast members during lighting set ups.

"VERSION" Crew List and Date

STUNTS

Responsible for safely planning and executing action that may pose a risk to principal cast members.

STUNT COORDINATOR
Designs the plan for safe stunt execution, hires and directs the stunt performers. They may also choreograph stunt sequences for stunt and principal performers with the Director.

TRANSPORTATION

Oversees trucking and transportation needs for all departments. This is often one of the largest departments on any production.

TRANSPORTATION COORDINATOR
When employed on a production, is the head of the transportation department. Secures all vehicle needs for the production including equipment trucks, department and cast trailers, passenger vans and other transport rentals, oversees department budget, logistics and staffing.

TRANSPORTATION CAPTAIN
Head of the transportation department in collaboration with or in place of the transportation coordinator. Often works with the "on" production crew to ensure proper parking placement and that all vehicles are maintained daily. Oversees all production drivers.

DRIVERS
Entry level transportation position. Drives any and all vehicles including production vans, trucks, trailer tows and other vehicles as licensed by the Department of Transportation compliance regulations.

VISUAL EFFECTS

Hired as needed per the demands of the script. Responsible for digitally creating imagery needed that cannot be done practically or has been determined to not be done practically. This team will supervise on set filming needs required to support the creation of the digital image using computer software.

A.2 – Office Supply List

OFFICE SUPPLY LIST

Basic Production Office start up list to be used as a guide. Individuals and departments will request items specific to their needs. Always consult with your PC before making any purchases.

CATEGORY	DESCRIPTION	QUANTITY
ADHESIVES		
	Tape dispenser refills	10 rolls
	Packing tape	5 rolls
	Packing tape dispenser	2
	2" black gaffers tape	1 roll
	2" white gaffers tape	1 roll
BINDING		
	Paperclips-Small	1000
	Paperclips-Large	1000
	Binder Clips-Small	50
	Binder Clips-Medium	50
	Binder Clips-Large	50
	Round head brass fasteners 1 ½"	200
	Staple removers	2
	Rubber bands	100
	Staple refills	2 boxes
CLEANING		
	Disinfecting wipes	2 containers
	Disinfecting Spray	1
	Paper towels	5 rolls
	Dish cleaning soap	1
	Dish sponges	1 package
COPY PAPER		
	8 ½" x 11" White	5 boxes
	8 ½" x 11" White 3 hole	1 box
	8 ½" x 11" Blue	1 box
	8 ½" x 11" Pink	1 box
	8 ½" x 11" Yellow	1 box
	8 ½" x 11" Green	1 box
	8 ½" x 11" Goldenrod	5 reams
	8 ½" x 11" Buff	If needed
	8 ½" x 11" Salmon	If needed
	8 ½" x 11" Cherry	If needed
	8 ½" x 11" Tan	If needed
	8 ½" x 11" Lavender	If needed
	8 ½" x 11" Gray	If needed
	8 ½" x 14" White	3 boxes
	8 ½" x 14" Blue	3 reams
	8 ½" x 14" Yellow	5 reams
	11" x 17" White	2 reams
DESK ACCESSORIES		
	Tape dispensers	5
	Staplers	5
	Desktop file trays	12

CATEGORY	DESCRIPTION	QUANTITY
DESK ACCESSORIES (cont.)		
	15" Guillotine style paper cutter	1
	3-hole punch	3
	Ruler	2
	Scissors	5
	Heavy duty 3 hole punch	1
	2 Hole punch	1
	Push pins	2 boxes
ENVELOPES		
	Mailing envelopes	1 box
	10" x 13" Manila clasp envelopes	100
FILING		
	Hanging file folders-Letter	50
	Manila file folders-Letter	100
	2" Three ring binders	5
	Binder tabs	5 sets
	File folder labels	1 package
	Sheet protectors	1 box
LABELING		
	P-Touch label maker	1
	Label maker tape refills-black on white	As needed
NOTEPADS		
	Writing pad-letter size	10
	3" x 3" sticky notes-Assorted colors	8 packs
	1 ½" x 2" sticky notes-Assorted colors	8 packs
POWER		
	Power strips	5
	Extension cords (10'-20')	2
	Cable covers	As needed
WRITING		
	Generic ballpoint retractable pens-Black	50
	Generic ballpoint retractable pens-Red	1 box
	Assorted multi-color highlighters	3 x each
	Sharpie fine point marker-Black	2 x box
	Sharpie fine point marker-Red	2 x box
	Correction /White out tape	10
	Mechanical pencils	1 x box
ADDITIONAL AS NEEDED		
	Clip boards-Letter	3
	Arch clip clipboard-Legal	6
	Printer toner	As needed
	Laminator	1

A.3 – Production File Organization Chart

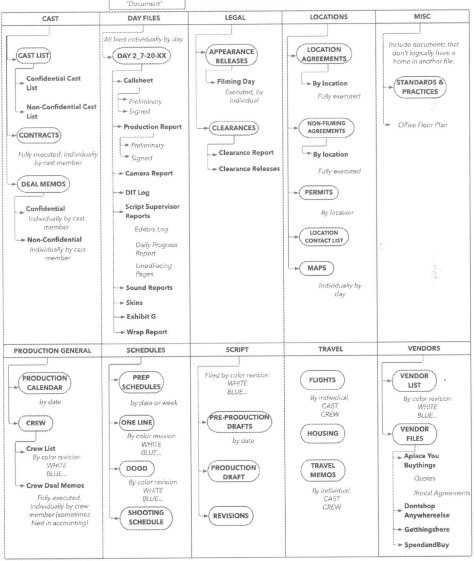

A.4 – Day File Labels

DAY 1 / 4-11-20XX	
FP&F-SEASON 2 — EPISODE 1	*HANGING FILE*
DAY 2 / 4-12-20XX	
FP&F-SEASON 2 — EPISODE 1	*HANGING FILE*
DAY 3 / 4-13-20XX	
FP&F-SEASON 2 — EPISODE 1	*HANGING FILE*
DAY 4 / 4-14-20XX	
FP&F-SEASON 2 — EPISODE 1	*HANGING FILE*
DAY 5 / 4-15-20XX	
FP&F-SEASON 2 — EPISODE 1	*HANGING FILE*
DAY 6 / 5-18-20XX	
FP&F-SEASON 2 — EPISODE 1	*HANGING FILE*
DAY 7 / 4-19-20XX	
FP&F-SEASON 2 — EPISODE 1	*HANGING FILE*
DAY 8 / 4-20-20XX	
FP&F-SEASON 2 — EPISODE 1	*HANGING FILE*
CALLSHEET — Day 1	
FP&F-SEASON 2 — EPISODE 1	*INSIDE FILE*
PRODUCTION REPORT — Day 1	
FP&F-SEASON 2 — EPISODE 1	*INSIDE FILE*
SOUND REPORT — Day 1	
FP&F-SEASON 2 — EPISODE 1	*INSIDE FILE*
CAMERA REPORT/DIT REPORT — Day 1	
FP&F-SEASON 2 — EPISODE 1	*INSIDE FILE*
SAG EXHIBIT G — Day 1	
FP&F-SEASON 2 — EPISODE 1	*INSIDE FILE*
SCRIPT SUPER REPORT — Day 1	
FP&F-SEASON 2 — EPISODE 1	*INSIDE FILE*

DAY FILE LABELS

A.5 – Production File Labels

A.6 – Mileage Log

THE FIGHTING PICKLE
PRODUCTION
MILEAGE REIMBURSEMENT FORM

NAME:			WEEK ENDING:		
			SOCIAL SECURITY #:		
ADDRESS:					
CITY, STATE, ZIP:					
POSITION:					
Dates	ODOMETER From	To	Destinations		Miles Driven
5/11/XX	96,783	96,788	PO > Market		5
5/11/XX	96,788	96,793	Market > Production Office		5
APPROVAL:		Total Miles:_____ x $.XX/mile = Total: $			

"From" is your starting mileage
"To" is your mileage when you arrive at the destination.

Include start and end location

"To" miles minus "From" miles

Each week, total your miles driven and turn this form in with your timecard.

A.7 – Script Title Page

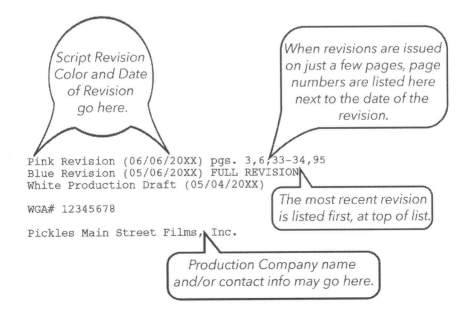

A.8 – Script Revisions

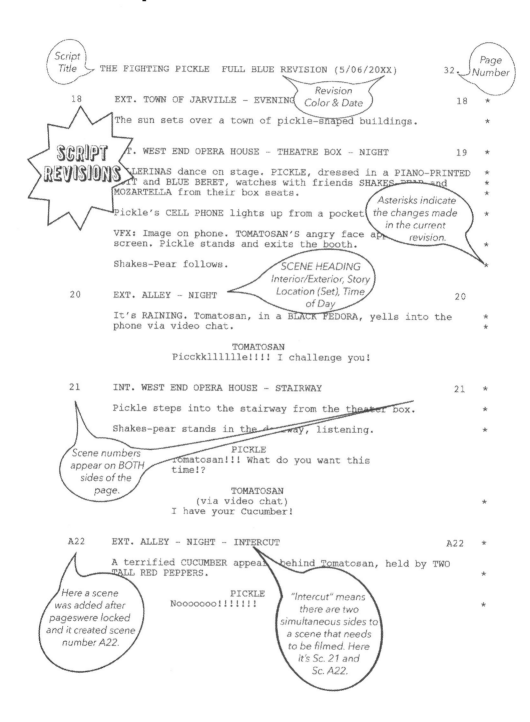

```
THE FIGHTING PICKLE   FULL BLUE REVISION (5/06/20XX)      32A.

                         TOMATOSAN                              *
                Meet me in the Alley! Now! Or you               *
                will never see your precious
                Cucumber again!

        INTERCUT:

        Tomatosan hangs up. Pickle puts the phone in hi
        steaming with anger. Pickle rolls up the suit s
        marches towards the back exit.

                         SHAKES-PEAR
                Pickle, Wait!                                   *

        Pickle is already out of earshot.                       *
```

(Annotation, left): *This label refers back to Sc. 21 and would be called out in the schedule as such.*

(Annotation, right): *After the script is locked, if a scene is changed and pushes onto an additional page, an "A" page will be created to avoid renumbering the entire script.*

```
         THE FIGHTING PICKLE      PINK REVISION (6/06/20XX)           33.
```

(Annotation: New revisions create a new color and date header.)

```
  22         EXT. ALLEY - NIGHT                                        22

              Pickle steps out into the Alley. The RAIN falls. Tomatosan
              stands ready for a fight.

                                  PICKLE
                        Tomatosan! Release Cucumber!

              The Two Red Peppers hold Cucumber behind Tomatosan.        *

                                  CUCUMBER
                        Pickle!!!! Please Help Me!                       *

              A flash of panic in Cucumber's eyes.

                                  PICKLE
                        Cucumber!

              Pickle looks up to the sky. Ennio Morricone's the GOOD THE
              BAD AND THE UGLY music plays. Pickle and Tomatosan face off.

              Pickle raises a hand to the sky, JUMPS in the air and comes
              down hard, fist to the ground, it shakes. Water splashes
              upward in SLOW MOTION.                                     *

              Tomatosan loses balance and wobbles backwards.

              The theater side door swings open. Shakes-Pear and Mozartella *
              jump out.

                                  SHAKES-PEAR
                        Yaaaaaaaa!

              Shakes-Pear and Mozartella head for the Two Red Peppers,   *
              waving their arms in the air.

              Pickle advances on Tomatosan. They leap, SLOW MOTION, into *
              the air at each other.

              VFX: POW! Tomato juice splashes against the theatre wall.  *

              The Two Red Peppers panic, they let go of Cucumber, and run *
              for their lives. Shakes-Pear and Mozartella cheer.

              Tomatosan is defeated.

              Pickle looks to Cucumber. Cucumber looks to Pickle. They run
              into each others arms. The rain has stopped.

  23         EXT. STREET - NIGHT                                        23  *

              Pickle, Cucumber, Shakes-pear, Mozartella walk arm in arm   *
              down the street, silhouetted in the street light.          *
```

```
            THE FIGHTING PICKLE    PINK REVISION (6/06/20XX)              34.

  24        EXT. ALLEY - NIGHT                                            24

            Tomatosan slumped against the wall, raises a fist to the air.

                                TOMATOSAN
                      This isn't over Pickle.... Not by a
                      long...

            The theatre door bursts open, Tomatosan is smooshed into the
            wall as PATRONS exit.

                                TOMATOSAN (CONT'D)
                      Ouch.

            Tomato juice oozes from under the door.


  25        OMITTED                                                       25    *
                                                                                *
```

When a scene is deleted after the script is locked, it's called an "OMIT."

A.9 – Phone Activity: Answering Common Calls

ANSWERING COMMON CALLS THAT COME INTO THE PRODUCTION OFFICE

Example activity!

The following practice calls will walk you through what to do when receiving specific types of callers in the production office.

1) THE GENERIC JOB SEEKER

RING! RING!

YOU/OFFICE PA	CALLER
"Production, this is _____"	"Hello, may I please speak with the production coordinator?"
"May I ask who is calling?"	"This is Sara Ineedajob."
"May I ask what this is regarding?"	"I emailed my resume earlier today and I wanted to follow up."
"May I put you on hold?"	

Contact information for the production office finds its way out into the world, you'll know when this happens because calls and emails from crew and actors looking for work will start coming in, in bulk.

WALK THROUGH THE CALL

WHO is calling? What do they *DO* or where are they *FROM*?	Sara Ineedajob, don't know, not from anywhere in particular.
Who are they calling *FOR*? What does that person *DO*?	The Production coordinator.
WHY is this person calling?	Following up on if their resume was received.
WHO should take this call?	You can.
Is who they are calling for *AVAILABLE* to take the call?	You are available.
Is there *SOMEONE ELSE* who can take the call?	Another PA, the production secretary.
Do you need to gather more details before passing the call on?	Not really, maybe confirm the email address it was sent to.
How *URGENT* is this call?	Not very.
Do you have *AUTHORITY* to give out the information being requested?	Yes.
What do you do?	LOOK for the resume in the production files, resume binder, or email inbox. NOTIFY caller if it was or was not received. Remember, this person could be you, so be kind.

2) THE AGENT'S OFFICE

RING! RING!

YOU/OFFICE PA	CALLER
"Production, this is _____"	"Hi this is Susie from WeRepFamousPeople Management, we represent Ani Actress."
"Ok, how can I help you?"	"Can you tell me what her call time is tomorrow and if Ani is working next Wednesday and if she will be available after 2pm Friday?"
"May I put you on hold?"	

Agents are notorious for calling the production office and asking for actor schedule information. Often they want schedule specifics days and weeks in advance. Call times are set by the AD department, the day prior to a work-day, so other than a general "yes" or "no" whether the actor is scheduled to work, an exact call time cannot be given until wrap on the day prior. Either way, this is **not** an answer you as the Office PA should be providing. (They also tend to talk really, really, fast so don't be surprised if you need them to repeat something!)

WALK THROUGH THE CALL

WHO is calling? What do they DO or where are they FROM?	Susie from WeRepFamousPeople Management, they represent cast member Ani Actress.
Who are they calling FOR? What does that person DO?	They didn't say. Think: Who is responsible for actor schedules? While the 1st AD will put the initial filming schedule together and manage it, once in principal photography the 2nd Assistant Director will handle information regarding actor schedules.
WHY is this person calling?	To get information about Ani's schedule.
WHO should take this call?	The 2nd Assistant Director.
Is who they are calling for AVAILABLE to take the call?	You will find out (by calling the person before transferring or checking in their office and asking).
Is there SOMEONE ELSE who can take the call?	The Production Coordinator or Line Producer. Anything regarding cast schedules can also be directed to the production coordinator or Line Producer.
Do you need to gather more details before passing the call on?	Not really.
How URGENT is this call?	Moderately urgent. If the request does not apply to the current day's work, it is not immediately urgent and the information they are requesting is likely not available yet.
Do you have AUTHORITY to give out the information being requested?	No
What do you do?	CHECK if the recipient is available. TRANSFER the call or take a MESSAGE. NOTIFY recipient & PC of the call.

3) THE CAST MEMBER

RING! RING!

YOU/OFFICE PA	CALLER
"Production, this is _____"	"Hi, Ani Actress calling. I received a garbled message on my phone. What is my call time tomorrow?"
"May I put you on hold?"	

While most cast members will call the 2nd Assistant Director directly to find out their call time, on occasion this call will come through the production office. Other than general crew call, the production office <u>does not</u> give out individual call times.

WALK THROUGH THE CALL

WHO is calling? What do they DO or where are they FROM?	Ani Actress, Cast Member on the show.
Who are they calling FOR? What does that person DO?	Didn't say. Think: Who has the answer?
WHY is this person calling?	She needs her call time for tomorrow.
WHO should take this call?	The 2nd Assistant Director.
Is who they are calling for AVAILABLE to take the call?	You'll find out.
Is there SOMEONE ELSE who can take the call?	The Production Coordinator (if unable to reach the 2nd AD).
Do you need to gather more details before passing the call on?	No.
How URGENT is this call?	Very. Cast members are considered VIP callers.
Do you have AUTHORITY to give out the information being requested?	No.
What do you do?	CHECK if the recipient is available. TRANSFER the call or take a MESSAGE. NOTIFY recipient & PC of the call.

4) THE STUDIO

Roles: Heather is the producer.
          Tia Greenlight is the studio executive.
          Nicole is the producer assistant.

RING! RING!

YOU/OFFICE PA	CALLER
"Production, this is _____"	"Hi, Heather please"
"May I ask who's calling?"	"I have Tia Greenlight on the line."
"Ok, let me try and reach them for you"	

More often than not an assistant to a studio executive will call the production office on behalf of the executive in order to connect them with someone in your office. When connecting a call from the executive's office you'll want to determine whether the executive themselves is on the line or if their "office" is on the line. This way the recipient can expect who will be on the other end of the phone when they pick up.

<u>WALK THROUGH THE CALL</u>

WHO is calling? What do they *DO* or where are they *FROM*?	Tia Greenlight's office, the Studio Executive
Who are they calling *FOR*? What does that person *DO*?	Heather the Producer
WHY is this person calling?	Don't know. In this instance, the reason for the call is secondary to connecting the studio executive to the producer.
WHO should take this call?	Nicole the assistant or Heather directly. Coordinate in advance with the producer's assistant on how calls that come into the production office for the producer are to be handled.
Is who they are calling for *AVAILABLE* to take the call?	You'll find out (through Nicole).
Is there *SOMEONE ELSE* who can take the call?	Nicole the assistant, or the Production Coordinator.
Do you need to gather more details before passing the call on?	No.
How *URGENT* is this call?	Very. The studio executive is a VIP caller.
Do you have *AUTHORITY* to give out the information being requested?	They aren't requesting any information.
What do you do?	CHECK if the recipient is available. TRANSFER the call or take a MESSAGE. NOTIFY recipient of the call.

5) THE 1ST AD

Roles: Moesha is the UPM
         David is the 1st AD

RING! RING!

YOU/OFFICE PA	CALLER
"Production, this is _____"	"Moesha please."
"May I ask who's calling?"	"David."
"Ok let me make sure she's available."	

This communication from the set to the office can be critical to the completion of the day.

WALK THROUGH THE CALL

WHO is calling? What do they DO or where are they FROM?	David the 1st AD on the show.
Who are they calling FOR? What does that person DO?	Moesha the UPM on the show.
WHY is this person calling?	Didn't say, however when an AD calls their boss from the set, this call could be potentially urgent.
WHO should take this call?	Moesha.
Is who they are calling for AVAILABLE to take the call?	You'll find out.
Is there SOMEONE ELSE who can take the call?	The Production Coordinator or Production supervisor.
Do you need to gather more details before passing the call on?	No.
How URGENT is this call?	Very.
Do you have AUTHORITY to give out the information being requested?	They aren't requesting any information.
What do you do?	CHECK if the recipient is available. TRANSFER the call or take a MESSAGE. NOTIFY recipient of the call.

6) THE PRODUCTION CREW JOB SEEKER

RING! RING!

YOU/OFFICE PA	CALLER
"Production, this is _____"	"Hi, have you hired a sound mixer yet?"
"Let me check."	"Ok thank you."

This call is similar to the generic job seeker, when prospective crew reach out in search of a position on the production.

WALK THROUGH THE CALL

WHO is calling? What do they DO or where are they FROM?	Didn't say, but probably a sound mixer or an agent.
Who are they calling FOR? What does that person DO?	Didn't say.
WHY is this person calling?	They want to know if we have a sound mixer for the show.
WHO should take this call?	You can.
Is who they are calling for AVAILABLE to take the call?	Sure, you are.
Is there SOMEONE ELSE who can take the call?	Another PA.
Do you need to gather more details before passing the call on?	No.
How URGENT is this call?	Not at all.
Do you have AUTHORITY to give out the information being requested?	Yes, usually but clear it with the PC before responding.
What do you do?	CHECK the crew list. If a sound mixer is listed, you can tell the caller one has been hired. Do not give out the name without approval. If a sound mixer is not listed, check with the PC or APC before responding to the caller.

7) THE PRODUCER

Roles: Heather is the producer
         Jamie is the producer assistant

RING! RING!

YOU/OFFICE PA	CALLER
"Production, this is _____"	"This is Heather. I need someone to pick me up from the car repair shop in Midtown."
"Sure, let me just get some more details from you..."	

Most of the time a producer will work through their assistant if they have one, however there are various reasons why a producer might elect to call the production office directly.

WALK THROUGH THE CALL

WHO is calling? What do they *DO* or where are they *FROM*?	Heather the producer on the show.
Who are they calling *FOR*? What does that person *DO*?	Anyone in the office.
WHY is this person calling?	They need to be picked up.
WHO should take this call?	You.
Is who they are calling for *AVAILABLE* to take the call?	Sure, you are.
Is there *SOMEONE ELSE* who can take the call?	Their assistant or another PA.
Do you need to gather more details before passing the call on?	Yes, get the details of the pickup, i.e. what time, the address, etc.
How *URGENT* is this call?	Very, they are the boss.
Do you have *AUTHORITY* to give out the information being requested?	They are not asking for information.
What do you do?	NOTIFY the PC of this request. NOTIFY Jamie (assistant) of this request and await further instructions.

8) THE UPM

Roles: Steve is the UPM
Carrie is the production coordinator

RING! RING!

YOU/OFFICE PA	CALLER
"Production, this is _____."	"Steve, for Carrie."
"May I put you on hold?"	

Short calls like this come in all the time. Knowing the names of the crew members will save valuable time when connecting callers.

WALK THROUGH THE CALL

WHO is calling? What do they *DO* or where are they *FROM*?	Steve, the UPM from the show.
Who are they calling *FOR*? What does that person *DO*?	Carrie the PC from the show.
WHY is this person calling?	Didn't say.
WHO should take this call?	Carrie.
Is who they are calling for *AVAILABLE* to take the call?	You'll find out.
Is there *SOMEONE ELSE* who can take the call?	The APC.
Do you need to gather more details before passing the call on?	No.
How *URGENT* is this call?	Very, they are the bosses.
Do you have *AUTHORITY* to give out the information being requested?	They aren't requesting any info.
What do you do?	CHECK if the recipients are available. TRANSFER the call or take a MESSAGE. NOTIFY recipient & PC of the call ASAP.

See, that wasn't so scary! Answering the phone is an ongoing task of any Office PA. Knowing how to connect callers quickly and efficiently will put you ahead of the game.

Glossary

10–1: The term used for going to or being in the bathroom.
1st Shot: The time the cameras rolled on the first shot of the day, as recorded by the Script Supervisor.
1st Shot After Lunch: The time the cameras rolled on the first shot after lunch, as recorded by the Script Supervisor.
First (1st) Team: The term used to identify principal performers.
2nd / "Second": The 2nd-in-command to a department head ("Key") in any department.
3rd / "Third": The third staffing level of a department's team. A skilled support position, not considered managerial.
Above-the-Line/"ATL": Refers to where production elements are traditionally located in a budget. Above-the-Line elements include Cast, Directors, Producers, and Writers, and are typically the more "high dollar" costs on a production.
AD Kit: The on-set Production Office toolkit used by the Assistant Director team.
AMPTP: The Alliance of Motion Picture and Television Producers, aka the major Studios. This is a trade organization that handles collective bargaining with Unions and Guilds on behalf of the major Studios.
Appearance Release: A legal document authorizing the use of your image and likeness, for the purposes defined in the release, such as behind-the-scenes documentation.
Background Breakdown: A summary of the background performers (aka "extras") that actually reported to work that day. Each performer is categorized by the time they reported to work, when they were dismissed, and their pay rate. The breakdown will also indicate any pay bumps/upgrades.
Below-the-Line/"BTL": Refers to where production elements are traditionally located in a budget. Below the Line elements include crew, equipment rentals, purchases, and everything else that supports the production.
Box Rental Form: The accounting document used in the event a crew member is renting personal, necessary, work-related items to the production. The form is completed on a weekly basis and submitted with their timecard. Also sometimes referred to as a "kit rental form." It requires an itemized list of all items being rented to the production and is not usually taxable.
Breakdown Process: The process of identifying the "non-dialogue" elements that comprise a screenplay and "breaking" them down into categories in order to accurately schedule and budget a project.
Call Sheet: This is the blueprint for each upcoming day of filming. It lists times for cast and crew members to report to work, what will be filming that day, any special departmental needs, equipment that will be used and the location where filming will take place.

Call Times: The times cast and crew are to report to work each day.
Camera House: The vendor where the camera equipment is being rented from.
Car Allowance: A stipend paid to crew members using their personal vehicles as transportation for work-related purposes (runs, deliveries, etc.). The stipend is intended to cover gas, tolls, and offset mileage usage.
Cast: The performers comprising the scripted speaking roles in a show.
Cast Deal Memo: The document that states the productions' agreed-upon employment conditions and pay rate for a performer.
Cast List: The list of performers with speaking roles and stunt performers that have been cast in the show, the roles they are performing, and either direct contact information or contact information for their representation.
Casting Sides: Script pages selected for use in cast auditions.
Check Request: The accounting form or process which requests a check authorized for payment to be made for a purchase or rental.
Cover Set: An interior set the production can use to film in the event of inclement weather.
Crew Base: The number of simultaneous productions that can be staffed with local crew members living in the area.
Crew Call: The general start time when crew is expected to report to work, unless noted otherwise on the call sheet.
Crew Deal Memo: This document identifies each crew member's terms or deal points for employment and serves as an employment contract.
Crew List: A list of names, titles, phone numbers, and email addresses of all crew members working on the film or television show.
Craft Services: This term is most commonly used to describe the snacks and beverages provided on a production. It is also the name of the department that supplies snacks and beverages on the film set.
Cross-Board: In television, this is when scenes from multiple episodes are scheduled together, in lieu of filming them exclusive to their episodic schedule. Often this means combining work needed at a specific filming location or to accommodate a performer's schedule. Feature films usually schedule filming in this way.
Clearance Report: A report that identifies potential legal rights use issues or concerns in regard to specific elements mentioned in a screenplay.
Content: The creative feature film and/or television product being produced for an audience.
Day Files: A method of organizing production paperwork generated for and during each day of filming. The files are kept and maintained by the Production Office.
Day Play: Employment on a day-to-day basis.
Day Out of Days / "DOOD": This document assigns each character in the script a number and is a chart of when they are scheduled to work based on the One Line schedule.
Daytime: Refers to the time of day an episodic television show airs, generally between the hours of 8 a.m. and 6 p.m., when a majority of audiences are assumed to be at work.
Department Head / "Key": The head or manager of a department.
DGA: The Directors Guild of America. A labor Union for Directors and their team, inclusive of UPMs, 1st AD's, 2nd AD's and 2nd 2nd AD's, as well as Stage Managers and Location Managers (NY/Chicago only).

Direct Dial: A phone number that connects directly to a person or department without an extension or connecting number.

Distant Hire: An employee that is working outside of a 60-mile radius from their place of residence and thus cannot return home safely at the end of a workday.

Distribution: The process of releasing a completed film, television, and/or media project to platforms for viewers to access and enjoy. Also known as "distro" in the Production Office, which is the process of sharing production-related documents with cast and crew members.

Drive-On: When working on a studio lot, this security permission allows visitors access to drive onto the lot.

Elements: The "non-dialogue" text in a screenplay, which identifies physical, tangible, and visual story needs such as cast members, props, wardrobe, and sets that need to be filmed. Often organized by department type and scene.

Episodic Television Series: Content written to be viewed in half-hour or one-hour time blocks, where a story unfolds over the course of a season. Designed to be viewed on a television or digital device, non-theatrical.

Expendables: Supplies and other consumable items purchased on a production by various departments.

Film Festival: Often a competition exhibition outlet where content can be viewed by potential distributors and the general public.

Fly: To "release" or distribute a document to the cast and crew.

Football: An accordion file folder used to "pass" daily paperwork between the set and office.

Form I-9: A federal employment form required as proof of eligibility to work in the US. Included as part of the start work packet.

Freelance: Project-based, short-term employment.

Greenlit: This is the approval or "go ahead," often given by the Studio that signals a project is financed and can begin official pre-production.

Half-Hour Episodic Television Sitcom: A situation comedy television program that is produced for a 30-minute time slot.

Hiatus: A temporary scheduled break from filming in principal photography. This can be of a short duration such as during the Christmas–New Year's holidays or for a longer period between physical production seasons.

High-Budget Feature Films: Feature films budgeted over $15 million are usually considered "high budget." Films above this size are often produced by large Studios.

Hollywood Industry Standard: A term for what has become common practice for content production in the entertainment industry.

Honeywagon: A large trailer with up to eight multiple rooms, including bathrooms, sometimes used for the AD Production Office on set, Producer rooms, or day performer cast members to rest or change.

Hot Lock: Used as a security measure for when a company is filming on a studio or soundstage lot. The hot lock is a list of production personnel authorized to have the stage open or closed.

IATSE: The International Alliance of Theatrical Stage Employees. The labor Union that represents most of the skilled craft labor on a production.

Infrastructure: The support resources that enable production operations in a region.

Insurance Certificate: A document that proves the Production Company is covered by an insurance policy. A "certificate" is often issued to rental vendors as a requirement to use their goods/equipment.

Limited Television Series: A television program that tells a story in a predetermined, limited number of episodes, without recurring seasons.

Local Hire: An individual employed on a production who lives within a specific radius of the production location and can easily travel home at the end of a workday.

Location Scouting: The period of time when members of the Locations department search for locations to match the visual aesthetic of the film per the Director and Production Designer.

Locked Script: Also considered the production draft and copied on white paper. This is the final script before official revisions begin.

Low-Budget Feature Films: Feature films budgeted under $15 million are considered low budget. This includes independent (non-studio financed) Union and non-Union films.

Mileage Log: A form used to track a drivers' mileage when doing runs. Used when a crew member is being compensated for mileage driven on the job in their personal vehicle.

Military Time: Also known as the 24-hour clock. Often used by the "on" production crew to report work hours.

Moving On / On the Move: A term used by the Assistant Directors to indicate when a scene has been completed and the company is moving on to the next scene. This may also indicate the company is moving to the next location.

Multi-Camera Sitcom: A type of episodic television situation comedy filmed with more than two cameras, often with a live audience.

Network: In television, this is the distributor, where the final show airs, and sometimes the producing entity of the project.

New Media: Often refers to content other than traditional television and feature films.

No Social Media Agreement: A written agreement between the Production Company and the cast or crew members to not post or publicize production-related content to social media.

Non-Disclosure Agreement / "NDA": A written agreement between the Production Company and the cast or crew members to not share or discuss production-related information with anyone outside of the production.

Non-Production City: A city where film and television production is not a substantial source of economic revenue, and thus does not have a large amount of local production resources or crew base available.

"Off" Production: The crew working off-set, taking care of everything that was just completed or is coming up.

Office Production Assistant: The entry-level position that works in the Production Office on a film or television show. YOU!!!

"On-call": Being available for work outside of scheduled work hours.

"On" Production: The crew members actively working on the set where principal photography is taking place.

One Line Schedule: Also referred to as the "strip board." Used to schedule a show, it identifies each scene in the script and a few corresponding elements for that scene, such as cast, set, day/night, interior/exterior, and a scene description. Basically, it briefly describes the elements of WHO, WHAT, WHEN, and WHERE.

One-hour Primetime Episodic Television Drama: An episodic television program of the drama genre that is produced for a one-hour evening time slot.

OTT (Over the Top): Content accessed using the Internet, such as streaming services.

Page Count: The number of pages in a script, divided into eighths per page. Used as a means to measure the amount of work intended to be completed each filming day.

P-Card: A purchasing card. Used in place of petty cash, it's a production-tracked credit card for production-only spending.

Petty Cash: A cash advance assigned to an individual on a production to be used for production-related purchases. The amount assigned remains as a consistent "float" regardless of the actual spending.

Physical Production: The period of time from pre-production through principal photography.

Pilot: In television, this is the first episode to be filmed. A Studio or Network may elect to pay for one "test" or single episode of a television show to be produced before committing to additional episodes.

Post House: Refers to the vendor the production is using to complete the editorial process, such as picture and sound editing, color grading, etc..

Prep Schedule: A schedule issued each day of pre-production, outlining meetings, fittings, and scouts happening that day or week to help prepare the show for principal photography. Also known as a "pre-production" or "pre-pro" schedule.

Pre-Sales: Selling the rights to a film or television show to an international or domestic distributor as a way to finance the project for production.

Preliminary Call Sheet: A draft version of the call sheet used as an advance look at the next days' work.

Pre-Production: The period of time from when the project has been financed and greenlit during which the production plan is created, prior to the start of principal photography.

Prep Meetings: Also known as pre-production meetings. Held in advance of principal photography to ensure alignment of departmental requirements for filming.

Primetime: Refers to the time of day an episodic television show airs. A primetime show will typically air after work hours, where viewership is expected to be higher.

Principal Photography: The period of time where the script is being performed and captured photographically.

Production: The period of time once a film has been financed, when it is creatively prepared and physically produced. Also is another name used when referring to a show.

Production Crew: The individuals that comprise the pre-production and principal photography team on a show.

Production Company: The producing entity on a television show or feature film.

Production Hubs: Also referred to as "production cities," these are geographic regions where a high volume of film and television production takes place.

Production Pattern: In television production this formula identifies the number of days/weeks an episode will spend in pre-production, principal photography and in post-production in order to complete the show by a pre-determined air date.

Production Plan: The result of the pre-production process. The production plan is the overall blueprint of how, where, when and for how long principal photography will take place.

Production Report: A reporting document that is a companion to the call sheet. It records cast and crew work hours, what was actually filmed, and any special incidents that occurred on each day of filming.

Production Schedule: The timeline that dictates the start of pre-production through principal photography and post production, ending with the air or release date.
Production Value: How the overall visual aesthetic of a show is measured.
Progress Board: A daily tracking whiteboard that reflects the progress of the filming day as reported from set and documented by the office.
Props: The handheld items used by cast members on-screen.
Purchase Order: When a payment account is set up with a vendor, this accounting document is used as a commitment for payment for the items needed for the production. The show agrees to pay up to that amount for the goods and services rendered when invoiced at a later date.
Push/Pull: When a call sheet has been approved and printed, it will be held for distribution until wrap each day. If production needs to change the next day's call time for any reason at wrap, they will use the terms "Push" or "Pull" in order to revise the work times immediately on the spot. Production may elect to PUSH the next day's call time *later*, in which case call sheets will be stamped, or handwritten with the phrase "Push Call X Hours" or "All Calls Pushed X Hours." Conversely, production may PULL forward a call time to start *earlier*, and call sheets will be stamped or handwritten with "Pull Call X Hours, or "All Calls Pulled X Hours."
Release Date: The date when content is available to viewers.
Release Platform: The means by which content is available to viewers, such as broadcast television, a streaming service, or movie theaters.
Release Schedule: The dates when the content is available to viewers.
Revisions: Used to refer to script pages that have been updated.
Runs: Errands.
SAG-AFTRA: The labor Union that represents cast members, stunt performers, and other specialty on-camera performers.
Safety Memo: AKA Safety Bulletin. A memorandum outlining safety protocols for actions such as stunts, special effects, location concerns, etc.
Screening: When a special viewing is arranged for a specific audience to see a film or television show.
Screen Credit: Names of individuals and their roles/titles on the production shown on-screen before or after a television show or feature film.
Script: The written story in a specifically formatted document that is the foundation of the content to be produced.
Scene Numbers: Numbers used to organize the scenes in the script in the order in which they appear.
Season: The number of episodes of a television show a Network orders and agrees to produce and air within the span of a year.
Set: Where the actual filming is taking place.
Set Dressing: Things like furniture and other decorative on-camera items that are added to a set in accordance with the needs of the script to create a fictional or realistic look.
Shop Steward: A Union crew member designated by their fellow crew members to represent them and serve as the liaison between production and the Union should any issues arise.
Short Ends: When content is photographed on film stock, the unused film left over in a magazine (the chamber where film is held before exposure) is called a "short end."

Shooting Schedule: A production paperwork document that categorizes all of the elements by scene in the script.

Show Budget: The document that dictates how much money the show intends to be produced for and/or is predicted to cost.

Sides: A mini version of the script pages scheduled to be filmed each day.

Signatory: An agreement between a Studio / Network / Production Company and a Union or Guild that confirms their collaboration and adherence to Union or Guild guidelines for the duration of their show.

Single Camera: In television, the term used to refer to the style of content produced using two or fewer cameras, often on one-hour dramas and non-audience shows.

Sitcom: Situational comedy, a type of television show often produced with a live audience.

Slate: The piece of equipment used by the 2nd Assistant Cameraperson. A small board that identifies each scene and take being filmed. The movable lever on top, that when "clapped" together makes a sound, assists post production in syncing the sound recording to the picture captured.

Spec Script: A script written in the style of an existing television show to reflect a writer's understanding of a show's structure and writing style. Can also be a feature screenplay written without prompting or presale that a writer intends to use as an example of skill.

Start Work Packet: The employer and payroll documents required to be completed by every cast and crew member on a production, in order to be paid.

Strike: Part of the wrap process. The removal and teardown of sets, set dressing, and other elements assembled for principal photography that are no longer needed.

Strips: What the one line schedule is comprised of, indicating scene number, day/night, Int/Ext, set, and a scene description.

Studio: Often the financing or producing entity of a production. The "studio" can also be a physical location, such as the studio lot where soundstages and offices can be found.

Tax Incentives: A state or city legislative action designed to promote film and television production in a specific location, which creates a tax credit or tax reimbursement for the production.

Teamsters: The below-the-line, skilled workers that are not members of IATSE.

Tech Scout: The process of showing department heads the practical locations selected for filming and reviewing how a scene will be filmed at the specific location so they can prepare.

To Set Box: A labeled box that lives in the Production Office, where items that need to be brought to set can be placed until they can be delivered.

Travel Memo: A detailed summary of all flight, housing, airport transfer, and ground transportation that have been arranged for a member of the cast or crew on a production.

Turnkey: A type of office where very little additional setup, such as furniture and utilities, is required before use.

Turning Around: A term used by the AD team to indicate to the crew that the next shot will face the opposite direction.

Turnaround Time: The time from when a cast or crew member is wrapped to when they are called to report to work the next day.

Union: A labor organization that protects workers' rights.

Vendors: Companies or individuals that provide goods and services to the film or television production.

Vendor List: A comprehensive contact list of companies that provide goods and services to the film or television production.

VPO: Virtual Production Office, digital web-based office management software.

W-2 Tax Form: Issued by your employer, this reports your earnings and taxes withheld for the year and is used to file state and federal taxes.

W-4 Tax Form: A federal wage and tax statement form. Part of the start work packet; it informs the payroll company how your paychecks will be taxed.

W-9 Tax Form: A taxpayer ID form, which can be used for an individual or company to identify that they are registered to pay taxes in the US but may be receiving a payment where taxes are not withheld. Thus, they are responsible for paying taxes directly to the IRS for any amounts received.

Walk Away: A lunch break where a meal is not provided by production; however, a full hour of time is allotted for the crew to take a break.

Wall Pockets: In the Production Office, a makeshift mail center for department distribution.

Watermarking: The process of digitally adding an embedded identifying label to production documents.

Wrap: The completion of principal photography where rented equipment is returned and the show closes down. The end of an individual filming day is also referred to as "wrap."

The Works: The process of cast going through hair, makeup, and wardrobe in order to be prepared for filming each day.

Index

Note: Page numbers in **bold** denote tables, page numbers in *italics* denote figures.

abuse; *see* harassment
accounting 91–97, 147, 150; policies and procedures 147, 150; *see also* check request; petty cash; purchase orders; purchasing "P" card
AD Kit **78–79**
advancement 158–160, *159*, 160
AMPTP 162, 171, 174, 176
Assistant Production Coordinator 15–16, 18
attitude 124, 141–142, 151, 162, 193, 201–204
availability 195–196

background breakdown 114, 120; *see also* morning paperwork
bankers box 47
basecamp 63
box rental form 147

call sheet 29, 57, 82,105–106, 111, *112–113*, 114–115, 118, 158
call times 32, *112–113*
camera reports 119; *see also* morning paperwork
cast contracts 121
cast deal memos 121
catering report 120; *see also* morning paperwork
cell phone 133, 135, 138; *see also* texting
check requests 95, *97*
clearance report 121
code of conduct 140, 143
competition 203–204
confidentiality 49, 127, 157
conflicts 142, 143
contact lists 12, 20, 33, 103, 106–107, 111, 121, 122, 154; cast list, confidential 107, 121; *see also* crew, list; location contact list 107; phone extension list 107; vendor list 107
cover letters 200–201
craft services (crafty) 43–44, 69, 74, 75–76

crew 7, 8–9, 11–12, 14, 20, 32–33, 106–107, 111, 127, 146–147, 154; base 7; call 32; deal memo 146–147; list 12, 20, 33, 106–107, 111, 154; organizational chart 8, *9*, *14*, 127; parking 63; structure 8–9, 11–12, 127
CSATTF 166, 171

daily checklist *86–91*, 155
daily prep schedule 65; *see also* meetings; scouts
daily progress report 119; *see also* script supervisor reports
daily time sheets 120; *see also* morning paperwork
damage 152–153, 156–157
day out of days 105–106, 108–110, *109*
day play 144
daytime 181, 184–185, 187–188
development *1*, **2**
DGA (Directors Guild of America) 163–164
digital workflows 47–48; *see also* virtual production office (VPO)
director's plans 121
discrimination 174–176, 179; *see also* harassment
distant hire 98
distribution **3**, 14, 16, 18, 35, 40–42, 44–45, 47–54, 178; electronic 51–54, 178; general distro 40; hard copy 44–45, 49–51, 178; tracking and managing 53; *see also* digital workflows
DIT log 119; *see also* morning paperwork
dress code 124, 141, 203
driving 153, 163, 165, 167–170
drop release 188; *see also* release, schedule

editor's log 119; *see also* script supervisor reports
emails 53–53; composing emails 52–53, *53*; sending and receiving emails 53

emergency action plan 166; *see also* production, safety plan
employer 193, 195–196, 200–201
employment 180, 184, 189–191
entry level 10, *11*, **12**
episodic television 180, 184
etiquette 131, 133, 138; office 131; phone 133, 138
Exhibit G 105, 119–120; *see also* morning paperwork
exhibition *1*, **3**
extras breakdown 114
extras vouchers 120

feature films 1, 10, 27, 30, 180–181, 187–188, 191; high budget 180–181; low budget 180–181
file storage 39
filing 39, 44, *45*–48, 106; day files 45, 106; digital 47–48; labels 39, 45–47; organization 39, *46*; *see also* digital workflows
film 192–194, 198–199, 202; commission 193–194; festivals 194, 198; office 192–193, 198; school 192, 194, 198–199, 202
filming xiv, 2, 29–31, *31*, 63
financing **2**
first aid 39, 168–169
first day 144, 154
football 106, 114, 120
freelance 29, 144, 152, 180, 196, 200

getting paid 145
gift baskets 100
guilds 162–164; *see also* DGA; PGA; SAG-AFTRA; WGA

harassment 140, 143,147, 154, 166, 170, 174–176, 179; sexual 174–175, 179; *see also* discrimination
hazard 166–168, 170–171, 174, 179; *see also* production, safety plan
hiatus 181, 190–191
holding/catering 63
holidays 146, 190–191
Hollywood industry standard xiii, 6, 8, 187, 248
human resources 175
hurry up and wait 123, 129
hygiene 141, 143; *see also* illness

IATSE (International Alliance of Theatrical Stage Employees) 163–164
illness 141, 152

IMDb 201
independent contractor 145–146, 148, 150, 152; *see also* freelance; getting paid
infrastructure 7
initiative 128–129
injury 152, 166, 170
injury illness prevention program 166, 170; *see also* production, safety plan
insurance 21, 145, 150, 152–153, 156, 198; certificate 21, 153; production 152–153, 156; unemployment 145, 150; workers compensation 152, 198
internships 195, 197–199
interview 196, 199–204

job 33, 192–195, 197, 200, 202, 205; search 194–195, 197, 205; skills and tools 33, 192–193, 197–202, 205; title 200

kaizen 131
keys 9, 11–12, 24, 35, 39, 45, 55, 102, 122, 143, 164, 179, 191, 205; creative 9, 11; logistical 9, 11; section 1–10, 12, 24, 35, 102, 122, 143, 164, 179, 191, 205; *see also* management

labor 10–12; skilled 10, *11*, **12**; specialized 10, 11, **11**; *see also* entry level
limited series 180, 188
Line Producer 19
lined script 119; *see also* script supervisor reports
local hire 98
location map *63*–64
logbooks 54–56, 91; cast contact info log 55; key Log **54**; morning distro log 55–*56*; PO logs **91**; script distro log 55–*56*; shipment-incoming **55**; shipment-outgoing **55**; to set log **55**
lunch 57, 61, 68, 70–74; catered meals 72–74; orders 71–73; walk away 70
lunch report 114–115, *118*, 118–120

management 10, **11**; creative **11**; executive **11**; support 10, **11**
marketing *1*, **3**
meetings 65–69, 110; pre–production meetings 65–67; set up 67–68; strike 68
mentors 199
menu book 71; *see also* lunch
mileage log 61
morning paperwork 105–106, 111, 114–115, 118–120
multi-camera 184

NDA (non-disclosure agreement) 127, 143
network 106, 114, 121
networking 192, 194–195
non-union 146, 163

office 37–40, 42–43, 57–79, 166, 168, 172, 174, 178; equipment 57–59; ergonomics 166; machines 38–40, 174, 178; operations 37, 57–79; safety 168, **172**; supplies 39, 78, 178; signage *42–43*
on the job 150–152, 154–155, 157
one line schedule 29, 105–*108*; see also schedules
OSHA 171, 179
OTT 187, **188**

parking 44, 63
payday 153–154
pay rates 145
payroll company 145–147, 150, 152, 155
personal: health 152; see also injury; property; see damage
petty cash 93, 94–95; see also accounting
PGA (Producers Guild of America) 163–164; see also guilds
phases of a show **1–3**
phone 135–137, 154, 195–197, 202; calls 135–*137*; see also cell phone
pickle i, 8, 54, 99, 150, 189, 190, 210–211
pitch 194
Post Production *1*, **2–3**, 10, 103, 110, 118–119
prep 29–*31*, 32, *111*, 180–181, 184, 189–190; see also pre-production
pre-production *1*, **2**, 29, 30, 65, 66
production: Assistant xii, 12, 13, 16, *28*, *36*, 145, 146, 162, 249; company policies 147; Coordinator 14–15, 18, 20, 65, 193, 195, 200, 204; crew 9–10, 33; hubs xiii, 3–4, 7, 129, 193; management 11; "off" *34–35*, 51; "on" *34–35*; paperwork 103–107, 110, 111, 115, 119–120, 122; pattern 180–182, *183*, 184, *185–186*, 189, 191; plan 13, 66; pyramid *23*, 125, 146, 158, 161; report 105, 115, *116–117*, 119–120; see also morning paperwork; safety plan 147; schedule 7, 27, 29, 181, 184, *187*, 189, *190*; Secretary 16, 18; staff 14; Supervisor 20; time *148*; vehicles 44
Production Office x, xii, xiii, 4–7, 13, 20, *22*, 24, 30–32, 35, 37–39, 57, 123–128, 130–133, 135, 137–138, 140–143, 152–154, 157–158, 160–161,163, 168, 170–172, 174–175, 177–178, 181, 190; floor plan 6; furniture 37–38; setup 37, 58;

staff responsibilities **18**; workspace 20, 37–38; wrap 44
primetime 181, 182, 184, 189–191
principal photography xiv, *1*, **2**, 5, 29, 30, 34; see also filming
political hire 204; see also competition
purchase orders 91, *92*, 93, 120; see also accounting
purchasing "P" card 93, 94–*96*; see also accounting

recommendation 204; see also references; referral
recycling 40, *177*–178; see also sustainability
references 200
referral 192, 204
relationships 196, 199, 204
release 181, 184, 187–189, 191; date 181, 184; day/date 188; platform 187–188, **188**; schedule 184, 188–189, *189*, 191
research 76–78
resources 130, 192, 194–195, 198; local 194; online 192, 195, 198
resume 192, 194–195, 199–203, 205; see also cover letters
runs 59–65; set runs 62–65

safeguards 151
safety 165–177; awareness *172–173*; bulletin 166, 168; culture 170; fire 166, 168; handbook 170–171; hotline 171; meeting 170; office 168, **172**; pandemic 174; plans 166; production 166, *167*, 168, 170–171; reporting 166, 171, 175–176; training 171, 177
SAG-AFTRA (Screen Actors Guild, American Federation of Television and Radio Artists) 163–164
schedules 29, 57, 82, 103, 105–115, 118, 122, 158; see also one line schedule; production calendar 110; prep 110, *111*; season production 110; shooting schedule 105–106, *109*, 110, 114; see also call sheet; day out of days
scouts 68–69, 110–*111*; director scout 68; location scout 68; tech scout 68–69
screen credit 198; see also job title
script 49, 79–81, 103–110, 80–82, 114–115, 118–119, 121–122, 145, 152, 155–156, 160–161, 164; breakdown *104*, 105; collating 81–82; locked 80; network draft 114; network outline 114; production 115; revisions 49, 79–81, 114–115; studio draft 114; studio outline 114

script supervisor reports 119; *see also* daily progress report; editor's log; lined script; morning paperwork
security 49, 52
set xiii, 5–7, 34–35, 51, 62–64; list 121; PA 17–18
sides 82–86; casting 82; sample *84*
single-camera 184
sitcom 184, **186**, 188
skins 120
social media 201
sound reports 118; *see also* morning paperwork
standards and practices 121
start paperwork 146–147
still photo breakdown 121
streaming 180, 184, 187–188; *see also* OTT
studio policies 170
Sue Ellen Crandell 211
sustainability 176–177; *see also* recycling

Teamsters (International Brotherhood of Teamsters) 163–164
texting 126, 129, 138
timecard 145, 147–149, *149*
to set box *41*
training programs 192, 196–199, 204; *see also* film, school; workshops
travel 98–101, 129; accommodations 99–100; airport transfers 98–99; Coordinator 16, 98–99; memo 98; rental car 153, 156
type of show 180–181, 189, 191

unions *see* IATSE; Teamsters
Unit Production Manager 19, 163

vendors 193–194, 198
vendor services 40; *see also* Production Office, setup
virtual production office (VPO) 47
visitors 69–70
voicemail 137–138; *see also* phone
volunteer 193, 199

wall pockets 40–*41*; *see also* distribution
welcome packets 100–101, 130; *see also* travel
WGA (Writer's Guild of America) 163–164; *see also* guilds
wrap 29, 30, *31*, 181, 184, 189–190
wrap report *118*, 118–119
working hours 31
work shifts *32*
workshops 193, 198
work trucks 63